-LLD

107 text?

Meaning-centered Grammar

Equinox Textbooks and Surveys in Linguistics
Series Editor: Robin Fawcett, Cardiff University

Also in this series:

Language in Psychiatry by Jonathan Fine

Multimodal Transcription and Text Analysis by Anthony Baldry and Paul J. Thibault

Forthcoming titles in the series:

Intonation in the Grammar of English by M. A. K. Halliday and William S. Greaves

Text Linguistics: the how and why of meaning by Jonathan Webster

The Rhetoric of Research: a guide to writing scientific literature by Beverly Lewin

Meaning-centered Grammar

Craig Hancock

LONDON   OAKVILLE

Published by

Equinox Publishing Ltd

UK: Unit 6, The Village, 101 Amies St, London, SW11 2JW
USA: DBBC, 28 Main Street, Oakville, CT 06779

www.equinoxpub.com

Meaning-centered Grammar by Craig Hancock
First published 2005
© Craig Hancock 2005

British Library Cataloguing-in-Publication Data
A catalogue record for this book is available from the British Library.

ISBN 1-904768-10-5 (hardback)
ISBN 1-904768-11-3 (paperback)

Library of Congress Cataloging-in-Publication Data
Hancock, Craig, 1948-
  Meaning-centered grammar : an introductory text / Craig Hancock.
     p. cm. -- (Equinox textbooks and surveys in linguistics)
  Includes bibliographical references and index.
  ISBN 1-904768-10-5 -- ISBN 1-904768-11-3 (pbk.)
  1. English language--Grammar. 2. English language--Syntax. 3.
English language--Usage. I. Title. II. Series.
  PE1112.H2865 2004
  808'.042--dc22
                          2004015041

Typeset by Catchline, Milton Keynes (www.catchline.com)
Printed and bound in Great Britain by Antony Rowe Ltd, Chippenham

Contents

Chapter 7 Verbs as adjectives, nouns, and as heads of non-finite subordinate clauses

Chapter 8 Coordination and compounding: appositional phrases

Acknowledgements

'Those Winter Sundays' Copyright © 1966 by Robert Hayden, from *Collected Poems of Robert Hayden* by Robert Hayden, edited by Frederick Glaysher. Material used by permission of Liveright Publishing Corporation.

'Asian Figures' by W. S. Merwin © 1973 by W. S. Merwin. Material used with the permission of the Wylie Agency Inc.

From *There are No Children Here* by Alex Kotlowitz, copyright © 1991 by Alex Kotlowitz. Material used by permission of Doubleday, a division of Random House, Inc.

'Silent Dancing' by Judith Ortiz Cofer is reprinted with permission from the publisher of *Silent Dancing* (Houston: Arte Público Press – University of Houston © 1990).

From *Hunger of Memory* by Richard Rodriguez. Material used with permission of David Godine, Publisher, Inc. Copyright © 1982 by Richard Rodriguez.

From *The Writing Life* by Annie Dillard Copyright © 1989 by Annie Dillard. Material used by permission of HarperColllins Publishers.

From *Pilgrim at Tinker Creek* by Annie Dillard Copyright © 1974 by Annie Dillard. Material used by permission of HarperColllins Publishers.

From *Coming into Country* by John McPhee. Copyright © 1977 by John McPhee. Material used by permission of Farrar, Straus and Giroux, LLC.

Preface

This text was designed to support a one semester introduction to grammar at the college level, in courses historically aimed largely at English teaching majors, though it is also an approach to grammar aimed at being useful to other students and in other contexts as well.

I am a writing teacher who has spent most of his working life on the front lines of composition, working for the last 18 years with Educational Opportunity Program students at the University at Albany. I have been well trained in approaches to teaching writing that help students build trust in their own language while putting it to work in the building of writing that they, too, find meaningful. Against the grain of my discipline, which has continued to think of grammar as a banal subject tied to archaic and banal teaching practices, I went in search of an approach to grammar compatible with meaning making approaches to reading and writing. The working premise has been that form and meaning are organically interconnected, that word choice and word arrangement are not neutral carriers of a pre-existent meaning, but a deeply important part of the meaning making enterprise. There is a long tradition of this in composition and aesthetics, though very few attempts to connect this with public grammar. Traditionally, grammar choices have been choices of 'correctness' or 'style'; for more experienced writers, revision is essentially a movement toward meaning. My question, from the first, was whether this functional notion of form could be extended to grammar. This book is a decade long positive answer to that question.

I am not, of course, the first or the last to be interested in this approach. Cognitive grammar builds a link between grammar and human cognition. Functional grammar, most notably Systemic Functional Grammar, sees language as a social semiotic, and describes the grammar of expression, interaction, and representation. Michael Halliday's *Introduction to Functional Grammar* has been an invaluable resource for this book. For many on this side of the Atlantic, Martha Kolln's *Rhetorical Grammar* has broken new ground in connecting grammatical choice with the making of meaning and with building a writer/reader connection. Thanks to her, rhetorical approaches to grammar are a respectful enterprise.

Generative grammar has generally shied away from pedagogical application, but has deeply established the truth that we are all innately wired for language, that language is learned rather than taught, that a language rich environment is the most important catalyst for language acquisition, that all human dialects are equally rule-driven, equally capable of rendering the world. The goal of this book is to bring that unconscious grammar to conscious light and to explore ways in which effective writing works in harmony with that natural language.

One principal goal of the book is to equip someone to participate in a public discussion of grammar, and for that reason I have tried to hold to as much of the traditional terminology of grammar as possible. Anyone wishing primarily to avoid error in the traditional sense of the term would still be well served by the much deeper and wider understanding offered here. A good deal of prescriptive grammar is highly questionable, even dysfunctional, and wider understanding gives us the insight necessary to make informed judgments. This is not a prescriptive grammar, but it does offer a perspective on prescriptive issues. More importantly, I think, it fully integrates the most functional aspect of traditional grammar, the conventions of punctuation, which do much to make written discourse effective and readable.

The last two chapters of the book, applications of grammar to reading and writing, were planned from the start, and many of the choices throughout the book have been made with the idea of making those chapters possible. The goal of this book has always been to equip someone to more fully enter the realm of real world language, to build a machine and then take that machine for a ride. Many of the sentences in the book are made up examples, but many are also drawn from the work of our best writers. It is a book about how grammar works when grammar works well, and I thought it important to draw on a diversity of voices from the best our language has to offer.

I have been blessed with students among the finest in the world; without their liveliness, diversity, curiosity, ambition, and innate language abilities, without their remarkable success despite all the standard predictions to the contrary, this book would never have been possible. I can't say thank you enough to my boss and mentor, Carson Carr, who has supported this project from my first tentative attempts to explain it, sometimes adjusting my workload to help make it happen. My colleague, Silke Van Ness, was the first to teach an early version of this, agreeing to that even before the draft was done. Without her patience and the enthusiasm of those first students, the project would not have gone on. Martha Kolln very graciously read an awkward early draft, giving invaluable encouragement and suggestions. Parts of it have been thoughtfully read by Jeff Weimelt (Southeastern Louisiana University), Barbara Stanford (University of Arkansas at Little Rock), Judy Diamondstone (formerly of Clark University), Joan Livingston-Webber (Western Illinois University), and Edgar Schuster (retired teacher and author of *Breaking The Rules: Liberating Writers Through Innovative Grammar Instruction*, Heinemann, 2003). Michael Cummings (York University, Toronto) has read the final versions of the text with both warm and critical eyes. Janet Joyce, my editor at Equinox, has supported this project in so many different ways since the first letter of inquiry. I want to thank my colleagues on the ATEG (Association for the Teaching of English Grammar) listserv and my colleagues in New Public Grammar – in addition to those listed above, most especially Herb Stahlke, Joanna Rubba, and Bill Spruiell – for deepening my understanding in so many ways in so many conversations. The team at Catchline has done yeoman service in getting the final version of this into print. Thanks to the Kinderhook Writing Group for keeping me focused and sane. Thanks especially to my late father, John Hancock, who found time for poetry in a busy life and passed on a grand love of language. Thanks to my partner, Laura Rogers, and to Rani, Zach, Nathan, and Aaron, who put up with a father with his head in a grammar cloud when it could just as well have been closer to home.

Chapter 1

Rethinking grammar

You are about to start on a difficult and wondrous exploration, a journey into the heart of your own language. You may expect that a grammar book will be about someone else's language, a 'correct' or 'proper' language that your own has often failed to measure up to. We will certainly talk about Standard English along the way, but our overall concern will be deeper and wider than that, focusing on the natural, inherent grammar of the language, the grammar you began to learn even before you began to talk. If you can read this sentence, you understand, not just the words themselves, but the roles they play, the meaning relations they establish among each other, though you have no doubt not spent much time contemplating that understanding. You already know far more grammar than any book or short-term study could possibly teach you. Coming to understand grammar is a lot less like learning a new language than it is like becoming aware of an old, familiar one. Of course, that familiar language is always growing. Most of our time will be spent bringing your current, growing language into conscious light.

When I tell people that I teach a college course in grammar, one common reaction is surprise that such a 'basic' subject is being taught in college. The assumption is that the course is somehow remedial, making up for failures or deficiencies at the *grammar* school or junior high level. The perspective presented in this book is that grammar is not a 'skill' or even an 'ability'; if it is, it's an ability that we all share by virtue of having been born human. We are considering grammar as a meaning-making system and are concerned with expanding our knowledge of that system, and since the system itself is extraordinarily rich and complex, learning about it will require a great deal of concentration, diligence, and patience. Since language is a living and dynamic phenomena, we will never fully understand or describe it. We will never have a complete grammar any more than we will ever have a complete physics or a complete biology, though we can certainly feel as if we are developing a deepening understanding.

Grammar is the natural, inherent, meaning-making system of the language, a system that governs the way words come together to form meanings; grammar is also the study of that system, the various theories or perspectives that attempt to understand and describe it. A popular idea of grammar – and one that we are discarding – is that grammar is the set of prescriptive rules that limit the language we have available.

Grammar is the natural, inherent, meaning-making system of the language, a system that governs the way words come together to form meanings; grammar is also the study of that system, the various theories or perspectives that attempt to understand it.

It may surprise you that there are competing theories and perspectives about grammar; you may have been taught that there is 'good grammar' and 'bad grammar' and that decisions about what is good and bad have been made once and for all by someone else. But there are competing perspectives about grammar, just as there are competing theories about biology, physics, and history. As a language user and a student of grammar, you should feel free to add your own insight to our common understanding.

When I say that you already know an astounding amount of grammar, I am saying that you have internalized for your own use the inherent grammatical structures that underlie the language. If I join with popular opinion in saying that most people do not know much grammar, I am talking about the theories that describe that system, the body of knowledge I am selecting from in constructing this book.

You cannot have meaning without grammar any more than you can have meaning without words. This is so much the case that linguists call the level of grammar the *lexico-grammatical level*, the word-grammar level. Words do not exist in isolation; and when dictionary makers isolate words for definition, they find it necessary to give a great deal of grammatical information, information about how that word works when combined in meaning-making ways with other words. Words do not mean apart from use, and use always evolves a grammar.

Grammar is not error and error is not grammar   1.2

We will explore the relationship between grammar and writing in detail in Chapter 10. At that point, we will have a great deal of grammar knowledge in common – as we explore the ways in which the grammar of writing draws from and differs from the natural grammar of speech and the conventional ways (like the punctuation system) through which grammar has come to be represented in a written form. But first it is useful to address some common misunderstandings of grammar.

Most of us confront grammar (and grammar problems) mostly in writing situations; for many of us, that has meant error and embarrassment and failure. For many people, perhaps most, *grammar* is *error* and *error* is *grammar*, so much so that the two words are often used as though they are synonyms for each other.

You should understand, first of all, that much of what we can call *error* in writing is not grammar at all. We can make errors in spelling, in vocabulary, in fact, in explaining too much or explaining too little, in being too business-like or not business-like enough. The possibilities are too enormous to list here. Because we are human, our efforts will always be imperfect. Perhaps the only way to avoid error is not to write at all. (Many of you may already write as little as possible.)

But the primary motive for writing is certainly not the avoidance of error. Good writers work very hard to try to make their writing purposeful (though those purposes may only become clear in the writing itself). For a good writer, writing decisions do not seem a hard and fast divide between correct and incorrect, but an attempt to bring their writing toward the goal of increased effectiveness. And when writing is working well, grammar will be an integral part of that. We will, in fact, be looking at grammar when grammar is working well for the great majority of this book. We will try to understand the contribution of grammar to the realization of meaning and of purposes.

A sentence is not a complete thought   1.3

When I ask beginning students what they know or understand about grammar, the most common response is that 'a sentence is a group of words that expresses a complete thought.' It's a definition they were first offered about the fourth or fifth grade by well-meaning teachers or textbooks because this notion can help you avoid sentence fragments, which can carry with them a sense of being incomplete. However useful this definition may have been in that limited context, if we hold on to it, it will ultimately do us more harm than good. We need to discard it before we can move on to a more mature understanding of the sentence.

Let's consider three sentences from three accomplished writers: the first by George Orwell, the opening sentence of *Shooting an Elephant*; the second by Toni Cade Bambara, the opening sentence from *The Lesson;* and the third by James Baldwin, the opening sentence of *Sonny's Blues.*

> *In Moulmein, in Lower Burma, I was hated by large numbers of people – the only time in my life that I have been important enough for this to happen to me.*

> *Back in the days when everyone was old and stupid or young and foolish and me and Sugar were the only ones just right, this lady moved on our block with nappy hair and proper speech and no makeup.*

> *I read about it in the paper, in the subway, on my way to work.*

One observation we can make about the Orwell and Bambara sentences is that they contain quite a bit of content and could quite easily be divided into a number of sentences with less content per sentence.

> *I was in Moulmein once. This is in Lower Burma. I was hated. Large numbers of people hated me. I was important. I had never been important enough to be hated by large numbers of people before.*

> *I once thought everyone older than me was stupid. I thought everyone younger than me was foolish. I thought me and Sugar were just right. A woman moved onto the block. She had nappy hair. She had proper speech. She had no makeup.*

If each of these is a complete thought, how is it that we once thought that a single complete thought held all these complete thoughts within it? The truth is that sentence boundaries are very flexible in writing, and sentences can vary widely in the amount of content they contain. Whatever the writer is aiming at may very well be and seem incomplete without the preceding and following sentences.

Both the Bambara and Orwell sentences, insofar as they work well, give us not a sense of completeness, but a sense of incompleteness, of wanting more. This effect is clearly evidenced (cleverly exploited) in the opening Baldwin sentence.

I read about it in the paper, in the subway, on my way to work.

The word *it* is a pronoun, a word that generally stands in for a meaning that has already been given. But this is our opening sentence. What did he read about? Clearly, Baldwin is attempting to create a sense of curiosity and anticipation. We cannot complete the meaning of this sentence without reading more. The story, in fact, continues to tease us through the next two sentences.

I read it, and I couldn't believe it, and I read it again. Then perhaps I just stared at it, at the newsprint spelling out his name, spelling out the story.

Here, we are further teased with *his* as a reference to a person who hasn't been named yet and *the story* as reference to a story that has neither been named nor identified. We do not know what these sentences mean until we read further.

One of the great difficulties of teaching grammar is that an understanding is so hard to develop; inevitably it requires looking at a great many sentences in isolation. If that is all we do, though, you may be left with a profound misunderstanding that will make it very difficult to ever put your understanding into practice. Sentences are not complete thoughts. They cannot usually be fully understood or appreciated apart from other sentences around them. And they cannot be fully understood, appreciated, or evaluated apart from the purposes of their writer.

If you are reading this sentence right now, it is because I have decided, rightly or wrongly, that it carries out the purposes of this book as they are being realized within this section of this critical first chapter. It is not a complete thought. It cannot be fully understood or judged in isolation.

Trust and distrust: conscious and unconscious knowing   1.4

No one can write in someone else's language.

That statement has become a mantra to me as a writing teacher. It may be hard to prove, but I have found it enormously helpful in practice.

I came upon the above formulation of the principle after a student came to me for help with a paper she was writing for another teacher. The teacher told her the paper she was writing was fine, even 'very good,' but that she should take it back and rewrite it 'with a better vocabulary.' There were no notations on the text, no places marked where the meaning wasn't clear or the words weren't carrying their weight. The student was understandably perplexed. She was probably also taken aback when I expressed how upset I was that a teacher – and this a literature teacher, who should certainly know better – should give such an absurd direction. Students are used to adapting to bad teaching; she was more prepared than I was to take it all in stride. 'It's an impossible assignment,' I told her. 'No one can write in someone else's language.'

When Nancy Sommers did research on ways approaches to writing differ between typical college students and experienced writers, she uncovered two very important differences. One is that naive, unpracticed writers tend to view writing as what Sommers calls 'linear' in nature; they believe they are somehow putting into words meanings that existed prior to, and independent of, the writing. To a professional writer, the process is more organic, more like a seed that grows and develops on the page. The second, related pattern is that naive writers, when they revise, tend to think in terms of improving the words and sentences, generally apart from any sense of developing or refining the meaning. Experienced writers, on the other hand, do not conceive of revising as ever extending beyond the task of exploring, discovering, and clarifying meaning, of bringing a meaning into focus for themselves and their readers. The idea of finding better words apart from a sense of purpose isn't within their frame of reference.

A wide vocabulary is certainly a positive thing, and writing, the pressure of creating meaning, will push us to draw in words that we might not normally use in everyday speech. And there is certainly something to be said for a teacher offering a student a word that seems to help bring a sentence or a thought into a much clearer focus. But you simply cannot write in a vocabulary not your own, and any attempt to do so is a prescription for disaster.

Equally disastrous is the prescription to write in someone else's grammar. Like vocabulary, the grammar you have available is the grammar you have available, pure and simple. Though vocabulary and grammar will expand over time, it is essential that you trust the language you have when you write. For this reason, a good writing teacher will often downplay the importance of grammar – though this in itself can be misleading. What is being downplayed is the pressure to write 'correctly', in accordance with elusive standards that you haven't internalized as your own. Since language is naturally and inherently grammatical, you are not dispensing with grammar when you put the pressure of correctness in abeyance, but simply allowing your own natural grammar to come into play.

If your preliminary sentences and thoughts, your first drafts or first attempts, seem very awkward, your experience is much the same as the experience of the best writers. Correcting the writing with better words (apart from the other sentences and your evolving purpose) and less surface error (apart from other sentences and your evolving purposes) may seem like an effective approach to writing, but that is not what good and successful writers do, and that will leave you with writing that is mediocre at best. The writing will need to be worked and shaped, as is true for all writers, but it is your own language, not someone else's, that will be worked and shaped into an effective text.

If learning to write well is primarily a matter of discarding your own incorrect language in favor of a correct one, as so many books would have us believe, you would expect writers to say just that, in particular those writers who come from less privileged backgrounds and less literate communities. You would expect something like the following: 'I could not become a successful writer until I left that terrible community language behind.' But what we find when we listen and ask is very much the opposite.

'If you say what is on your mind in the language that comes to you from your parents and your street and your friends you'll probably say something beautiful,' says Grace Paley, herself a critically acclaimed fiction writer whose narrators often speak in the rhythms of a Yiddish influenced English. The fine black fiction and non-fiction writer John Edgar Wideman claims his success as a writer was only possible 'after fighting for years to believe again in my primal perceptions, my primal language, the words, gestures, and feelings of my earliest memories. At some point I taught myself to stop translating from one language to another.'

That Mr. Wideman defends Black English in such masterful prose only seems ironic. This is not an either/or choice. He writes to us now in a language fully nurtured and grown through wide reading and extensive practice, but it is a grown language and not a learned one. We have no choice in this matter other than a choice between embracing and failure, for a fully mature language can only be built on the foundation of our earliest speech. Any five- or six year-old child enters our public schools with a language far too sophisticated to be replaceable. This is a scientific judgment, insofar as our science has carried us and not a political one; it should not surprise us that the insights of linguistics are reaffirmed by our finest writers. Like William Stafford, they see writing more as a matter of 'trust' than of 'skills':

> It remains mysterious, just as all of us must feel puzzled about how we are so inventive as to be able to talk along through complexities with our friends, not needing to plan what we are going to say, but never stalled for long in our confident progress. Skill? If so, it is the skill we all have, something we must have learned before the age of three or four.

It would be wrong, of course, to accuse these writers of abandoning standards. Their work is a great gift to all of us, a communal treasure built out of stubbornness and integrity, an ability to discount false and misleading standards in favor of highly demanding personal standards and a disciplined listening to their own internal voices.

A writer with important things to say will look for a language to say them, and her language will grow to meet that challenge.

But if writers learn to trust their own language, they also learn to distrust any particular output of it. They allow themselves plenty of room to fail precisely because a failure is a discarded possibility and openness to many possibilities is an essential part of exploration. A new discovery will make initial thoughts obsolete and the whole text will be adjusted to make room for it. Meaning and form often evolve simultaneously and the writer arrives at a level of confidence where final decisions can be made, even down to the level of the grammar. Good writing is purposeful, though those purposes are not usually clear at the start.

Many educators who believe that grammar is inherent and natural have used this as an argument against the teaching of grammar. If we already know grammar, why do we have to study it? The key here would be what is meant by 'know' and what is meant by 'have to.' We learn grammatical forms and develop a highly functional repertoire of those forms in the language of our everyday lives, but we are not naturally and inevitably conscious of that language, and many of us feel we are not as effective in our language use as we would like to be. We are, perhaps, no more in need of becoming conscious of this than we are in need of becoming conscious of the underlying elements of any other human activity, but being conscious is in many ways what makes us more fully human. The question is perhaps not whether we 'have to' know about language, but whether knowledge of language, including the grammar of language as it enters into our real world interactions, is enriching or useful.

Educators have been in the awkward position for some time of recognizing that attempts to teach grammar in isolation have not resulted in better writing (if better writing is described as producing fewer 'errors'). There also seems to be a unanimous understanding (I have yet to hear a serious objection) that knowledge of grammar is useful. (Those of us who know grammar find it enormously useful.) This book can be thought of as an attempt to bridge that gap between knowledge and useful teaching, an attempt to help you know what I know in the hopes that you'll find useful ways to put it into practice in your own language-rich lives.

How much conscious knowledge of grammar is necessary or useful in reading and writing? That's hard to say. It may be best left as an open question that each of you can answer in your own way as your own conscious knowledge of grammar expands through this study. It also would be a wonderful question to ask someone you already respect as a somewhat accomplished writer: How much grammar do you know and what knowledge of grammar do you find yourself using when you write? A good writer certainly pays attention to words and to the arrangement of words and makes an enormous number of grammatical decisions. They may say, like Joyce Carol Oates, 'I would fiercely defend the placement of a semicolon in one of my novels.' How many of their careful choices are intuitive and how many could be consciously explained may differ enormously from writer to writer.

What is a meaning-centered grammar?   1.5

A meaning-centered grammar is, first of all, a grammar that pays respect to what linguists have learned about the way language is acquired and learned. We now know that most language is not acquired through direct teaching, but simply learned naturally and easily if the conditions are right. We know that a child entering school already knows most of an adult grammar. In the years of greatest language learning, a typical child learns more than ten new words a day, a rate that cannot be explained by direct instruction. In the words of Noam Chomsky:

Acquiring language is less something that a child does than something that happens to the child, like growing arms instead of wings, or undergoing puberty at a certain stage of maturation.

In our meaning-centered grammar, we will pay homage to that natural grammar and consider it the primary focus of our exploration. This is not an attempt to change your language (though that may happen), but an attempt to bring it to consciousness. It is a language awareness approach, not an attempt to change language habits or even skills (other than analytical). The assumption is that you will have many purposes of your own that cannot be predicted and that a wider and deeper understanding of how language works will help you in accomplishing those purposes.

This is also a meaning-centered grammar in that, unlike prescriptive approaches to grammar, we will assume that all language use is rich and interesting, that all language forms, the non-standard as well as the standard, are available to us as meaning-making resources. Certainly knowing about Standard English is important – we are not likely to wish it away any time soon – but we don't need to be limited by it as language users or as students of language. The notion that we should limit ourselves to Standard English is belied daily by the work of our best writers. We do not write exclusively for elitists. If we purged our shelves of non-standard English, we would lose *Huckleberry Finn* and *A Catcher in the Rye*. We would lose much of the work of Langston Hughes, August Wilson, and Alice Walker. The list could go on almost endlessly. We would lose much of the best contemporary fiction, non-fiction, and poetry.

Consider the testimony of Amy Tan, who tells us in *Mother Tongue* that she failed as a fiction writer as long as she tried to write sentences that proved she had 'mastery over the English language.' 'Fortunately,' as she says, she abandoned that and:

> began to write stories using all the Englishes I grew up with: the English I spoke to my mother, which for lack of a better term might be described as 'simple'; the English she used with me, which for lack of a better term might be described as 'broken'; my translation of her Chinese, which could certainly be described as 'watered down'; and what I imagine to be her translation of her Chinese if she could speak in perfect English, her internal language, and for that I sought to preserve the essence, but neither an English nor a Chinese structure. I wanted to capture what language ability tests can never reveal: her intent, her passion, her imagery, the rhythms of her speech and the nature of her thoughts.

If you have come to know and admire *The Joy Luck Club*, you know that the book could not have been written in any other way.

This is also a meaning-centered grammar in that we will try our best not to study grammar in isolation. One of the central arguments of the book will be that grammar cannot be fully understood in terms of isolated sentences, that the kinds of choices a writer makes are never made on the basis of sentences in isolation. Though we will look at isolated sentences throughout the book, that will not be an end in itself. The final chapter, in fact, will focus on an extended look at longer passages, a process that you will be preparing for concept by concept and chapter by chapter.

It should be emphasized, though, that this is not a rhetoric and not a writing text. (Though I certainly hope your teachers ask for journals and/or papers.) If this is a meaning-centered grammar, it is also a grammar. Our central focus will be on the natural grammar of the language as a meaning-making system.

Any grammar text, and especially a text meant to be a one semester introduction to the subject, has to be highly selective. Since you can't cover it all, you need to make highly difficult decisions about what to include and what to leave out. I have decided to make ideas about grammar the central focus and to bring in details only when they help bring these ideas into focus. Ultimately, though, ending the book with a close look at real world grammar argues in its own way for inclusiveness; the course could be made much easier, as happens with many grammar books, if the kinds of sentences you are exposed to were controlled. The ultimate test of any grammar is in how useful it is when applied. Anyone who dutifully moves through this book should find the analysis of longer passages from our best writers a significant challenge, but doable and rewarding.

Nothing would please me more than knowing that you disagree with this book in some substantial way. Ultimately, it is your own understanding that is important.

The more I learn about language, the less comfortable I am in telling anyone else how to use it, though dialogue about work in progress can be helpful and delightful. Just as the living world cannot be enclosed in a biology book, a single book cannot enclose the living world of language. Let's try to pay respect, every step of the way, to its magic and its mystery and its power.

Chapter 2
Section Exercises

Page 27
Identify prepositional phrases and tell whether each is adjectival or adverbial.

Page 29
Identify prepositional phrases and draw a slash (/) between subject and predicate. Tell whether each prepositional phrase is adjectival or adverbial.

Chapter Practice

Page 31
Identify subject and predicate. Underline each prepositional phrase, tell whether it is adjectival or adverbial and tell what word group it modifies.

Basic principles of grammar

The mords slobly bordled a slom don in the nox.

I was given a sentence quite like the one above in my own undergraduate linguistics course. It worked for me, so I typically give my grammar classes my own version very early in the semester. I like to write it on the board and watch their reactions as they filter into class and try to figure out what language it is written in. Grammatically, it is a typical English sentence, though it has, as you may have guessed, a number of made up words. The made up words have the effect of highlighting the grammar, especially the internal, hidden, unconscious grammar that is the prime focus of this book. When my students tell me they don't know what it means, I tell them they do know a great deal about what it means and try to convince them of that by asking questions like the following:

1) Who did it?
2) How many of them were there?
3) What was done?
4) Who or what was it done to?
5) How many of them were there?
6) How was it done?
7) Where was it done?
8) When was it done?
9) What was the don like?

Try to answer the questions yourself before reading on.

Typically, the answers are as follows:

1) *The mords* did it.
2) I'm not sure how many, but there were more than one.
3) What the mords did was *slobly bordled a slom don in the nox*; or what the mords did was *bordle*.
4) This was done to *a slom don*.
5) There was one *slom don*.
6) This was done *slobly*.
7) This was done *in the nox*.
8) This was done sometime in the past.
9) The don was *slom*.

Once this is accomplished (with surprising agreement), I ask what is perhaps the more important question: how do you know these things? Again, try to come up with your own answers before reading on. Typically, for each of the questions the answers are as follows.

1) We know that the mords did it because *mords* follows the word *the* and comes at the beginning of the sentence.

2) We know there is more than one mord because the word ends with an *s*.

3) What the mords did was everything that follows them in the sentence, but if we have to pin it down to one word, that word would be *bordled* because of the *ed* ending.

4) We know it was done to a slom don because *slom don* is preceded by *a* and follows the action word in the sentence.

5) We know there is only one slom don because of the *a* and because there is no *s* at the end of don.

6) We know it was done slobly because of where the word comes and because of the *ly* ending.

7) We know it was done in the knox because *in* is a word that is usually followed by a place.

8) We don't know exactly when it was done, but the *ed* ending on *bordled* tells us that it was done sometime before it was written about.

9) We know that the don is slom because *slom* comes between *a* and *don*.

This is a very sophisticated grammatical knowledge and it comes to us, not because we remember reading about it somewhere in a book, but because we have consulted our own internal grammar. That internal consultation is very important to our enterprise, and it's very important that you learn to tap into it and trust it. We also need to take that process slowly and assimilate what we know into conscious patterns. In this case, we can divide our observations into three groups, three principal ways in which grammar communicates to us through physical clues: word order, changes in the form of a word (what grammarians call inflections) and the presence of grammatical or function words (like *a*, *the* and *in*).

There are three principal ways in which grammar communicates to us through physical clues: **word order**, changes in the form of words (**inflections**), and the presence of grammatical or **function words**.

2.1.1 *Word order*

Word order is tremendously important in English grammar. English is a language that has become heavily dependent on word order for grammatical meaning. If you doubt that, we need simply to change the order of the above sentence in slight ways to accomplish a significant difference in grammatical meaning:

A slom don slobly bordled the nox in the mords.

In this version, the actor has become *a slom don*, the receiver of the action has become *the nox* and the place where it happened is now *the mords*. A significant number of other changes are possible by simple shifts in word order. *Slobly*, for example, despite its *ly* ending, can just as easily relate to an actor as an action, as in *the slobly mords*. (Think of real words like *silly* or *sly*.) Even *bordled*, which seems clearly an action, can come to suggest a quality of a thing in a word group like *the bordled nox*. Clearly, word order is enormously important to the grammar and the meaning. English depends on it heavily.

2.1.2 *Inflections*

Changes in the form of a word for grammatical purposes, inflections, are also very important. These usually take the form of changes in word ending, but are not limited to this. *Mice*, for example, is a word we can recognize as a variation on *mouse*, *caught* is clearly a grammatical variation of *catch*, etc. Over the years, English has come to rely less and less on inflections and more on word order, but inflections are still a significant part of the meaning making system we call grammar.

2.1.3 *Function words*

Also extremely important are grammatical terms or function words, which seem to carry primarily grammatical meaning. In traditional grammars, these are often described as belonging to the structure classes (as opposed to nouns, verbs, adjectives and adverbs, which are thought of as members of the form classes. We will look closely at these in the next chapter.). Grammatical terms include words like *a* and *the* (determiners), auxiliary verbs like *is, do, have*; pronouns like *he* and *she* and *we*; conjunctions like *and, but, or*; prepositions like *in, out, beyond, after*; and finally qualifiers like *very* and *so* in word groups like *very kind* and *so sadly*. We will examine all these categories again, so don't worry about memorizing them here. The important point to understand now is that some words, partly because of their enormous familiarity, seem to carry out purposes that are more related to grammar than they are to vocabulary (what grammarians call the lexical meaning). To a native speaker, they are so familiar as to be almost invisible; they are words you can look up in a dictionary, but words that a native speaker would probably never find occasion to look up. Because they carry so much weight in the grammar, however, we will give them a great deal of attention throughout the book.

In summary, even when we don't know the meaning of many words in a statement, a great deal of grammatical meaning is available to us. For the most part, we are not consciously aware of that meaning, which comes to us not from having learned it in a book, but from our natural, internal grammar. Becoming aware of that grammar is very important to our enterprise. The most important ways in which grammar reveals itself to us through physical clues are word order, inflections, and grammatical or function words.

2.2.   Constituency

One way to define grammar is as the study of what happens when words come together to form meanings.

One way to define grammar is as the study of what happens when words come together to form meanings. When words come together, they don't simply add up their individual meanings, but establish relationships with each other and take on roles. Meaning cannot happen without that, and meaning shifts when the relationships shift among the words.

In the previous section, we examined a typical English sentence with made-up words in order to highlight its grammatical meaning. Now examine the following:

suitcase man the big the dog hit a with

In the above sequence of words, we do not have a grammatical sentence and, in fact, know less about its meaning than we do about *The mords slobly bordled a slom don in the nox* even though we now believe we know the meanings of all the words involved. This is, in fact, an example of what happens when a sentence is divided into individual words, those words are mixed up and then randomly selected. Word order is so important to building the grammar of a sentence that entrusting this to a process of random selection is almost inevitably going to leave us with nonsense. It's worth trying, because the chances of coming up with a meaningful arrangement by chance are slim. Yet all of us are capable of creating a meaningful arrangement out of these words; I have used them with a number of classes over the years, and no student that I am aware of has ever failed to do so. A meaningful arrangement of these words is also a grammatical arrangement. We don't know the meaning of these words until we know how to group them together and know what roles those word groups play in the larger structure (sentence or statement) that they are a part of.

We can, in fact, come up with a number of meaningful arrangements, though fewer occur when we feel constrained to come up with an arrangement that makes the most sense based upon what we know about the world. (Based on what we know about men, dogs, hitting, being big, and suitcases.) It is perfectly grammatical, for example, to say:

The suitcase hit the dog with a big man

but this is not an expected choice because it is more difficult to imagine it happening. Among the most usual sentences my classes have come up with are the following:

The man with a suitcase hit the big dog.
The man hit the big dog with a suitcase.
The big man hit the dog with a suitcase.
The man hit the dog with a big suitcase.
The man with a big suitcase hit the dog.

The funniest combination came from a student who first asked me if he could change the word endings:

The man suitcased the dog with a big hit.

There are a few reasons for the most common choices. The only action word seems to be *hit* and the most likely candidate to do the hitting is *man*. (If you substitute *bit* for *hit*, you'll see what I mean. The most likely candidate for carrying that out would be *dog*.) The word *big* seems to float fairly easily among *man*, *dog*, and *suitcase*. We recognize *big* as a quality, meaning something like large in size or better yet, larger than usual. (A big ant is much smaller than a little elephant.) We look around for something to assign *big* to – *suitcase*, *dog*, and *man* are the most likely candidates since they can come in different sizes. Traditionally, grammarians call words like *suitcase*, *dog,* and *man* nouns and a word like *big* an adjective. (We will examine these in more detail in the next chapter.) For a word like *big* to act like an adjective, it needs to find a noun to modify. We establish its constituency by placing it within a word group (like *the big man*) and describe its role (or function) when we say that it modifies *man*. Another way of saying that is that we don't know what *big* means in this sentence until we know what word or word it combines with and what role it takes on within that word group. *Big* will alter (or modify) our view of the man, suitcase, or dog when we assign it a meaningful place. Words like *hit* that convey an action, we call verbs and any word that typically modifies a verb (alters or changes our view of the action) is called an adverb. Adverbs are also traditionally used to designate words that typically modify an adjective or another adverb. Verbs are not always just action words, which we will explore in some detail in later chapters; but this idea will do for now. Typically, adverbs convey when, where, how, or why something is done. They can also tell us the conditions under which it happens or the extent or duration of its happening. In traditional grammar, adverbs include words that typically qualify or intensify, though we will place those words within another category (qualifiers).

When we ask what word or words a word hooks up with or combines with, we are asking about its constituency. When we do so, we are looking not just at the typical form class of the word, but at how it is functioning within a particular use. Constituency is a very important concept, and it's the main concern of this section. It's very important that we take time to explore it and get a solid working feel for it before we move on.

Words become part of word groups. A group of words that acts like a group is a constituent group. Constituency is not a careless or arbitrary classification, and it's not something imposed upon the language by grammarians, but something discovered or noticed. For this, it's important to remember our idea of an internal grammar, not only internal for you as a language user, but internal to the language itself as it is shared by other language users. It was there long before grammar books were made and will be there tomorrow even if every grammar book disappeared and all the grammarians were shipped off to Mars in spaceships. (The world would probably change less than you imagine.)

Let's examine two possible sentences from the string of words that started this section.

The man with a suitcase hit the big dog.
The man hit the big dog with a suitcase.

How are they different in structure? How are they different in meaning? Take your time with these questions and answer carefully before you read on.

You probably noticed that the constituent group *with a suitcase* has changed sentence position from sentence one to sentence two and that an important change in meaning comes with that change in structure. Most people would agree that the first sentence says that the man had a suitcase, but it doesn't say for sure what he hit the dog with. He may, for example, have been carrying the suitcase in one hand while hitting the dog with the other. The second sentence implies that the man actually hit the dog with a suitcase, that the suitcase was an instrument of the hitting.

It's also possible with the second sentence that the dog had the suitcase when the man hit him, though that seems less likely given what we know about dogs. When two or more meanings are possible with a single word arrangement, we call that ambiguity and say that the statement is ambiguous. Sometimes ambiguity is lexical – having to do with two or more possible meanings of a word – and sometimes grammatical, as it is here – having to do with two or more ways of assigning grammatical relationships. If we wanted to imply that the dog was carrying a suitcase, against our reader's expectations, we would likely use a word arrangement that was less ambiguous, as in *The man hit the dog that was carrying a suitcase*. But let's discard that possibility and consider these two sentences as having the meanings we most naturally assign them.

Ambiguity
When two or more meanings are possible with a single word arrangement, we call that ambiguity. Sometimes ambiguity is lexical, and sometimes grammatical.

What's important to note for our discussion of constituency is that we do not know what the constituent group *with a suitcase* means until we know what other words it combines with. In that sense, it's very much like the word *big* in our discussions above. Like *big*, it is a modifier. Either it acts like an adjective and modifies *the man* or it acts like an adverb and modifies the verb *hit*. (We say it is either adjectival or adverbial. These are terms that relate to the way a word or word group functions within a statement.)

A **prepositional phrase** typically consists of a preposition followed by a noun plus its modifiers. It is almost always adverbial or adjectival in function.

Those of you who know some grammar may recognize the constituent group *with a suitcase* as a prepositional phrase. A phrase is the first level of constituency above the level of the word; every word in a statement is part of a phrase, even if it's occasionally the only word within that phrase. Prepositional phrases typically consist of a preposition followed by a noun and its modifiers. A list of words that very commonly act as prepositions is included at the end of the chapter, in Section 2.7. (If the concept is new to you, you may want to look at the list now.) With very rare exception, prepositional phrases are always adjectival or adverbial. ('Prepositional phrase' describes its structure and 'adverbial' and 'adjectival' describe its role.) Even though they usually include nouns, they are not free to act like nouns. The role of the preposition, in fact, is to establish a relationship between the noun phrase in the prepositional phrase and some other word group, usually a noun phrase or verb phrase, in the sentence. It is only because we recognize that relationship, as ordinary language users, that we are able to process its meaning.

A **phrase** is a constituent group that does not rise to the level of clause.

A **clause** is a word group with a subject and predicate structure.

You may have noticed that I am using the word 'phrase' for the prepositional phrase as well as for the noun phrase contained within it. Shouldn't another classification be used for the larger group? A case could certainly be made for that, especially since some word groups (phrases) seem to act like expanded words and others seem to act like diminished clauses. (Clause is explained below.) We will simply follow the more conventional practice of using phrase to refer to constituent groups that do not rise to the level of a clause. A phrase is a group of words that acts like a group. It differs from a clause (also a constituent group) in that a clause has a subject and predicate structure, whereas a phrase does not. (We will cover subject and predicate in the next section.) A phrase can include other phrases and even, as we will see in later chapters, other clauses, but it may help to think of a clause as a larger group than a phrase or as higher up on the ladder of constituency. Again, every word in an English sentence belongs to a phrase, even if it is the only word in that phrase.

If we think of a constituent group as a meaningful arrangement, we can even extend the idea of constituency above and below the sentence. In the interest of a meaning-centered grammar, it is very useful to do this because it highlights a fundamental way in which the mind works in relation to language.

A word is a group of one or more sounds (or letters). Think of *I* or *a* as examples of single sound words. (I am using common language terms here rather than linguistic terms. A phoneme is the smallest unit of sound that language users recognize as distinct and a morpheme is the smallest combination of sounds that carries meaning, including grammatical meaning. The study of the sound system and the study of the combination of sound into words are called phonology and morphology respectively. Sounds, letters and words will do for our own purposes.)

A phrase is a group of one or more words. We call a single word a phrase when it acts just like a multiword group would in the same language slot, in other words, when it acts like a phrase.

A clause is a group of two or more phrases that carries (or implies) a subject and predicate. (There are examples of single phrase clauses, like the commands *shut up* or *leave*, but grammarians get around this by saying that the subject *you* is implied.)

A sentence is a group of one or more clauses. By using the word 'sentence', we are talking about writing and not speech. Speech certainly uses clauses and clause clusters, but the term 'sentence' is relevant to writing. A word group followed by a period that does not include both subject and predicate is looked down upon by traditional grammarians as a sentence fragment. For the first part of this course, we will limit ourselves to examining single clause sentences and look at the way these are constructed of phrases that are themselves made up of words.

A paragraph is a group of one or more sentences. (You may have been discouraged from writing single sentence paragraphs, but good writers do so when they have good reasons. There is certainly no rule against it, even in traditional grammar.)

A section (or chapter) is a group of one or more paragraphs.

A whole text (story, editorial, essay, report, plea bargain, whatever) is a group of one or more sections.

Constituent groups

A word is a group of one or more sounds.

A phrase is a group of one or more words.

A clause is a group of two or more phrases that carries a subject and predicate.

A sentence is a group of one or more clauses.

A paragraph is a group of one or more sentences.

A section is a group of one or more paragraphs.

A whole text is a group of one or more sections.

What one hopes for as a listener/reader at each of these levels is that the arrangement is not accidental or arbitrary, that the form and the meaning are intimately and purposefully connected. At the level of sound especially, but at the level of the grammar as well, many of these choices are made unconsciously with more awareness of meaning than of form, though a good writer will tell you that the ear never stops listening and making choices. And it may well be that different principles are involved in combining sounds into words than in combining words into sentences. Perhaps a good rule of thumb is that the larger the constituent group, the more conscious we are of the relationship between form and meaning. We simply could not use our language efficiently, perhaps not at all, if we had to construct the sound of each word consciously before we moved along. You may still remember how difficult it was to write back in kindergarten or first grade when the construction of each letter of each word was such a task, far more awkward than the smooth flow of words and the complex grammar you had already mastered when you talked.

In summary, then, a constituent group is a group of words that acts like a group. It is not arbitrarily or analytically imposed, but an inherent structure of language that we are noticing or observing.

Examples of constituent groups include phrases and clauses. A clause has a subject and predicate structure. A phrase may seem like an expanded word or a diminished clause; it's a term applied to word groups that do not rise to the level of a clause.

Words that typically modify nouns are called 'adjectives' and any word or word group functioning as a modifier of a noun is called 'adjectival'.

Words that typically modify verbs are called 'adverbs' and any word group functioning as a modifier of a verb is called 'adverbial'.

Prepositional phrases are made up of a preposition followed by a noun phrase. Like other modifiers, they need to combine with other word groups before we can assign their meaning. Most typically, they are either adjectival or adverbial.

Underline each prepositional phrase in the following sentences and tell whether each is adjectival or adverbial. Some sentences will have more than one.

1) *You are standing on my foot.*
2) *The man in the moon is a product of our imagination.*
3) *That idiot under the tree is my brother.*
4) *My idiot brother is sleeping under the tree.*
5) *She served the meal of my dreams with grace.*
6) *A bird in the hand is worth two [birds] in the bush.*
7) *He often reads in the chair by the window.*

The basic structure of a clause: subject and predicate 2.4

We will designate the two basic constituent groups within a clause as subject and predicate, following a pattern long used within traditional grammar. For those of you who have had some experience of grammar already, it should have the benefit of familiarity. This way of looking at a clause isolates an element (the subject) as something which has been chosen as the basis for a statement or proposition. The predicate is whatever is being said (predicated) about it. The single clause sentence

My family eats lots of sweet corn in the summer

for example, can be looked at as a statement about *my family* (the subject). What it says (predicates) about the subject is *eats lots of sweet corn in the summer*. For purposes of analysis, once you have isolated the subject, the predicate is whatever else is left over. This view of a clause as a logical proposition has some shortcomings which will be addressed later in the book. It's a good way of looking at a clause, though not a complete one. We will reexamine the idea of subject in Chapter 4.

Some linguists designate the two basic constituent groups within a clause as noun phrase and verb phrase (rather than subject and predicate). This is a very tempting analysis, because it highlights the fact that the verb dominates the predicate and that the very nature of the predicate is determined to a great extent by the kind of verb that it carries. We will deal with this in some detail in Chapter 6. From this view, the predicate consists of a verb phrase plus its complements and modifiers. (A complement is a necessary element, a word group that completes the meaning of the verb in some essential way. We will look closely at these in Chapter 6.) The verb phrase is at the heart of the predicate. When we call it *a* predicate, we are not describing its internal structure so much as its function in relation to the subject. We are taking a step back and looking at the role of this constituent group within the clause.

In order to see how subject and predicate work in practice, let's look again at the two sentences from the previous section.

The man with a suitcase hit the big dog

can be divided between a noun phrase (NP) subject, *The man with a suitcase*, followed by a predicate phrase (Pred P) *hit the big dog*. The subject phrase can be identified as the answer to the question 'What are you talking about?' (*The man with a suitcase*.) Which can be followed by another question, 'What are you saying (predicating) about him?' (A subject, of course, won't always be a he or even a person.) And that second question would likely be answered by '*He hit the big dog*.'

You may be wondering (since you're so smart and such an active reader) why we don't divide the sentence into three parts, as follows:

The man with the suitcase / hit / the big dog.

There are two basic reasons for this. One is that we can generate sentences like *The man with the suitcase laughed* (or *danced, fell, died, disappeared...* there are many others) that don't have anything past the verb phrase to constitute a third part. The fact that:

The man with a suitcase hit

does not seem grammatical or complete has much more to do with the VP *hit* than it does with the nature of the subject. The VP *hit* seems to require something to complete it (a complement), something to receive the action of the hitting. The particular kind of complement exemplified by *the big dog* is direct object, but don't worry about remembering that now. We will come back to it again in Chapter 6. For now, one important point to keep in mind for future reference is that the predicate phrase is dominated by its verb phrase.

If I asked you what is the most important word in the NP (noun phrase) subject, most people would say *man* simply because it's the one word that is indispensable to the sentence. We will call *man* the head of the noun phrase.

Head is a term we can use for other structures as well. In the NP *two very small children*, for example, there are two heads – *small* and *children* – because *very* qualifies *small* and *very small* modifies *children*. We can say that the NP *two very small children* is made up of an adjective (*two*), an adjective phrase (*very small*, itself made up of the qualifier *very* and the adjective *small*) and the head noun *children*.

The **head** of a phrase is grammatically the most important word in that phrase. The kind of phrase is determined by the head.

Constituency means that words group together. They do so at various levels. And within a constituent group, an element or elements will often be of greater grammatical importance and can be thought of as heading the group. These three principles – grouping, level and heading – are the core principles of constituency.

2.5

Section

Exercise

For each of the following sentences, underline each prepositional phrase and draw a slash (/) between subject and predicate. If there is more than one prepositional phrase in a sentence, assign each a number. Tell whether each prepositional phrase is adjectival or adverbial.

1) *The man with a suitcase hit the big dog.*
2) *The man hit the big dog with a suitcase.*
3) *You are standing on my foot.*
4) *The bruise on my foot is very sore.*
5) *Two very small children were playing near a busy street.*
6) *A boy with little money became a man of great wealth.*
7) *Sarah kept her diary in a locked box.*
8) *Two very important friends helped me in college.*
9) *The diary in the locked box is Sarah's (diary).*
10) *The locked box with the diary is Sarah's (box).*

2.6   Using tag questions

If you are having difficulty finding the subject of a sentence, a trick that usually works is to append a tag question at the end. *The man with a suitcase hit the dog, didn't he?* You can then ask yourself what the pronoun in the tag question (in this case *he*) refers to (*The man with a suitcase*). In *The dog was hit by a big suitcase, wasn't it?* the tag pronoun *it* would refer back to *The dog*. The reason why this works is revealing. The grammatical subject is a very important part of what makes a statement either a direct statement (presenting information) or a question (asking for information). The tag question is a useful way to draw on your internal grammar. It only works because you have been constructing subjects and predicates, statements and questions, including tag questions, for as long as you have been using the language.

2.7   Frequently occurring prepositions

The following words commonly act as prepositions. With very rare exception, prepositional phrases are always adjectival or adverbial.

about	*beside*	*near*	*unlike*	*inside of*
above	*besides*	*of*	*until*	*instead of*
across	*between*	*off*	*up*	*out of*
after	*beyond*	*on*	*upon*	*up to*
along	*by*	*onto*	*with*	*by means of*
against	*despite*	*over*	*within*	*by way of*
as	*down*	*since*	*without*	*in addition to*
amid	*during*	*through*	*across from*	*in front of*
around	*except*	*throughout*	*aside from*	*in order to*
at	*for*	*till*	*along with*	*in spite of*
before	*from*	*to*	*away from*	*on behalf of*
behind	*in*	*toward*	*because of*	*on top of*
below	*into*	*under*	*due to*	
beneath	*like*	*underneath*	*except for*	

For each of the sentences below, place a slash between subject and predicate. Underline each prepositional phrase, tell whether it is adjectival or adverbial, and tell what word group it modifies.

1) *His boss does everything by the book.*
2) *People with drug problems should seek counseling.*
3) *The big break for the home team came after half-time.*
4) *That tree by the river has been dying for some time.*
5) *He bought a book about basketball for his son.*
6) *The speeches after lunch will last for three hours.*
7) *A cat with fleas has an owner with a problem.*
8) *Her belief in herself carried her to success.*
9) *The students in the dorm often sleep until noon.*
10) *Members of the group will meet on the first Wednesday of each month.*
11) *The early part of the day is a good time for studying.*
12) *The quietest students often sit near the front of the class.*
13) *His deepest feelings were echoed in that song.*
14) *The key to her heart is kindness.*
15) *The quarterback always looked to the sidelines for the next play.*

Chapter 3
Section Exercises

Page 47
Draw phrase structure tree diagrams for noun phrases, verb phrases,
prepositional phrases and whole sentences.

Chapter Practice

Page 53
Draw phrase structure tree diagrams for sentences from Sir Arthur Conan Doyle's
The Hound of the Baskervilles.

Chapter 3

Elements of the simple clause

Later in the book, we will look closely at sentences that contain more than one clause. Our focus here, in this third chapter, will be to look at all the structures that can occur within a single (simple) clause. Another way of phrasing the opening questions would be What kinds of phrases (in addition to predicate phrases and prepositional phrases) are possible within a simple sentence? What kinds of words show up in those phrases? We will also practice phrase structure tree diagrams, a way of diagramming or showing these relationships. Being able to use these diagrams for single clause sentences is an outcome of the chapter, but it's also important to keep in mind that diagramming is not and should not be thought of as an end in itself. It is a way of articulating or showing our understanding of the language we are examining.

What kinds of phrases are possible within a simple sentence? What kinds of words show up in those phrases?

Certain kinds of phrases will seem like an expanded word (an expansion of the head word of the phrase). And so one way of determining the kinds of phrases possible is to ask ourselves which words are capable of expansion. The quick answer would be the kinds of words often thought of as members of the four form classes: nouns, verbs, adjectives, and adverbs. Other kinds of words (often called the structure classes) can be thought of as expanders, fulfilling subsidiary (largely grammatical) roles. The form class word groups can be thought of as very open to new members; new nouns and verbs and adjectives and adverbs are being added to the language all the time. The structure groups (including auxiliary verbs, pronouns, prepositions, determiners, and qualifiers) are much more closed; it's not that their membership doesn't change, but that it doesn't change quickly, often, or easily. These words are so familiar to us that we are barely conscious of their presence in a sentence. They add considerable, largely grammatical meaning, but do so below the level of our conscious attention. Since we are exploring the grammar of the language, it is worth slowing things down and spending considerable time bringing their meanings into conscious attention.

Four form classes
nouns
verbs
adjectives
adverbs

Consider the following four word sentence, which includes a word from each of the open (form class) words. (We will look at these groups in more detail later on, so don't be overly concerned about being able to name them here.) *People often feel confused.* Using our Chapter 2 analysis, we can certainly say that the sentence includes a subject (*people*) and a predicate (*often feel confused*) and has no prepositional phrases. What evidence do we have that it includes other phrases as well? The most compelling evidence is that each of these words is capable of expansion.

Young people very often can feel highly confused. We now have a noun phrase (*young people*), an adverb phrase (*very often*), a verb phrase (*can feel*), and an adjective phrase (*highly confused*). Those phrases were, in fact, present in the shorter version, though as single word phrases. A phrase structure diagram for both versions would be as follows:

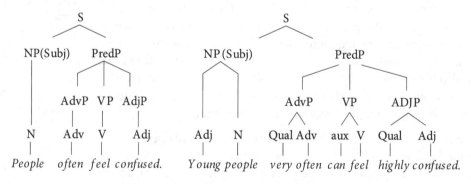

Just above the words are abbreviations for the individual words: N (noun), Adv (adverb), V (verb), Adj (adjective), Qual (qualifier), and Aux (auxiliary verb). At the next level, we begin to see ways in which the words combine together into phrases; the abbreviations here are phrase abbreviations: NP (noun phrase), AdvP (adverb phrase), VP (verb phrase), and AdjP (adjective phrase). The Subj abbreviation (in parentheses) is a description of function; it also helps us to divide our simple sentence into two important parts, the subject and predicate. Notice that the subject is a simple noun phrase (that won't always be the case) and that the predicate phrase has three phrases within it. The places where the word groups come together are called nodes. S (for sentence) is the highest node of the diagram because it includes everything.

The elements of noun phrases   3.2

In looking at how to diagram noun phrases, we are also exploring ways to understand them. Again, the understanding is more important than the diagramming, which is only one way to express that understanding.

Elements that frequently occur as part of a noun phrase are nouns, pronouns, determiners, adjectives, adjective phrases, and, as we have seen already, prepositional phrases that follow the head noun as adjectival modifiers. Later in the book, we will explore other word groups that can fill that after the noun (postnominal) adjectival role, but this will be more than enough to get us started and to understand the nature of noun phrases in a sophisticated way.

> Elements that frequently occur as part of a noun phrase are nouns, pronouns, determiners, adjectives, adjective phrases, and prepositional phrases that follow the head noun as adjectival modifiers.

3.2.1 *Nouns*

If I ask you what you currently understand about nouns, you might tell me that a noun is 'a person, place, or thing.' This is all right as a starting point, but doesn't explain a great many nouns that seem more like concepts, words like *courage, justice, peace, destruction*, or *organization*. It does tend to explain what grammarians usually call 'proper nouns', nouns that give unique names to a particular person, place, and, in our increasingly brand-name age, things. *Samuel Smith* is a proper noun; despite the fact that we may find several Samuel Smiths listed in the phone book, we have the sense that the two words name a particular person. *The Empire State Building* is a proper noun, as are the *Hudson River* and *Quaker Oatmeal*.

> **Proper nouns** give unique names to particular persons, places, or things.

A great many nouns fall into the class of common nouns, which don't designate things so much as groups or classes of things: words like *cow, animal, tree, banana, fruit*, and *baseball*. Some of these are more general (and abstract) than others, meaning they represent larger classes. *Thing*

> **Common nouns** designate something as a member of a group.

is more general than *machine*, which is more general than *car*, which is more general than *sedan* and so on. One reason why level of abstraction is important is that a great many modifiers of nouns, including the determiners, serve to help us narrow down or restrict the noun rather than just give us additional information about some thing that has already been identified. It helps to see that a noun is as much an idea as a thing, a way of classifying the world, of dividing the 'things' of this world, including 'things' we can't physically touch or see, into meaningful categories.

A noun is as much an idea as a thing, a way of classifying the world into meaningful categories.

Nouns are also often divided into count nouns and non-count nouns. Count nouns can be made plural and can be modified by numbers. We can have *a cow*, *many cows*, *two cows*, etc. Non-count nouns seem more like concepts than categories of things; if they are things, they are only so in an abstract and metaphoric way. (There are exceptions to this, non-count nouns like *rice* or *milk* that can only be counted in units, like *a pound of rice* or *gallons of milk*.) We can't have *two courages* or *many peaces*, though we can have *much courage* or *extensive peace*, not just because *two courages* and *many peaces* are ungrammatical (which they are), but because we understand *courage* and *peace* as concepts that cannot be counted. (We can, of course, talk about *two acts of courage* or *many periods of peace* because we understand *acts* and *periods* as concepts that can be finitely numbered.)

Count nouns
Count nouns can be made plural and can be modified by numbers.

3.2.2 *Pronouns*

Nouns are an unlimited (open or form) class: that is to say, a group of words that can be and is being added to all the time, just as older members of the group can fall out of use. Pronouns, on the other hand, are a limited (closed or structure) class, a small number of words that are not likely to change or be added to.

Pronouns
are a limited (closed or structure) class, a small number of words that are not likely to change or be added to.

You may already think of pronouns as words that take the place of or stand in for a noun and that is an acceptable definition to start with, one that we will expand on in the next chapter, though there are indefinite pronouns, like *anybody* or *somebody*, that are hard to explain in that way. The idea of standing in for a noun is certainly true of the personal pronouns: *I, you, she, he, it, we,* and *they.* These are generally classified by person and number, a classification that will be very useful when we explore verb endings in Chapter 5. Each of these personal pronouns also has variations to show possession (possessive pronouns) or when used as object of a preposition or verb (often called objective case). The following chart lays that out.

			possessive		objective	
person	singular	plural	singular	plural	singular	plural
1st	I	we	my	our	me	us
2nd	you	you	your	your	you	you
3rd	she	they	her	their	her	them
3rd	he	they	his	their	him	them
3rd	it	they	its	their	it	them

There are also demonstrative pronouns (*this, that, these,* and *those*), which we will discuss again, along with possessive pronouns, as determiners; and interrogative pronouns, which we use to ask questions like *who is going?* or *what will you do?*; relative pronouns (usually *who, which,* or *that*), which we will explore later when we explore relative clauses; and reflexive pronouns, like *myself* or *himself,* which often show up in a predicate phrase as a way of standing in for the subject, but in a predicate phrase role (*I saw myself* or *John hurt himself*).

Because they are so familiar and because they generally stand in for a meaning that is already given (established), we can think of pronouns as basically grammatical in meaning. If I say *Pete is a friend of mine; I have known him since second grade,* a reader or listener barely notices the *I* or *him* in the second sentence. They are there to fill grammatical slots so that the new information (...*known* ...*since second grade*) can be added on. We will revisit these concepts in the next chapter.

Pronouns
can be described as follows:

personal
possessive
demonstrative
interrogative
relative
reflexive

When standing as the single word head of a noun phrase, we give pronouns the abbreviation *Pro.*

```
                 S
              ___|___
      NP(Subj)        Pred P
         |            __|__
         |          ·VP    NP
         |           |      |
        Pro          V     Pro
         |           |      |
         I          like   him
```

In this sentence, *I* and *him* are not only pronouns, but single word NPs.

3.2.3   *Determiners*

Determiners help us designate or understand or determine which member of the noun class we are talking about.

If we think of nouns as designating classes rather than things, we can begin to understand the role of determiners in a noun phrase. They help us designate or understand or determine which member of the noun class we are talking about. Since adjectives also take on that role, it can be difficult to draw a clear line between determiners and adjectives in a noun phrase. One help in analysis is that various kinds of determiners, adjectives, and noun modifiers all have set slots in the noun phrase.

A (and its variant *an,* used when the following word begins with a vowel sound) and *the* are determiners. They are also called 'articles', with *a* being an indefinite article and *the* being a definite article. If you are a native speaker, you use these freely and naturally, though they can seem absolutely baffling to someone whose first language (like Mandarin or Cantonese) doesn't have them.

A is always singular. In general, it designates a member of a class when the member has not been identified or differentiated yet, as in *I sat down next to a girl. The* can be singular or plural and means, in general, the member of the class that you and I both know I am talking about. Consider how awkward the following two sentences seem: *I sat down next to a girl. A girl spoke to me.* In the second sentence, we expect *the girl* (to designate that it's the same girl mentioned in the first sentence) or *another girl* (to designate that it's not). Though *a* is always singular, we don't generally use it for proper nouns, since they imply a class with only one element in it. (We don't usually say *an Empire State Building* or *a Hudson River* because that would imply that there are more than one.)

The class of determiners that fills the same slot filled by *a* and *the* also includes the *demonstrative pronouns: this, that, these,* and *those. This* tends to designate something you are holding or something you are close to. *That* tends to designate something you are pointing to or something you have some distance from. Closeness or distance can also be an expression of attitude, as in *This proposal is a great one, but that proposal is flawed. These* is plural for *this* and *those* is plural for *that.*

This group (words that fill this slot) also includes the possessive personal pronouns we discussed above: *my, our, your, his, her, its,* and *their.* Again, the role of a determiner is to narrow down or determine which member of a class we are talking about. *Don't just give me a book; give me my book*. This slot, as you might be beginning to suspect, can also be filled by any possessive noun. *Give me Paul's book.*

The determiners we have described so far can be thought of as primary determiners. Determiners that would come before primary determiners in the noun phrase are sometimes called 'predeterminers' and words that come after the primary determiners are often called 'postdeterminers'. Words in the predeterminer group are basically quantifying in function. They can occur without the primary determiners, as in *all friends* or *both brothers*. These words tend in some way to quantify the head noun; they tend to tell us how many members of the group (from *none* to *all*) are being included.

When these words are followed by *of*, as in *each of the boys* or *many of my friends*, words like *each* and *many* are better understood as pronouns and as the principal head of the noun phrase, with *of the boys* and *of my friends* (in these examples) now functioning as adjectival prepositional phrases. One reason for doing so is that the verb agrees with these pronouns rather than with the noun phrase that follows the *of*. The notion of agreement will be clearer when we look closely at subject/verb agreement in Chapter 5. In common practice, though, we would say *Each of the boys plays a different instrument* (where *plays* takes its cue from the singular *each*) and *The boys play different instruments* (where *play* takes its cue from the plural *boys*). To further complicate the problem, *of* is sometimes explicitly rendered and sometimes not. (*All the boys were here. All of the boys were here.*) In other words, these words sometimes act like the pronoun head of the noun phrase and sometimes act like part of the determiner system.

Numbers are pretty much frozen in position in a noun phrase, coming after any of the primary determiners but before any of the freer adjectives. Of these, the *ordinal numbers* (*first, second... ninth ...thirty-eighth*, etc. and including *next* and *last*) come first and the cardinal (regular) numbers (*one, two ...nine ...thirty-eight*, etc.) come next. One reason for including both within the determiner system is that they are frozen in position within the noun phrase, ahead of the other (sometimes called 'movable' or 'coordinate') adjectives. These can also move to the head of the noun phrase as pronouns, as with the predeterminers above. *The first of twelve songs. The second of his three wives. The last of his obsessions.* (In terms of pronoun or verb agreement, all three would be thought of as singular.)

By now, it should be clear that determiners can pile up in a noun phrase, as in *all my brother's first attempts*. In this case, *my* is a determiner in the noun phrase *my brother's*, which is itself a determiner in the whole noun phrase (*my* modifies *brother's* and *my brother's* modifies *attempts*), but that level of analysis is something that we may sometimes wish to avoid. If there are two or more words working together as determiner in a noun phrase, it would be fine for our purposes to diagram them as a single unit, using a triangle in the diagram, as follows:

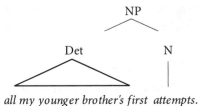

all my younger brother's first attempts.

Here's an example of a sentence with a noun phrase subject that includes all of the above types of determiners in their natural sequence. *All the first seven applicants were female. All* is predeterminer, *the* is primary determiner, *first* is ordinal numeral postdeterminer and *seven* is a regular number postdeterminer. Again, we can triangle them out in our diagrams, which would look like the following.

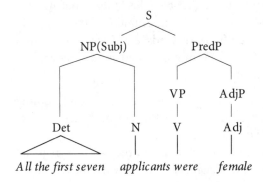

All the first seven   applicants were   female

Determiners are a kind of adjective and the line between them gets very fuzzy at the margins, particularly when adjectives are acting like determiners, acting to restrict down the meaning of a noun so that we can tell which member of a class is being referred to. Consider, for example, *the blue house on the corner* in the sentence *Deliver this to the blue house on the corner.* The only true determiners in that sentence are the two *thes*, though the adjective *blue* and the adjectival prepositional phrase *on the corner* are clearly acting to help us understand which house out of many possible houses should be delivered to. The classification of adjectives and adjectival structures as restrictive or non-restrictive is a very important one and we will come back to it a number of times during the book.

3.2.4 *Adjectives*

In diagramming adjectives, we diagram them differently when they act as single word adjectives in a noun phrase than we do when they act as adjective phrases on their own (or as adjective phrases within a noun phrase structure). These three possibilities are shown below.

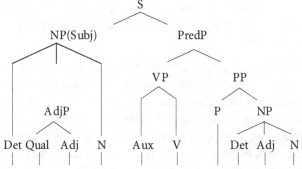

Two very small children were playing near a busy street.

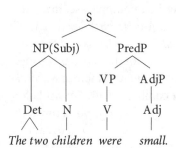

The two children were small.

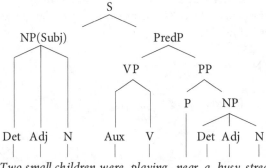

Two small children were playing near a busy street.

In the first sentence, *very small* is treated as an adjective phrase because *very* qualifies *small* and *very small* acts as a unit in modifying *children*. In the second sentence, *small* is treated as a single word adjective phrase because it acts independently as a complement of the verb *were*. In the third sentence, *small* is treated as a single word adjective in the noun phrase *two small children*.

3.3   Nouns as modifiers: compound nouns

Words often function in ways we would not predict solely from their form classes. Nouns, for example, can function as modifiers.

It may surprise you that nouns can act as adjectives, but English gives us that kind of flexibility quite often. Here, we are making a distinction between the form class that a word seems to belong to when we consider it in isolation and the function that it serves in a particular group of words when actually used.

The language, in fact, has a great many noun plus noun combinations that act like a single word and are conventionally written that way: words like *stairway*, *doghouse*, and *birdbath*. The conventions for writing these as one word and not two can seem terribly arbitrary. (I'm always looking them up myself because I lack confidence in my memory. Why should *clambake* be one word, but not *clam chowder*? Why should *citystate* be one word but not *city council*?)

At any rate, when nouns pile up together in a noun phrase, they often combine in complex and interesting ways. *A prize birthday cake* is not the same as *a birthday prize cake*. *A road hazard sign* is not the same as *a hazard road sign*. *The town speed limit* is not the same as *the speed town limit*. All of this indicates to us that *birthday* combines with *cake* before it is modified by *prize*, that *road* combines with *hazard* before that two word combination modifies *sign* and so on. Sometimes the structure will be inherently ambiguous. Is *a small animal hospital* a small hospital for animals or is it a hospital for small animals? When we find it important, we can make that kind of careful constituency analysis. If not, we can simplify the process through the use of a single triangle, as with the noun phrases below.

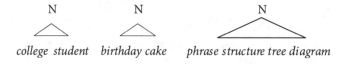

N   N   N

college student   birthday cake   *phrase structure tree diagram*

If we are unsure whether a modifier is a noun modifier, we can use some form of the verb *to be* between the terms and reverse their order as a test. It seems terribly awkward to say *This student is college* or *This cake is birthday* or *This diagram is phrase structure tree* or *This structure tree diagram is phrase*. For regular adjectives, the test will give you a sentence that seems fine. In *The small children*, *small* is clearly a separate adjective because it seems fine to say *The children are small*.

Verb phrases   3.4

When diagramming verb phrases, the diagram should include all the auxiliary verbs, but not any verb phrase internal adverbs, which often occur as interrupters of the verb phrase elements. The exception to this will be *not*, which we will call an *adverb*, as traditional grammar does, but understand as a very special adverb, changing the polarity of the verb phrase from positive to negative. It's presence in the verb phrase is not simply an interruption, and placing it elsewhere would radically change the meaning. For now, we will simply use the abbreviation *Aux* to designate an auxiliary and postpone explaining those auxiliaries until Chapters 4 and 5. The following are examples of what typical verb phrase diagrams would look like. Again, don't worry about how the various auxiliary verbs function. We will spend some time on that in Chapter 4.

Not is a special adverb which changes polarity from positive to negative.

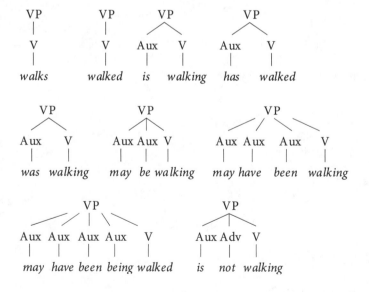

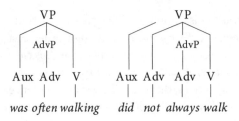

3.5   Adverb phrases

Adverb phrases are among the most moveable of all phrases.

Adverb phrases are not always bound up within a verb phrase. They are, in fact, among the most movable of all phrases. *She was entering the room very quietly. Very quietly, she was entering the room. She was very quietly entering the room. She was entering, very quietly, the room.*

The following two sentences include diagrams for two word and single word adverb phrases.

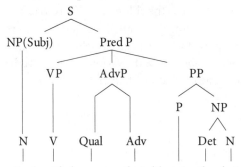

*Paul settled **very comfortably** into the chair.*

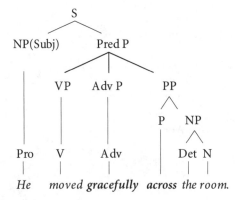

*He moved **gracefully** across the room.*

The most common element in an adverb phrase (other than the head element) is a qualifier of some sort, often a word that intensifies or diminishes an adverb or adjective. *So cool. So quickly. Slightly bald. Very swiftly. Highly suspect.* Traditional grammar calls these adverbs (any word that modifies a verb, adjective, or other adverb). 'Qualifier' seems a term more suited to the word's function. It's worth noting here, though, that an adverb can modify an adjective without being a qualifier, as in phrases like *quietly confident* or *wisely silent.*

Qualifiers generally intensify or diminish an adverb or adjective.

Prepositional phrases   3.6

A prepositional phrase is simply a preposition plus noun phrase, so once you know how to diagram a noun phrase, prepositional phrases by themselves don't constitute a much greater level of difficulty. When they appear in a sentence, though, they can be adjectival or adverbial (you may have had some difficulty with this in Chapter 2) and it can be difficult to understand exactly where to draw the phrase structure tree lines from prepositional phrase nodes in a diagram.

Consider the following two sentences, which are quite different in their constituency, though that difference is not readily apparent from the way they appear on the page.

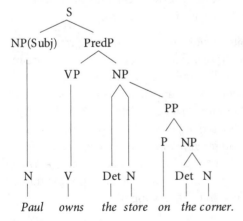

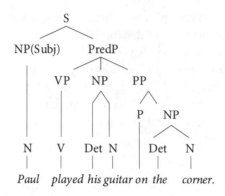

In the first sentence, *on the corner* is an adjectival modifier of *the store*. The phrase structure lines are drawn in such a way as to show that relationship. In the second sentence, *on the corner* is an adverbial modifier of the VP *played*; by convention, its constituency line is drawn directly to the predicate phrase, meaning it is being designated as a modifier of the verb. The only way to come to those decisions is to step back and consider the meaning of the whole sentence. You have to draw on your internal grammar. In the first sentence, *on the corner* tells us about the store. (It is *a corner store*, not *a corner owning*.) In the second sentence, *on the corner* tells us about the playing, about where the playing took place. (It's not *a corner guitar*, but it is *a corner playing*.) If you're having trouble with that, think of the prepositional phrase as the answer to a hypothetical question. (What store does he own? The store on the corner. Where did he play the guitar? He played on the corner.)

Since prepositional phrases often modify noun phrases and prepositional phrases include noun phrases, it seems logical that the noun phrase in a prepositional phrase can also be modified by another prepositional phrase in series. In fact, this does often happen, and there is no limit to the number of prepositional phrases that can be strung along like that. (There's a popular children's book that plays with prepositional phrase sequences in that way: *a bird in a nest in a branch of a tree in a hole in the ground...* Even young children have that grammar available.) When this happens, the whole noun phrase becomes the object of the initial preposition. It gets diagrammed in the following way:

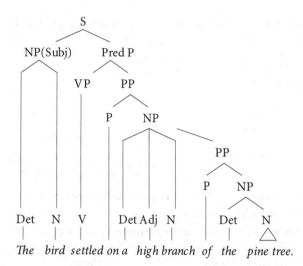

The bird settled on a high branch of the pine tree.

3.7
Section
Exercise

Draw phrase structure tree diagrams for the following:

1) Noun phrases: *They, a dog, a green frog*
2) Verb phrases: *listens, has listened, will not listen*
3) Prepositional phrases: *over the wall, a piece of cake in the back of the closet*
4) Whole sentences: *He ate the big birthday cake with two hands. He changed his tone very quickly.*

A special problem in constituency: particle verbs 3.8

In English, verbs often draw in words that are usually prepositions to become, in effect, part of the verb phrase. We call these verb particles. The resultant combinations are often called phrasal verbs. If you're not alert when diagramming, it is easy to mistake them for prepositions.

Sometimes the boundary between them becomes fuzzy. Consider the following sentence pairs. In one, the underlined word is a verb particle;

Phrasal verbs
In English, verbs often draw in prepositions to become part of the verb phrase. We call these verb particles. The resultant combinations are often called phrasal verbs.

in the other, the same underlined word is a preposition. Can you tell which is which? Try it on your own before you read on.

Before climbing, the hikers looked <u>up</u> the hill.
We looked <u>up</u> the word in our dictionary.

The skater turned <u>on</u> the ice.
My brother turned <u>on</u> the light.

He tried to point <u>out</u> the window.
He tried to point <u>out</u> our problems.

In each case, the first sentence includes an underlined preposition and the second sentence includes an underlined particle. A good test for it (not always foolproof) is to see if the preposition or particle can be moved past a noun phrase that follows it. If it can, the word is definitely a particle. If it can't, it's probably not.

We looked the word up in our dictionary.
My brother turned the light on.
He tried to point our problems out.

Each of these sentences passes the movability test. Phrasal verbs that fail the movability test include *look for* and *look into*. *He looked for a way out. He looked into the problem last week.* I would call these phrasal verbs solely on the basis of a strong feeling that they act together as verbs. *Looking for* seems like seeking. *Looking into* seems like investigating. One good way to help solidify your understanding of these phrasal verbs is to look at the verb entries for common verbs in a good dictionary. You will find many listed and defined.

A verb particle should be diagrammed as follows:

VP
/\
V   Prt
We looked up the word in our dictionary.

Because you have read this far in the book, you have picked up an enormous amount of grammar in a very short time. I encourage you to begin looking at real world sentences, including your own, in this analytical way. But you will find very quickly when you do so that a good deal of what you find will still be confusing. The sentences in this chapter have been carefully controlled to allow you to build a comfort level with certain core concepts before moving on. One way they have been controlled (and you'll find this out very quickly if you examine sentences somewhere else) is that none of the constituent structures have been compound. Our NP subjects, for example, have all been single NPs, whereas real world sentences will frequently have more than one NP as subject. (*Mom and Dad will be there.*) We will deal with compounding in some detail later in the book, but the phenomenon is so common that it makes sense to at least introduce the concept early.

As a general rule of thumb, any constituent group and any member of a constituent group can be compounded. When analyzing and diagramming, you need to be careful about which elements are being joined.

When elements are compounded, they are equal in status. They also join together to form a single constituent within the larger clause they take part in. The sentence above can serve as an illustration:

Compound structures contain joined elements that are equal in status. they form a single constituent within a larger clause.

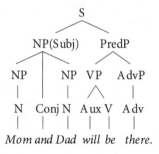

In this sentence, we have a NP (*Mom*) and a NP (*Dad*) that combine together to form the NP *Mom and Dad*. The same can be true for verb phrases, predicate phrases, prepositions, objects of prepositions, verb phrase auxiliaries – again, pretty much any sentence element can be compounded. Here are a few examples that can begin to suggest the range of possibilities. In each case, compound elements are underlined.

He threw the ball and *broke the window*.
Compound predicate phrase sharing the NP subject *He*

They went over, under and *around the fence*.
Compound prepositions, sharing the object of preposition *the fence*.

He often impresses or *irritates his listeners*.
Compound verb phrase, sharing the complement *his listeners*.

The police searched through the cabinets and *the closets*.
Compound NP as object of preposition *through*.

Each of these sentences is diagrammed below.

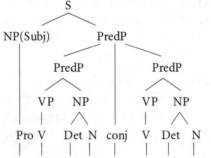

He threw the ball and broke the window.

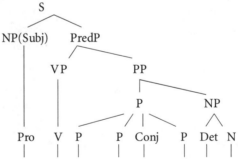

They went over, under, and around the fence.

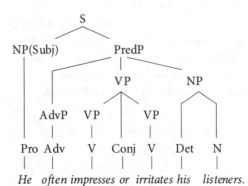

He often impresses or irritates his listeners.

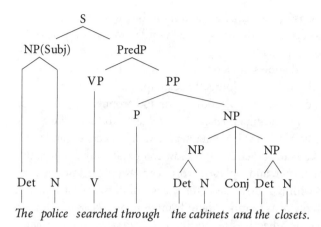

The police searched through the cabinets and the closets.

Form, structure and function 3.10

If nouns, verbs, adjectives, and adverbs carry most of the meaning in a clause, why do we call them members of form classes and not members of meaning classes? The answer can help us understand differing approaches to grammar and help us make important distinctions between membership in a word group, participation within a constituent group, and function.

You may have been given meaning based (semantic) definitions for words like 'noun' (a word that names a person, place, or thing) or 'verb' (a word that expresses action or a state of being) when you were in school. Chances are, you were also given functional definitions for words like 'adjective' (a word that modifies a noun) and 'adverb' (a word that modifies a verb, adjective, or other adverb). If your experience is typical, you were expected to know (learn) the 'parts of speech' with somewhat unclear definitions and explanations. If you were good at it, it may very well have been a result of close attention to your own internal grammar.

The problem is that these definitions tend to break down in application in ways that you are probably already able to describe. If a noun is a person, place, or thing and a verb expresses action, how do we classify words like *wrestling* or *contemplation*? If an adjective is a quality held by a person, place, or thing, how do we account for words like *honesty, courage,* or *talent,* none of which seem to have existence apart from living beings? If something becomes an adjective by virtue of modifying a noun, how do we deal with modifiers in phrases like *college student* or *stone wall*?

The term form class grew out of an attempt to be more scientific, more accurate in classifying words into groups. Words can generally be ruled into these groups on the basis of passing certain form tests. One kind of test is if the word allows inflections (changes in the form of the word for grammatical purposes). Nouns, for example, and only nouns, can be made plural or possessive by adding *s* or apostrophe. Regular verbs can change tense by adding an *ed* ending and all verbs can take an *ing* ending for progressive aspect (see Chapter 5). Many adjectives (and some adverbs) can take *er* and *est* endings to show comparative and superlative meanings (*high*, *higher*, and *highest*). Words can also sometimes be confidently placed within a form class on the basis of derivational suffixes, endings added to words to move them from one form class to another. Nouns can become adjectives by adding *ous* (*courageous*, *outrageous*, etc.). Adjectives can become nouns by adding *ness* (*happiness*, *lightness*, etc.). A third way words can be tested for form class is to see if they can co-occur with certain words, like some determiners (*a* and *the*) and auxiliary verbs (like *is*, *have*, and *do*). Occasionally, a word will seem to resist passing any of these form tests, and we can fall back on common sense (our own internal grammar).

> Nouns, verbs and adjectives can often take new endings. The words may move into new form classes as a result.

When we say that a word is a noun, we say that it belongs to the form class noun. If it appears in a sentence, it may be the head of a noun phrase, which is one of many structures (constituent groups) that typically appear in a clause. If we say that the noun phrase is acting as subject, object of preposition, or the like, we are making an observation about the function of the phrase within a particular use. We have seen already that a noun can also modify a noun, that it can be adjectival in function.

> **Form class** designates the potential of a word.
>
> **Function** describes how it is acting within a particular text.

You may have started this book believing that words are parts of speech which find their way into sentences. Now you are adjusting to the notion that words participate within phrases and clauses and often function in somewhat unpredictable ways. In the words of M. A. K. Halliday, from his *Introduction to Functional Grammar*:

> Class labels are, so to speak, part of the dictionary; they indicate the potential that the word, or other item, has in the grammar of the language. Function labels are an interpretation of the text; they indicate the part that the idea is playing in the particular situation under consideration (27).

Structural grammar seems to me primarily interested in the classification of words and often seems to consult practice as a way of fine-tuning the classification. In that sense, it is much like traditional biology, with a functional or meaning based grammar being more like an ecology, a greater concern with how elements interact in practice. From the perspective of a writer, for example, interested in the production of meaning and not the production of forms, the interest is in the resources available to carry out certain purposes. The perspective we take will often govern what we find and what we determine to be important. If we look at sentences in isolation from each other and in isolation from the speaker or writer's purposes, much will be missed. We will continue that important discussion in the next chapter.

3.11

Chapter Practice

Draw phrase structure tree diagrams for the following sentences from Sir Arthur Conan Doyle's *The Hound of the Baskervilles*.

1) *I could read his fears upon his wicked face.*
2) *The light beneath him was reflected in his small, cunning eyes.*
3) *We rushed over the brow of the hill.*
4) *A lucky, long shot of my revolver might have crippled him.*
5) *He might have been the very spirit of that terrible place.*
6) *It came with the wind through the silence of the night.*
7) *The night air was heavy with the smell of damp and decay.*
8) *The light still burned steadily in front.*
9) *A boulder of granite concealed our approach.*
10) *We had heard the creak of a step in the passage.*

Additional practice sentences:

1) *Your name came up during our recent discussion.*
2) *Hard work and determination will get you through college.*
3) *Two fine proposals were made during our first meeting.*
4) *One man's drink is another man's poison.*
5) *The college students at the graduation dinner were very tired but very proud.*
6) *We ran all the way to our house.*

Chapter 4
Section Exercises

Page 65
Identify theme, grammatical subject and actor in given sentences; make
transitive sentences passive by using a three step transformation process.

Page 66
Study of *I Have a Dream* by Martin Luther King, Jr. Questions on how grammar and
meaning work together: questions on emphasis, themes and marked themes,
given and new elements, and the use of repetition.

Page 78
Identify finite and lexical verbs; rewrite sentences as questions.

Chapter Practice

Page 73
Identify theme, grammatical subject and actor in given sentences; draw phrase
structure diagrams of sentences with marked themes; make sentences passive
using a three step transformation process.

Chapter 4

Context based meaning in a sentence

I frequently ask beginning college students what they understand about grammar. The most common 'understanding' of sentence is somehow connected to the idea of a 'complete thought,' an idea I began arguing against in Chapter 1. In this traditional or 'common sense' view, a sentence is a group of words that expresses a complete thought. Even though this view of the sentence has some practical use (in trying to cure beginning writers from the accidental use of sentence fragments), it is also fundamentally inaccurate and misleading in important ways.

Another frequent commandment that you may have been exposed to is that a writer should not repeat words or meanings. A text, in other words, an article or paper or essay, should consist of a string of complete thoughts that are all new, unrepeated statements.

Taken together, these two commandments, to write complete thoughts and not repeat them, can make an ordinary writing assignment seem enormously intimidating. If you are being asked to write, say, 1,500 words on a subject (about five typed pages, depending on the margins and font size), you may imagine you are being asked to produce, say, 100 sentences (about 15 words per sentence), each saying something complete and separate from the rest. You may feel, very rightly, that you do not have 100 things to say about the subject, and the essay now becomes a daunting task in somehow not running out of things to say. You may even try to avoid writing about the subject right away for fear of running short once you do, a practice I call 'coming down from the clouds.'

A practiced writer, on the other hand, may feel that 1,500 words is very little and look for significant ways to cut the subject down so that it can be covered meaningfully in such a short space. A practiced writer is likely to feel that he/she should find one or two significant things to say about the subject, using a succession of sentences to bring that significance home. (He or she will also be open to new ideas or changes in thinking, knowing new drafts can be shaped to accommodate this evolving understanding.) His or her idea of a sentence, in other words, will be very different from the common sense view of the unpracticed writer unduly influenced by traditional writing instruction and traditional grammar. The experienced writer is likely to come at the subject directly and cultivate a considerable carry over of words and meaning as the essay or paper progresses. Whatever the complete thought (or unified perspective) is that this writer wants to present, the reader will clearly benefit from having it portioned out in much smaller units, within various paragraphs and sentences, with considerable overlap between them. In revising the sentences, the writer may do considerable shifting of sentence boundaries. These sentences will not be ends in themselves or judged solely on the basis of their individual, isolated completeness. They will be shaped to work in harmony with other sentences toward the realization of higher purposes.

Cohesion in writing requires considerable carry over of meaning.

In place of the traditional, common sense misunderstanding of the sentence as a complete and isolated thought, we can substitute the following propositions:

A sentence is not a complete thought.
A sentence is a move in a series of related moves.
Sentence boundaries are very flexible.
A sentence does not exist in isolation from other sentences.
A sentence does not exist in isolation from larger purposes.
Sentences can vary widely in the amount of content they contain.
Sentences can vary widely in the way their content is organized.

One way to examine the rightness of a sentence is to measure it against norms of grammaticality or correctness. If it is grammatical, it is a sentence that a native speaker would be likely to say. (Someone just learning the language, a child or someone not native to the country, might formulate sentences that are ungrammatical in this way: *My plants growed; We saw two cow.*) If it is 'correct', then it conforms to certain shifting standards of correctness, some useful, but some strangely arbitrary and impractical, asserted by handbooks and traditional grammarians. In this chapter, however, we will be exploring ways in which sentences function effectively in the creation of extended meaning. If the content of a sentence can be arranged in varying ways, all of which are both grammatical and correct, how would a writer choose among those varying versions? How can an understanding of grammar help us produce writing that is meaningful and effective and not simply grammatical or correct?

If we look at how grammar functions within rhetorical context (in real world writing), we end up with a very different understanding. Again, we should not revise sentences as if they are isolated, self-contained thoughts. We want our sentences to work in harmony with other sentences, and we want these sentences to work together in the realization of complex purposes, purposes which may or may not be fully clear to the writer at various stages of the writing process, purposes which change and evolve as the writing itself changes and evolves.

> Effective sentences work in harmony with other sentences and in harmony with the purposes of the writer.

Three kinds of repetition   4.2

Perhaps a good rule of thumb is that successful writers do not avoid repetition, but cultivate it and exploit it. It would be silly, of course, to say that good writing simply repeats itself over and over again. As the writing moves forward, the expectation is that sentences will add something new. If the writing is to remain coherent, though, if it is to hold together in any kind of meaningful way, it will also carry something already given from previous sentences in the text. The repetition of content, the 'given' in a sentence, may escape our attention as we attend to what the writer wants us to attend to. Much repetition is invisible to the eye, but no less valuable because of that. Without a carry over of meaning (the given in a new statement), coherent discourse is impossible.

> Without a carry over of meaning, the **given** in a new statement, coherent discourse is impossible.

To bring that point across, I sometimes give my students two sentences like the following and ask them what they think the next sentence might be. You might want to look at the two sentences and think about the question before you read on.

The price of bananas has risen recently. My mother was born in Canada.

I'm usually amused by the dialogue of the students, who sometimes get angry at me once they realize they are being set up. They always spend time trying to establish connection between the two sentences in order to anticipate what might come in the third. Perhaps bananas are even more expensive in Canada? Perhaps it's important that both bananas and my mother are imports? They offer sentences like *My mother never ate bananas until she came to the United States.* I have never had anyone in a class offer the suggestion that the next sentence should be just as unrelated as the first two, something like *The Unabomber shouldn't be given the death penalty.* That two consecutive sentences should relate in some way is something we have grown so used to that we take it for granted, generally assuming that when the connection isn't immediately apparent, there is something wrong with us as readers or the writer has made some sort of error or the connection will be made apparent later on.

Coherence is built through interweaving given and new, continuing and expanding meaning almost simultaneously.

A more typical pattern would be something like the following: *I gave my mother a graduation gift. It was a big surprise. I graduated on time.* Here we have three sentences that build a meaning together. After the first sentence, a reader would not be surprised to see *I*, *she*, or *it* in the grammatical subject slot for the following sentence or sentences. This pattern of given and new is very common. *Graduated* echoes *graduation* from the third sentence to the first. Coherence is built through an interweaving of the given and the new, a continuation of meaning and an expansion of meaning almost simultaneously.

Quite often, the given in a sentence will be carried out through pronouns. We can think of pronouns as taking the place of a noun (person, place, or thing), but that is misleading in some ways. It's certainly better to think of the pronoun as standing in for all the meaning in its antecedent noun phrase, but when meaning begins to build, the pronoun stands in for a more complex meaning as well.

Consider the following two sentence sequence.

When I was a junior in high school, a young girl helped me believe I could be attractive. She was two years younger.

The *she* in sentence two is given, *two years younger* adding additional information. It stands in here, though, not just for 'young girl', but for everything we have learned about her, something like 'the girl who made me feel I could be attractive.' If we add a third sentence opening with *she*,

she will then stand in for *the girl two years younger than me who made me feel I could be attractive. She looked up to me in the way girls often do to older guys they barely know.* Something new is certainly being added here, but something old is also carried over. These are not complete thoughts (independent of each other), but moves in a series of related moves, a portioning out of (a building of) a connected meaning. Without the given, without a carry over of meaning, the sequence won't cohere.

When repetition carries over a given meaning from one sentence to another, the words themselves become almost invisible. They are more grammatical than lexical in their meaning, acting almost like place-holders. At other times, repetition will have the opposite effect, with a repeated word emphasizing meaning and calling lots of attention to itself. Thus in *government of the people, by the people and for the people*, we have *people* occurring three times when it's only needed once. (*Government of, by, and for the people.*) Was Lincoln being inefficient and wordy? Or was he telling us, by the form of his words as well as their content, that people are most important? In this case, *people* is not so much a given as emphatically expressed content. We can call it lexical repetition. What we want from a writer is a compatibility between form and purpose; we want repetition of words to lead us to the heart of the message, to emphasize and unify.

Another kind of repetition is grammatical repetition, the repetition of grammatical structures. …*of the people, by the people and for the people* is a good example, not only repeating words (*the* and *people*), but repeating the structure of preposition, determiner and noun phrase. We can find countless examples in poems and songs, in part because the repetition of these structures is pleasing to the ear. They also aid in the processing of meaning. We will find them in commercials, in public speeches, in the words of our best orators. *Give me liberty or give me death*, not *give me liberty or I want death.*

The following example is a sentence from E. B. White about the circus in an essay called *The Ring Of Time*:

> *Out of its wild disorder comes order; from its rank smell rises the good aroma of courage and daring; out of its preliminary shabbiness comes the final splendor.*

In this three clause sequence, all three kinds of repetition are being used here to great effect. The pronoun *it* keeps the circus (given) in focus. All

Repetition

'Carry over' repetition reinforces core meaning.

Lexical repetition adds emphasis.

Grammatical repetition can be found in the chorus parts of songs and as a rhetorical device in speech making. It pleases the ear and aids in the processing of meaning.

three begin with prepositional phrases followed by verb phrases, and the same verb phrase (*comes*) is repeated in the first and third clauses. *Out of* is given twice. In all three, you may have noticed, the subject follows the verb phrase (a highly unusual, highly marked structure). In all three, there is movement from negative to positive, from *disorder* to *order*, from *smell* to *aroma*, from *shabbiness* to *splendor*. None of these fine repetitions would be worth much, though, if they didn't move the meaning forward in a harmonious way. You need to look at their place within the whole paragraph and the whole essay to fully appreciate their effectiveness.

4.3　Clause ending emphasis (tonic prominence)

Tonic prominence, an intonation based message structure emphasis, usually falls on the last constituent group within a clause.

One major place of message structure emphasis in a clause is the end, the final element. This is a borrowing from the tone group structure of speech, where the final element is the unmarked place for the rise or fall in pitch that signals importance. In speech, we can vary that, but in writing, unless we use the boldface capabilities of our word processors, we cannot. I'll give you a few quick examples to help bring that home.

Suppose someone asks you, *Have you seen the new Star Trek movie?* You may very well answer *Yes, I have seen it twice* with *yes* and *twice* being placed in the natural slots for message structure emphasis, the beginning and the end. You would not be likely to say *Yes, twice I have seen it* because *I have seen it* is given information. It adds nothing new, and the clause ending position of emphasis is generally reserved for new information.

Or consider the following as two possible sentences in a letter of recommendation from one of your teachers. Which would you rather have in the letter? Why?

Her writing was always excellent, but usually late.
Her writing was usually late, but always excellent.

Most people would prefer the second sentence because it seems to present excellence as a primary message. The first seems more a message about lateness. Yet nothing has changed about the sentence except the placement of the contrasting elements. Whatever comes at the end seems to gather emphasis and importance.

Emphasis can be added to middle of the clause elements, sometimes by varying the normal order of the sentence, generally in conjunction with the placement of commas (which govern, not so much pauses, as waves of attention). We will be giving more attention to that in later chapters of the book.

Subject functions   4.4

When we use language, we don't simply do so to create grammatical structures, but we do so to carry out purposes (however vague those purposes may be when we begin). Classical rhetoric and functional grammar give us a similar breakdown of those purposes, a breakdown very useful for us here in our study of language, and that breakdown of purpose was mentioned in Chapter 1: language is a message, an interaction, and a representation. We can look at a written text, for example, in terms of the message the writer is trying to express (or in terms of what is expressed unconsciously). We can look at it as an interaction with an audience (or even with many different audiences); and we can examine ways in which the text is a structure that represents the larger world. Even if this analysis is never carried down to the level of the grammar, it is a very useful way to look at your own writing or someone else's writing. It's important to recognize that language conveys different kinds of meaning and that it conveys those meanings simultaneously.

> We can look at the meaning of a text as a message, interaction, and representation.

These rhetorical purposes may be easier to understand if we think in terms of a particular (hypothetical) text, for example a job letter. You may concentrate in a job letter in conveying the message that you are interested in a job and are highly qualified; you may be careful in creating a tone of quiet confidence and enthusiasm. The letter is clearly an interaction, because you dearly hope that your audience on the other end will actually do something (hire you) as a result, and you may spend considerable time wondering about who will read it and how they will think and feel as they read it through. And you will no doubt spend some time as you write trying to represent a world (carefully selected references to that world) in which you have already accomplished and experienced important and relevant things; perhaps you will even spend time representing an imagined future world in which you will do useful things for the organization. All this time, you will be constructing noun phrases and verb phrases and clauses and sentences, though you may not be at all aware of that. Those are means to an end and not the end in itself, and the success of the letter will reside, not in isolated words or phrases or even sentences, but in how well they all work together to accomplish your larger purposes.

To further the process of seeing how rhetoric gets built into the grammar, we will reexamine the idea of subject that we began in Chapter 2 and think in terms of subject functions. In functional grammar, each of the three kinds of meanings we have described above – message, interaction, and representation – is woven into the structure of a clause. Rather than a single subject function within a clause, we have three – theme, grammatical subject, and actor (we will expand the term later) – to correspond with message structure (theme), interaction or exchange (grammatical subject), and representation (actor and other terms we will add in Chapter 6).

The idea of subject we established in Chapter 2 is very traditional. It's a little hard to pin down – we'll look at it in more detail later in this chapter – but it's the idea of a subject you may have been exposed to early in grade school, and it's the idea of a subject that you will find in a traditional handbook. We will call it 'grammatical subject' in this chapter, but when the term subject is used later in the book, it will be this traditional notion of subject that it refers to. It's important to keep in mind that a grammatical subject is part of a clause structure and requires a predicate to be a subject. *The man with a suitcase* is not a subject by itself, but in *The man with a suitcase hit the big dog*, it takes on a subject role. As grammatical subject, it is a word group, typically a noun phrase and typically the first word group in a clause, about which something is being predicated.

Grammatical subject requires a predicate to be a subject. It is a word group about which something is being predicated.

If you found yourself somewhat adept at recognizing grammatical subjects by the end of Chapter 2, that is largely because the concept isn't new to you; you have been using subjects that way all your speaking life. You and I therefore share an understanding that is hard to explain or define.

To more fully understand the idea of three subject functions, let's look closely at a sentence quite like those we explored in some detail in previous chapters.

A drunk driver killed my dog the day before Christmas.

We can begin by analyzing the sentence as we did in Chapter 3, using a phrase structure tree diagram to help us along.

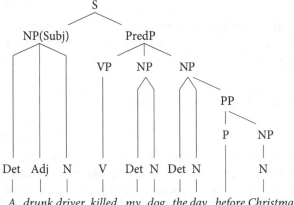

A drunk driver killed my dog the day before Christmas.

The sentence consists of a NP subject, including a determiner (*A*), adjective (*drunk*), and a head noun (*driver*). It has a single word verb phrase (*killed*) heading the predicate. The verb phrase is followed by a NP, including a determiner (*my*) and a head noun (*dog*). This is followed by another noun phrase, including a determiner (*the*), a head noun (*day*), and an adjectival prepositional phrase (*before Christmas*). It's a fairly straightforward sentence, much like the sentences we looked at closely in Chapter 3.

In this particular version of the sentence, *A drunk driver* is not just grammatical subject, but also theme and actor.

Theme is a starting-off point or stepping-off point for the message structure, and it is always realized in an English clause by coming first. It's important to understand that theme is not defined by being first, but recognized and realized in that way. Coming first is just one way, in English, that a constituent group is given a message structure emphasis. When the word group that constitutes the theme is also grammatical subject and actor, we say that it is an unmarked theme (apart from questions about whether or not it is given information). It's a sort of normal or default selection and doesn't generate as much attention or emphasis. A marked theme, on the other hand, since it's a change in the usual order, does draw attention and emphasis.

In this sentence, *A drunk driver* is not just theme and grammatical subject, but also actor. In a material process clause (more on that in Chapter

Theme is a starting-off point or stepping-off point for the message structure, and it is always realized in an English clause by coming first.

6), actor can be identified as the answer to the question *Who did it?* The clause represents an action or happening in the world, and the actor has a role in that event.

When two or more functions are combined within the same word group, as they are here, we say that the functions are 'conflated'. This is a term we will use in other places as well.

If we simply change around the order of the word groups, as we did in Chapter 2, we can shift the actor role:

> *My dog killed a drunk driver the day before Christmas.*

Theme, grammatical subject, and actor can be carried out by the same word group (conflated). When a word group other than grammatical subject opens a clause, it is a **marked theme**.

But the imaginary person who generated this sentence is not likely to be comfortable with that change because the language now represents the happening in a way that may not seem accurate. 'No, no,' we can imagine him saying: 'It didn't happen that way. The drunk driver did it. My dog was the victim.' But English does give us a way of focusing on the dog without altering the representational meaning:

> *My dog was killed by a drunk driver the day before Christmas.*

This allows us to construct a sentence which still represents the same event, but directs our attention differently. When this happens, there is a three part transformation:

1) The receiver of the action is moved into the grammatical subject slot. (This can only happen if a receiver of the action is already present. We will cover this in more detail in Chapter 6. This can only happen in a transitive sentence; the change is a change from active to passive.)

2) Some form of the verb *to be* is added to the verb phrase. (In this case, *killed* becomes *was killed*.)

3) The actor is moved into the predicate phrase and preceded by the preposition *by*. In this new sentence, *My dog* has become grammatical subject and theme, but *a drunk driver* remains the actor. (It is still the doer of the action even if it is no longer the starting point for the message structure or the constituent group about which something is being predicated.) It's also possible to leave the actor out: *My dog was killed the day before Christmas.*

Not every constituent group can open an English sentence. Consider, for example, the following, which is clearly ungrammatical: *Killed my dog a drunken driver the day before Christmas.* But adverbial structures tend to be very movable, and our adverbial noun phrase *the day before Christmas* can easily move into thematic (clause opening) position for either of the two sentences (active and passive) that we have already generated.

The day before Christmas, a drunk driver killed my dog.

In this sentence, *The day before Christmas* has become theme and *a drunk driver* is grammatical subject and actor.

The day before Christmas, my dog was killed by a drunk driver.

In this version, the three subject functions are fully separate. *The day before Christmas* is marked theme. *My dog* is grammatical subject. And *a drunk driver* is actor.

As a good rule of thumb, pretty much any element of a statement can be made the thematic (or message structure focus) of another statement, though that may require a change in structure. As you can see from the following examples, the grammatical subject can also become very complex.

Who was the driver that killed your dog?
The driver that killed my dog was a stranger.
How did having your dog die in this way make you feel?
My dog being killed just before Christmas by a drunk driver made me feel terrible.

This flexibility is enormously important to a writer trying to write a connected and coherent text.

I. Identify theme, grammatical subject, and actor for each of the following sentences:

1) *A truck smashed our oak tree during the big blizzard.*
2) *Our oak tree was smashed by a truck during the big blizzard.*
3) *During the big blizzard, our oak tree was smashed by a truck.*

II. Make the following transitive sentences passive by using the three step transformation process described above.

1) *Paul owns the store on the corner.*
2) *That song echoes my deepest feelings.*
3) *Our cat caught three mice in one day.*

4.6

Section

Exercise

The following are the two opening paragraphs to Martin Luther King, Jr.'s famous *I Have a Dream* speech, given in Washington, DC in 1963. The sentences have been numbered for convenience.

> 1) *Five score years ago, a great American, in whose symbolic shadow we stand, signed the Emancipation Proclamation. 2) His momentous decree came as a great beacon light of hope to millions of Negro slaves who had been seared in the flames of withering injustice. 3) It came as a joyous daybreak to end the long night of captivity.*
>
> 4) *But one hundred years later, we must face the tragic fact that the Negro is still not free. 5) One hundred years later, the life of the Negro is still sadly crippled by the manacles of segregation and the chains of discrimination. 6) One hundred years later, the Negro lives on a lonely island of poverty in the midst of a vast ocean of material prosperity. 7) One hundred years later, the Negro is still languishing in the corners of American society and finds himself an exile in his own land. 8) So we have come here today to dramatize an appalling condition.*

Read these paragraphs aloud and listen to how they sound. Are they easy to listen to? Why? Think about the meaning. To answer the questions you will need to consider how grammar and meaning work together.

1) Look at the last constituent group for each of the sentences. Do they all end on material that deserves a natural emphasis? Explain.

2) We could think of the first paragraph as a thematic stepping-off point for the whole speech. Is it an effective way to begin?

3) There are marked themes (something other than grammatical subject) in sentences one (*five score years ago*) and four through seven (*One hundred years later* repeated). Are they effective? Why?

4) Why does the second paragraph begin with *But*? Why does the last sentence begin with *so*?

5) Sentence five is passive. Theme, grammatical subject, and actor are separated elements. *The life of the Negro* is grammatical subject and *the manacles of segregation and the chains of discrimination* is actor (compound). Within the context of the whole paragraph, is that effective? Explain.

6) What are the given elements in each sentence and which elements are new? For each, do they tend to come at the beginning or end? Why?

7)   What do you see as the most important or most effective repetitions? (Look for grammatical patterns as well as lexical terms.) Is repetition more important in a speech than in a written text? Why?

There are no 'correct' answers to these questions; they are designed to encourage your critical thinking.

Clause as interaction   4.7

Language, of course, is not merely a message, but an exchange or interaction with a listener or reader or with listeners or readers. We use language to offer and request information or request goods and services, to plead or order, to inform, move, entertain, or persuade, for interactive purposes too numerous to include, often more than one at once. For now, we will focus on key concepts, from how grammatical subject is related to the notion of exchange, to the kinds of interactive meaning carried out in a clause.

Grammatical subject and finite verb together form the mood element because variations in their arrangement are what determine the mood of a sentence, whether declarative (a statement), interrogative (a question), or imperative (a command). *Open the window*, an imperative statement, has *You* as an understood subject. It's also possible (and I think useful) to think of *must* as part of what is understood. (*You must open the window.*) Imperatives seem to me very close to the modal category of obligation. (We will cover modal auxiliaries later in the chapter.) Another mood, the subjunctive, has to do with conditional statements, with statements about situations that are hypothetical or wished for. *If I were President, I would feed the hungry*. Compare this to *If I am President, I will feed the hungry*, which makes it sound as if you are an actual candidate.

Mood element
Variations in the arrangement of the grammatical subject and finite verb form the mood of a sentence.

When a statement is a statement in written English, it almost always follows a subject/verb order, even when the grammatical subject is preceded by other thematic elements.

The child slept quietly in her crib.
In her crib, the child slept quietly.

In both cases, *the child* is grammatical subject and *slept* is the verb phrase. In the second sentence, *In her crib* has become theme, but that does not effect the usual subject/verb order.

In speech, we have two ways of making a word group a question, one having to do with sound and the other having to do with word order. When writing, we use word order and punctuation (a period or question mark).

In speech, we make a yes/no question a question by raising the pitch of our voice at the end. (For pitch, think of a musical scale. The note is higher.) We make a statement a statement (or command) by lowering the pitch at the end. In both cases, the voice rises in volume (it gets louder). The rise in volume usually comes on new information, on what we want to emphasize, most often at the end. (In writing, without a voice to guide us into alternative choices, it comes at the end, its usual place, by default.) Thus, *You will be there tomorrow* can be expressed in its usual way as command, with higher volume and lower pitch on the stressed syllable of *tomorrow*, or it can be made into a question simply by raising the pitch at the end. (In writing, we can use a question mark. *You will be there tomorrow?*) In general, a raised pitch denotes uncertainty and doubt, a lowered pitch its opposite – certainty and confidence. A speaker, who can vary both pitch and volume, has more control over emphasis.

Tone is the overall emotive quality of the language, with feelings and attitudes expressed by the author and/or evoked in a listener or reader.

Another term we should talk about here is tone, which has to do with the overall emotive quality of the language: the feelings and attitudes expressed as well as feelings and attitudes evoked in a listener or reader. (There's no certainty a reader will share the attitudes and feelings.) Pitch and volume are one way that tone is built, but tone can be built in other ways as well – for example through the connotations of (feelings and attitudes associated with) the words we choose. Technically speaking, tone is not simply an aspect of the grammar, but it is an aspect of meaning that grammar works in harmony with as a writer achieves unity of purpose. Again, we want to be careful not to look at grammar in isolation.

The other way a word group becomes a question in both speech and writing is through inverting the order of grammatical subject and finite verb. (This is true for yes/no questions, questions that can be easily answered with a simple yes or no. Other questions, called Wh- questions, also invert grammatical subject and finite verb, but also add a term like *where, when,* or *what* to give additional focus to the question. They call for specific information rather than a simple yes or no in response. The Wh- element gives a thematic focus to the kind of information asked for.)

The **finite** element in a verb phrase grounds the statement in time and/or attitude and helps give a statement a propositional status.

The finite is the part of the verb that carries tense (and sometimes modality). If there are auxiliaries to the verb, the finite auxiliary is always first. The lexical verb, the word we would look up in the dictionary if we wanted to know the verb's vocabulary meaning, always comes last. In simple present tense or simple past tense (more on that in the next chapter), finite and lexical verbs are conflated (combined together in a single word). In order to form a question, though, they have to be separated out so that the finite verb can float to the head of the clause and leave the lexical verb behind. The following are examples.

She is walking.
is is finite, *walking* is lexical.

Is she walking?
subject and finite verb reversed in order.

She walks.
walks is both finite and lexical.

Does she walk? Is she walking?
Finite and lexical verbs are split in order to carry out the question transformation. Notice that the *s* gets dropped from *walks*. It no longer carries tense.

The same patterns hold true for past tense.

She was walking.
statement.

Was she walking?
question.

She walked.
statement, with finite and lexical conflated.

Did she walk?
Again, finite and lexical separate, with the finite moving into clause opening position. The *-ed* ending is dropped from *walked* because the tense function has shifted to the auxiliary.

Modal auxiliaries carry the form of tense and generally do convey some sense of time in context within a whole clause, but strictly speaking, they function more as conveyors of attitude and judgment. They include *may, can, will, shall, should, would, could, might, must,* and occasionally two word combinations like *ought to.* They convey a speaker's attitude or judgment about possibility, probability, desirability, or obligation.

> **Modal auxiliaries** help convey a writer or speaker's attitude or judgement about possibility, probability, desirability, ability, opportunity, or obligation.

She can go to Paris.
She is able to go.

She may go to Paris.
She has permission to go or her going is a possibility.

She should go to Paris.
It is desirable for her to go.

She must go to Paris.
She is obligated to go.

She will go to Paris.
It seems certain to happen.

Modal auxiliaries may appear to be present and past tense forms of each other (*will/would, shall/should, may/might, can/could*), but they don't act like that in practice (with the exception, perhaps, of *can* and *could* when used to mean something like *be able*). To say *I shall go* rather than *I should go* is not to take the same lexical meaning and simply change the time reference. Both seem like present time (time of the speaking) expressions of attitude. *Shall* implies that the speaker is committed to going. *Should* simply says that the speaker feels an obligation. The verbs seem to have floated free of each other in terms of their lexical meanings and seem to have floated somewhat free of the usual meanings of tense. *Must* is the past tense form of a word that has disappeared from the historical record. Because it conveys a sense of deep obligation, it often gives a time of the telling attitude about future happenings.

> In many ways, modal auxiliaries seem to have floated free from what we normally think of as tense.

One invariable rule in English is that modals cannot be followed by a verb or auxiliary that carries normal tense, as in *She must walked* or *She could was walking*. This is because tense and modality are two ways of filling the same slot in the verb phrase and two ways of fulfilling the same function, which is to make a clause something you can agree with or disagree with. The tenses simply assert the historical happening of an event, somewhat qualified in relation to time in ways we explore further in Chapter 5. The modals qualify a statement in terms of the speaker's attitude. They posit levels of certainty, desirability, or obligation.

Like the tense carrying auxiliaries, modals are the auxiliaries that float to the head of a clause when we want to ask a yes/no question.

She must walk home.
statement.

Must she walk home?
question.

With statement or question, we can agree or disagree by amending the statement or answering a simple yes or no.

In addition to the modal auxiliaries, a speaker or writer has available adverbial phrases that can act like modal adjuncts. These would include words like *possibly, certainly, hopefully, perhaps,* and *maybe* that can be thought of as sentence adverbials rather than simply verb phrase modifiers because they tend to qualify the whole statement. It is not just a statement about the world, but a statement qualified by a writer's level of confidence in the truth of the statement or the likelihood of something happening. Words like *sometimes, always, often, never,* though generally not sentence modifiers, can be thought of as acting in asserting attitudes about likelihood, desirability, and obligation. (*He sometimes cheats. You should always brush after eating. It is often better to avoid a harsh truth.*) Other phrases that would mitigate a statement in these ways would include phrases like *It is possible* or *I suspect* or *It may be* or *I have come to believe.*

Finite auxiliaries, in combination with the grammatical subject, are essential elements in making a statement a full proposition or in asking a question. This notion is very much what traditional grammar has in mind when it says that a sentence must be a complete thought. A word group like *students studying well into the morning hours for finals* doesn't seem like a complete thought because it lacks a finite verb. *Were studying well into the morning hours for finals* doesn't seem like a complete thought because it lacks a grammatical subject. Including a grammatical subject and finite verb gives a sense of completeness: *Students were studying well into the morning hours for finals.* Or *It's not good practice to stay up late before an important test.* We feel like we understand the perspective of the writer and how he or she wants us to view things. We feel like we can answer *yes* or *no,* in whole or in part.

A clause that contains a finite verb phrase is called a finite clause. Later in the book, we will look closely at non-finite clauses. We will also look closely at finite clauses that do not convey a sense of complete thought. These are called finite subordinate clauses. Here is an example: *Because students were studying well into the morning hours for finals.* It has a grammatical subject (*students*) and a finite verb phrase (*were studying*). Why is it not an arguable proposition?

As a writing teacher, I can't resist adding the admonition that a good writer should show, not tell. Writing teachers across the country are probably saying that in harmony with me right now, and that is because beginning writers tend to think in terms of expressive meaning and not enough in terms of the interactive. Quite often it's the detail of a text that engages the reader, provoking thoughts and feelings, not just expressing them. Expressing your own thoughts and feelings is no guarantee that your reader will share them or even care about them. Again, we want our understanding of grammar to harmonize with larger purposes.

It may be that traditional grammar overemphasizes the exchange function in its idea of a sentence, just as writing in school perhaps overemphasizes thesis writing (an argument structure) at the expense of other purposes. We will return to these questions in our chapter on punctuation.

4.8

Section Exercise

I. In the following sentences, underline the finite verbs and circle the lexical verbs. If both are conflated in the same word, circle the word and write 'both' above it.

1) *The baby slept quietly in her crib.*
2) *The baby can sleep through a great deal of noise.*
3) *She was sleeping through a great deal of noise.*
4) *She should be sleeping already.*

II. Rewrite each of the above sentences as questions.

4.9   Diagramming marked themes

A predicate phrase constituent group can be given thematic emphasis by being moved to the front of a clause. Unless the element is being promoted to grammatical subject (as we do with passive constructions), the element will retain its predicate phrase constituency. In other words, an adverbial predicate phrase modifier will stay an adverbial predicate phrase modifier even though it has been moved to the front of the clause. When that happens, you should diagram it out as follows:

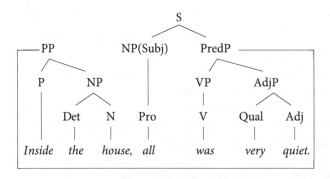

A lengthy line has been drawn from the highest node of the prepositional phrase (adverbial modifier) *Inside the house* all the way around to the PredP node of the diagram. This diagram allows us to describe constituency (*Inside the house* as an adverbial modifier of VP *was*) while keeping message structure order intact. It should be clear from the diagram that *Inside the house* is given a special emphasis by being moved out of its routine position. The AdjP *very quiet* has also been given additional emphasis by being placed in clause ending position.

4.10
Chapter
Practice

I. Identify theme, grammatical subject and actor in these sentences:

1) *The children often swap sandwiches during lunch.*
2) *During lunch, the children often swap sandwiches.*
3) *Sandwiches are often swapped by the children during lunch.*
4) *I was warned about that teacher by several students in my dorm.*
5) *Several students in my dorm warned me about that teacher.*
6) *About that teacher, I was warned by several students in my dorm.*

II. Draw phrase structure diagrams for sentences 2 and 6 above.

III. Make the following sentences passive using the three step transformation process.

1) *The jazz singer sang an old blues song.*
2) *A volunteer crew cleaned up the campus before Parents' Weekend.*
3) *Paul provided much needed information about the subject.*

IV. In the following sentences, underline finite verbs and circle lexical verbs. If both are combined within a single word, circle the word and write *both* above it.

1) *Our train will be leaving at three o'clock.*
2) *His careful planning left little to chance.*
3) *Everything possible is going wrong.*
4) *Did someone in this class borrow your book?*
5) *My grandfather walked four miles to school.*

Chapter 5
Section Exercises

Page 86
Give past tense forms for given verbs; tell whether each verb is regular or irregular; analyse sentences from *Proverbs of Hell*, from *The Marriage of Heaven and Hell* by William Blake, for tense (or modality), subject/verb agreement, and aspect.

Chapter Practice

Page 87
Examine sentences from Louise Erdrich's *Love Medicine* and Annie Dillard's *Pilgrim at Tinker Creek* and *A Writing Life* in terms of tense or modality, subject/verb agreement, and aspect.

Chapter 5

A closer look at verb phrases

A typical English verb has four forms (irregular verbs may have as few as three and as many as five) and combines, in addition to the modal auxiliaries, with the principle auxiliaries formed from the verbs *be*, *have*, and *do*, sometimes in sequence with each other. If you're a native speaker, you probably use these forms quite easily, with only occasional trouble, but understanding them and analyzing them might seem, at first glance, like a hopelessly complex task. Why, you might wonder, does the system have to be so complicated? Perhaps the best answer is that, with the exception of the presence of irregular verbs, which we owe more to patterns of change in the history of the language than we do to function, the system is no more complex than it needs to be to form and convey important nuances of meaning. A simpler system would limit what we are able to understand and say.

If English is not your native language, the complexity of verb forms may be an area of great difficulty, not just for analysis, but for everyday use. Over years of working as a writing teacher with students like yourself, I have come to find that a functional approach is very effective. If we keep our attention on function, a formal understanding will fall into place. You want to create, after all, not just correct forms, but clear and thoughtful meanings.

We will be aided in this process by one invariable rule in verb phrase formation in English: no more than one grammatical function can be carried out within a single term. English adds auxiliaries in order to add grammatical functions. We saw, in the last chapter, that in the verb phrase of a declarative statement, the finite verb always comes first and lexical verb always comes last. This predictable orderliness also carries through in verb phrases of greater complexity. We can start with the simplest forms and then see how additional meaning is built in.

The most important functions we will cover are tense and aspect. These are accomplished, often in combination, through changes in the form (inflections) of the lexical verb and the addition of auxiliaries.

Verb forms
We can identify 5 verb forms: infinitive, third person singular present tense, past tense, present participle, and past participle

A typical verb has four forms and a few have as few as three or as many as five. (The verb *to be* has eight, a particularly radical exception.) It's probably easiest to think in terms of five forms, each with different roles, with the understanding that for most verbs two of those forms are identical. These forms are the infinitive, sometimes called the 'base form' or 'plain form' (*walk*); a form for third person singular, present tense, formed in almost all cases by adding *s* to the base form (*walks*); past tense form, formed for regular (weak) verbs by adding *ed* to the end of the base form (*walked*) and formed for most irregular (strong) verbs by a change in the internal vowels; the present participle form, formed in all cases by adding *ing* to the base form (sometimes the final consonant is doubled, as in *cutting* or *controlling*) (*walking*); and the past participle form, which is identical to past tense in the vast majority of cases (*walked*).

A **regular** verb forms past tense by adding -ed to its base form. **Irregular** verbs form past tense through some other pattern, generally a change in internal vowels.

When we classify verbs as regular or irregular, as many traditional grammars do, we are highlighting the structure of the verb. Regular verbs follow a more recently developed pattern. When we classify the same verbs as weak (for regular) or strong (for irregular), as some linguists do, we are highlighting a pattern of historical change. The vast majority of English verbs are regular, but it might not seem that way because irregular verbs are used so frequently. It is, in fact, that frequency of use (and the age of the verbs) that accounts for their irregularity. Because of frequent use, these strong verbs have held on to the older way of doing things, essentially forming the past tense by more radical and less predictable changes in the word. Thus *break* becomes *broke*, *catch* becomes *caught*, *strike* becomes *struck*, etc. A few strong verbs, like *hit* and *cut*, do not change at all from present to past tense forms. We will follow the pattern of calling these verbs regular and irregular, though weak or strong are useful terms as well.

Basic forms for a prototypical regular verb (*walk*) and three types of irregular verbs (*cut*, *catch*, and *break*) are given below.

walk cut catch break
infinitive

walks cuts catches breaks
third person singular, present tense

walking cutting catching breaking
present participle

walked cut caught broke
past tense

walked cut caught broken
past participle

Tense   5.2

Contrary to popular thinking and contrary to the classifications of traditional grammar, it is best to say there are only two tenses in English, present tense and past tense. There is no future tense; this is not to say that English cannot convey a sense of future time, but that it doesn't use a verb tense to accomplish this. Even with present and past, it is wrong to assume that there's a pat, easy relationship between the grammatical category of tense and the real world category of time. Past tense comes closest, or at least closer than present tense, in accomplishing that.

> English has two verb tenses, **present** and **past**. There is not an easy, pat relationship between the category of **tense** and the representation of time.

Present tense, in fact, can routinely narrate past, present, or future time events. It's not the usual, but a writer can narrate past time events in present tense in order to convey a sense of being there, a sense of immediacy:

It's 1975, and I am on my way to Kindergarten for the first time. I am terrified as I walk up the steps, holding the patient hand of my mother.

Present tense here becomes a point of reference, with events before this starting point narrated in past tense and events after this starting point spoken about as if they have not happened yet.

I went to daycare for two years, but daycare was small, and this place is vast and confusing. It will be months before I am comfortable.

Present tense often conveys habitual or future happenings.

When simple present tense is used to narrate present time occurrences, more often than not it doesn't denote a particular moment, but habitual or routine action. If someone says *I drive to work*, we would interpret that as meaning that driving is their usual way to get there. If they call us up from their car on a cell phone, they might say *I am driving to work* (using the present participle), meaning it's happening right now, as they speak. *I drive to work now* would seem awkward and confusing. Present tense can also be used to convey future time events, as in *I leave for Paris on Tuesday*.

Modal auxiliaries often seem like future tense auxiliaries; that may be because the attitudes they convey (desirability, possibility, ability, permission, or obligation) often have to do with a world that hasn't come to be yet. Whether they seem to refer to past or future time events, perhaps they are best understood as present time assessments by the writer or speaker. (*She should have gone* or *She should go*. In either case, the modal is an expression of attitude.) One exception to this understanding would be the rather soft modal *would*, which often functions by denoting past time actions as routine or habitual, much the same sense often conveyed by a simple present tense. If I say *She would drop the kids off at daycare on the way to college*, I'm implying that this was a pattern, not just a one time occurrence, and that this pattern is true of past time. The same effect can be created in a more informal way with *used to*, as in *She used to eat hamburgers all the time*.

For our purposes, we should determine whether a finite verb phrase carries tense or modality and think of those as separate categories. As discussed in Chapter 4, the modals seem to have floated free of meaning ties between past and present forms of each other and seem to have floated free of the usual meanings created by a shift in tense. If modal, then we will ignore the category of tense. If it conveys tense, that tense will be either present or past.

Present tense uses the infinitive (base) form of the verb for all but third person singular. For this, you may want to review our pronoun paradigms in Chapter 3. We will say *I walk*, *you walk* (whether singular or plural), *we walk*, and *they walk*. The *s* (or occasionally *es*) ending is added for *he*, *she*, *it*, or any grammatical subject that can be replaced by those pronouns. *He walks*, *she walks*, *it walks*, *Harry walks*, and *the elephant walks*. When this happens, we say that the verb agrees with the subject in person (third person) and number (singular). The grammatical category, which you will find in any good handbook, is subject/verb agreement.

Any good handbook will help you deal with occasions in which the choice seems uncertain, as with subjects like *a herd of cows*. Some spoken dialects of English routinely drop that s inflection. This can be thought of as a natural evolution in the language (English has been dropping and regularizing inflections for centuries), not a breaking of the rules, but following alternative rules, though the chances of getting most people to recognize that and respect those differences seem pretty slim. If you grew up speaking one of those alternative dialects and are interested in writing Standard English, you will probably not be able to trust your ear, at least at first. Both *she walk* and *she walks* may sound fine. Unlike other speakers, who can simply write it the way it sounds right, you will need to approach the task analytically.

Most changes in the verb to **agree** with the subject occur in present tense with third person singular subjects.

When finite and lexical verbs are not conflated, tense shifts to the primary auxiliaries (*be*, *have*, and *do*). For all verbs but the verb *to be* (see below), past tense forms are identical regardless of person or number.

Aspect   5.3

In addition to past or present tenses (or modality), verb phrases can carry one of two (or both) aspects, the progressive and perfective. Progressive aspect uses the present participle form of the verb in combination with some form of the verb to be. *She is walking*, for example, is present progressive. When this happens, it is the auxiliary verb (*is*) that picks up the present tense and agrees with the subject in person and number (in this case, third person singular). *She was walking* would be past progressive, with *was* carrying the tense (past) and the present participle form of the verb carrying the progressive aspect.

Aspect
Verb phrases can carry one of two (or both) aspects, the progressive and perfective.

In general, progressive aspect tends to convey a more continuous action. This may seem in contradiction with what was stated above, that *I am driving* seems more connected to the here and now than *I drive*, but the notion of continuous action is different from the idea of a pattern of action. If I say *I am driving*, I convey the sense that I am in the midst of a continuous process. If I say *I drive*, I am conveying the sense that driving is something I routinely do. If I say *I picked up my books*, I convey the sense that an action was over and done with. If I say *I was picking up my books*, it conveys the sense of an action that was ongoing. This would routinely be followed by *when* or *while* or *as*, as in *I was picking up my books while thinking about what I would say in class today.*

Progressive aspect uses some form of the verb *to be* as auxiliary plus the present participle form of the verb. It tends to denote a continuing or ongoing action.

Perfect aspect uses some form of the verb *have* as auxiliary plus the past participle form of the verb. It tends to denote a sense of completion.

Perfective aspect is created through the use of some form of the verb *have* as auxiliary in combination with the past participle form of the lexical verb. (You should recall that past participle form is identical to past tense for the vast majority of verbs.) Again, it is the auxiliary that picks up the finite work of tense and agrees with the subject in person and number (when appropriate).

> *I have walked. She has walked.*
> present perfect

> *I had walked. She had walked.*
> past perfect

Present perfect gives us a way to speak about actions recently completed, with the sense that this completion carries relevance into the present. If a friend phones you and asks what you're doing, you might say **I** *have studied chemistry and now I'm studying grammar. Have studied* conveys the sense that the studying of chemistry is just completed. You'd be very unlikely to say it if you had studied chemistry the week before.

Past perfect is to past tense as present perfect is to present tense. Once we begin a narrative in past tense, it gives us a way to place events as prior to that initial point of reference. Like present perfect, we tend to do so when those previous events have relevance to the events that have been chosen as a central focus. A short passage might help make that clearer.

> *Paul was studying chemistry. <u>He had failed</u> the last test, and he wasn't going to let that happen again. It was the only test he <u>had failed</u> in two years of college, and the blow to his ego still left him shaken.*

If you look closely at the passage, you can see how the two past perfect verb phrases help us keep clear the relation between the moment in his life we are attending to (his studying of chemistry) and the previous event (failing the previous test) that was influencing it.

5.4   Modals and aspect

Verb phrases that carry a modal auxiliary as primary auxiliary can also be progressive or perfective, though they require an additional auxiliary to accomplish this. We can't say *must walking* or *must walked*, but require the verb *to be* or *have* as auxiliary, though this time in the infinitive form(*must be walking* or *must have walked*.) The reasons for this are worth taking our time with.

One invariant rule with modals is that they are always followed by the infinitive form of a verb. We say *she walks* in simple present, but *she must walk* in modal form, dropping the *s* from *walks* in the second sentence because *must* has now taken up the role of finite, which can only happen once in a verb phrase.

This combines with the rules above that say a verb phrase becomes progressive by adding a verb *to be* auxiliary and the present participle form of the verb and that a verb phrase becomes perfective by adding a verb *to have* auxiliary in combination with the past participle.

In combination with the modals (which soak up the finite role), the aspect auxiliaries (*be* and *have*) revert to their infinitive forms.

This may appear confusing, but the patterns themselves should be clear from examples.

She walks.
simple present

She is walking.
present progressive, with *is* carrying the burden of tense and subject agreement

She has walked.
present perfect, with *has* carrying the burden of tense and subject agreement

She walked.
simple past

She was walking.
past progressive, with *was* picking up the burden of tense and agreement

She had walked.
past perfect, with *had* picking up the burden of tense

She must walk.
modal. no tense or subject agreement, since modals are invariant.

She must be walking.
modal progressive; no tense or subject agreement

She must have walked.
modal perfect; no tense or subject agreement

5.5   Aspect in combination

A verb phrase can also be both progressive and perfective. As usual, the first auxiliary (*have*) carries the burden of tense and subject agreement. The second auxiliary (*be*) reverts to past participle (to complete the requirements for perfect aspect) and the *ing* (present participle) is carried by the lexical verb. It's not as hard to spot as it sounds if you take each auxiliary at a time. Examples are given below.

> *She has been walking.*
> present plus perfect plus progressive; *has* carries the present tense plus subject agreement

> *She had been walking.*
> past plus perfect plus progressive; *had* carries tense

> *She must have been walking.*
> modal plus perfect plus progressive; no tense or subject agreement, since modals are invariant

If we are native speakers, the forms and subtle meanings of verb phrases are available to us unconsciously. We are once again bringing complex natural occurences to conscious light.

By now, you may be wishing you had taken up an easier subject (like quantum physics) or a more exciting one (like accounting). Let's step back, though and remember that these complex steps, as difficult as they are analytically, are usually effortless for anyone who uses the language. We're not making up rules, but simply observing them as complex, natural occurrences. What a wonderful mechanism the human mind is that a child learns these rules so well that he/she has the luxury of taking them for granted; what that child learns, of course, is not just the correct forms, but the subtle nuances of meaning that each conveys. Without that facility, we would be stalled forever in even the simplest of conversations.

5.6   Passive structures

If you recall from Chapter 4, a transitive active clause can be made passive through a three step process, part of that including a transformation of the verb phrase.

As you recall, a clause is passive when the receiver of the action is moved into the grammatical subject slot. This allows us to shift the message structure of the clause without confusing or altering the representational meaning.

Your dog ate my dinner.
actor and grammatical subject are combined

My dinner was eaten by your dog.
passive version

Just for review, the three step process is as follows:

1) The receiver of the action is moved into the grammatical subject slot;

2) A verb *to be* auxiliary is added to the verb phrase and the lexical verb changes to past participle (For regular verbs, past tense and past participle forms will be identical.);

3) The actor moves into the predicate phrase with the help of the preposition *by*.

To further complicate things (or make them rich and interesting), passive verb phrases can also carry tense or modality and aspect. No matter how complex the verb phrase, though, the lexical verb in a passive verb phrase will always be past participle and the verb *to be* will always be its closest auxiliary.

Your best bet, though, may be to recognize the passive through attention to meaning, by seeing that the receiver of the action is also grammatical subject. A close look at the structure of the verb phrase can help confirm that judgment. At any rate, examples of passive verb phrases are given below.

My dinner is eaten by your dog.
present passive

My dinner is being eaten by your dog.
present plus progressive plus passive

My dinner was eaten by your dog.
past passive

My dinner was being eaten by your dog.
past plus progressive plus passive

My dinner has been eaten by your dog.
present plus perfect plus passive

My dinner had been eaten by your dog.
past plus perfect plus passive

My dinner has been being eaten by your dog.
present plus perfect plus progressive plus passive

My dinner had been being eaten by your dog.
past plus perfect plus progressive plus passive

My dinner must be eaten by your dog.
modal plus passive

My dinner must be being eaten by your dog.
modal plus progressive plus passive

My dinner must have been eaten by your dog.
modal plus perfect plus passive

My dinner must have been being eaten by your dog.
modal plus perfect plus progressive plus passive

An **agentless passive** is a passive clause without an explicit actor or agent.

Passive clauses can get trickier to recognize when the actor is left out of the predicate phrase, leaving us with what is called an agentless passive. This is frequently the case when we can see the results of an action, but we aren't sure who or what did it. We may say something like *My radio was stolen* or *My car was broken into*, without adding the rather unhelpful phrase *by someone.*

5.6.1   *The special case of the verb to be*

The verb *be* has a first person singular form in present tense (*am*) and a form for first and third person singular in past tense (*was*).

For every verb but the verb *to be*, the finite verb is inflected to agree with the subject in one case only, third person singular, present tense. The verb *to be*, though, has three forms in the present tense (rather than the usual two) and is the only verb to have two forms for past tense:

Present tense forms: I *am* (first person singular); you, we, they *are* (second person singular and plural, first person and third person plural); he, she, it *is* (third person singular).

Past tense forms: I, he, she, it *was* (first and third person singular); you, we, they *were* (second person singular and plural, first and third person plural).

5.6.2   *Do as auxiliary*

In Chapter 4, we explored the use of forms of the verb *do* as finite auxiliary when asking questions. I gave *Is she walking?* and *Does she walk?* as examples of the way *She walks* might be transformed into a question form. Now that we know about aspect, however, it should be clear that *Is she walking?* is not just interrogative in mood, but progressive as well. *Does she walk?* is closer to the original. *Do*, in fact, functions primarily as a neutral finite when a finite is needed, either to ask a question (as we covered in Chapter 4) or to negate a statement. As when asking a question, a statement can't be negated when finite and lexical verbs are conflated. We can't say *She not walks* or *She not walked*. To negate the sentence, we need to split finite and lexical verbs and the auxiliary *do* gives us an ability to do that without adding aspect. *She does not walk* or *She did not walk*. This seems to imply that it is the finite and not the lexical verb that is being negated. Negation should be thought of as a central part of the exchange function. When presenting or coming to understand the perspective of a statement, whether the statement is positive or negative is of central importance. In a declarative statement, *do* can also give a sense of emphasis or insistence. To say *I did wash the dishes* might imply that the action has been questioned.

Do is primarily a neutral finite, used to ask questions or add negation. It can also add insistence.

Do, as auxiliary, cannot combine with other auxiliaries. We don't say *She does be going* or *We did have gone*. Again, *do* gets called into service when no other finite auxiliary is present. We can use it to negate a statement or ask a question without adding aspect. When *have* or *be* are present as auxiliaries, they can take on the role of finite and *do* is not needed.

5.6.3   *Modals in combination*

There seems to be a rule in the language that prohibits most modals from combining with each other. We don't say *She must can* or *She might may*. But there are what are called 'periphrastic forms' for most modals, two or three word combinations that can be used in place of modals and allow us to string more than one modal notion together or to combine with tensed auxiliaries (like *is able to* or *was allowed to*). These are worth examining because they will confuse you in analysis if you're not alert to them. We can say *She must be able to* or *She may be allowed to*. Other examples would include *ought to*, *have to*, *be supposed to* and *be going to*.

5.7

Section
Exercise

I. Give past tense forms for each of the following verbs (you will have to consult your own internal grammar) and then tell whether each verb is regular or irregular.

1) *seek*
2) *know*
3) *wrap*
4) *stir*
5) *explore*

II. Finite verb phrases have been underlined in the following sentences. Analyze each for tense (or modality), subject verb agreement and aspect. Remember that all categories may not apply. If a category doesn't apply, you don't need to say so. Your decision procedure should be as follows:

1) If the finite verb is modal, say so and move to step four. If the finite verb carries tense, move to step two. (A verb phrase that begins with a modal will be outside the category of tense and not have subject verb agreement.)

2) Tell whether the tense is present or past.

3) Tell whether the finite verb is inflected to agree with the subject in person and/or number. For all verbs but the verb *to be*, this will only occur for third person singular in present tense. If the finite verb is *am*, this will include first person singular. If the finite verb is *was*, the verb phrase is singular. (You won't know from the verb phrase alone whether the subject is first or third person.)

4) Analyze the verb phrase for aspect. Look for perfective first and progressive second, since that is the order they will come in if both aspects are present.

5) Determine from meaning and structure whether the verb phrase is passive.

The five sentences are from *Proverbs of Hell*, from *The Marriage of Heaven and Hell* by William Blake.

1) *The eagle never <u>lost</u> so much time as when he <u>submitted</u> to learn of the crow.*
2) *The fox <u>provides</u> for himself, but God <u>provides</u> for the lion.*
3) *If the lion <u>was advised</u> by the fox, he <u>would be</u> cunning.*
4) *The nakedness of woman <u>is</u> the work of God.*
5) *If others <u>had not been</u> foolish, we <u>would be</u> so.*

Finite verb phrases have been underlined and numbered in the following sentences from Louise Erdrich *Love Medicine* and Annie Dillard *Pilgrim at Tinker Creek* and *A Writing Life*. The sentences also include verb forms in other roles that we will discuss in later chapters; for now, you should ignore those and concentrate on the verb phrases that are underlined. Describe each in terms of tense or modality, subject verb agreement (where appropriate) and aspect (where appropriate). If the verb phrase is passive, say so. Remember that all categories may not apply.

1) *The morning before Easter Sunday, June Krapshaw <u>was walking</u>[1] down the clogged main street of oil boomtown Williston, North Dakota, killing time before the noon bus <u>arrived</u>[2] that <u>would take</u>[3] her home.*
2) *He <u>looked</u>[4] familiar, like a lot of people <u>looked</u>[5] familiar to her. She <u>had seen</u>[6] so many come and go.*
3) *Although the day <u>was</u>[7] overcast, the snow itself <u>reflected</u>[8] such light that she <u>was</u>[9] momentarily <u>blinded</u>.[9]*
4) *He <u>ordered</u>[10] a beer for her, a Blue Ribbon, saying she <u>deserved</u>[11] a prize for being the best thing he'<u>d seen</u>[12] for days.*
5) *Her hair <u>was rolled</u>[13] carefully, sprayed for the bus trip, and her eyes <u>were</u>[14] deeply watchful in their sea-blue flumes of shadow.*

(Louise Erdrich)

1) *I <u>had been reading</u>[15] about locusts. Hordes of migrating locusts <u>have</u> always <u>appeared</u>[16] in arid countries, and then <u>disappeared</u>[17] as suddenly as they <u>had come</u>.[18] You <u>could</u>[19] actually <u>watch</u>[19] them lay eggs all over a plant, and the next year there <u>would be</u>[20] no locusts on the plant.*
2) *I <u>can watch</u>[21] a muskrat feed on a bank for ten minutes, harvesting shocks of grass that <u>bristle</u>[22] and <u>droop</u>[23] from his jaws, and when he <u>is</u>[24] gone I <u>cannot see</u>[25] any difference in the grass.*
3) *Outside, everything <u>has opened</u>[26] up.*
4) *I <u>am sitting</u>[28] under a sycamore by Tinker Creek.*
5) *When you <u>write</u>,[29] you <u>lay out</u>[30] a line of words. The line of words <u>is</u>[31] a miner's pick, a woodcarver's gouge, a surgeon's probe. You <u>wield</u>[32] it, and it <u>digs</u>[33] a path you <u>follow</u>.[34] Soon you <u>find</u>[35] yourself deep in new territory. <u>Is</u>[36] it a dead end, or <u>have</u>[37] you <u>located</u>[37] the real subject? You <u>will know</u>[38] tomorrow, or this time next year.*

(Annie Dillard)

Chapter 6

Section Exercises

Page 96
Identify copular verb phrases.

Page 106
Identify sentences as copular, intransitive, transitive, di-transitive, or complex transitive.

Page 114
Identify process types in clauses.

Chapter Practice

Page 115
Identify verb phrases and tell whether they are copular, intransitive, transitive, di-transitive, or complex transitive; diagram given sentences; identify process types for verb phrases.

Chapter 6

Transitivity: clause as representation

In Chapter 4, we explored expressive (message structure) and interactive (exchange) meanings in some detail, postponing a more detailed look at representational meaning until this chapter. In this chapter, we will explore ways in which language holds a mirror (or lens) up to the world. Though it should be emphasized that the world directly represented in language is often an internal world, the world of our sensing and feeling and thinking, as well as the physical world around us. We will explore the different kinds of representational meaning the language makes possible, especially as these meanings are built through the transitivity system of the grammar.

You may also remember from Chapter 2 that we discussed subject and predicate structure and said that the verb phrase is the heart of the predicate. In that discussion, we briefly explored the existence of verb complements, constituents in the predicate phrase that seemed to complete or complement the verb. We will explore those complements in some detail in this chapter as aspects of representational meaning.

Verb complements
This chapter explores verb complements: constituents in the predicate phrase that complete or complement the verb.

We will start with categories, sentence types, that have deep roots in traditional grammar. We will then use some of the insights of functional grammar to help smooth out the useful, but rough understanding those traditional classifications give us.

Representational meaning is what people usually refer to when they talk about the meaning of a sentence. From a purely representational view, it is possible to talk about two different sentences as conveying the same meaning. You may remember our understanding of a sentence, that sentences can vary widely in the content they contain and can vary widely in the way that content is organized. From a functional perspective, a change in form (the arrangement of that content), however slight, is always a change in meaning; if nothing else, it brings about change in the message structure of the clause, in what is given heightened importance or emphasis. But the sense of a representational meaning existing independently of our manipulation of it into different messages is extremely important. In exploring representational meaning, we need to rely on that intuition very heavily.

6.2   Basic clause types

Let's begin by looking at three sentences, which no doubt seem awkward to you and ungrammatical.

Paul rose the window.
Paul is sleepily.
Paul noticed very smart.

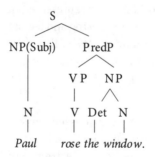

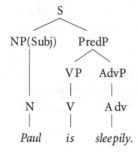

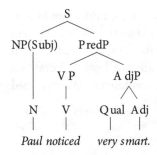

Look at the sentences carefully and see if you can explain what's wrong with them before you move on. The answer won't come from a purely structural analysis, as you can see from the diagrams of these sentences above. All three exhibit patterns that are very common.

You may have discovered that if you shift the constituents that come after the verb phrases from sentence to sentence, you can come up with three sentences that are very acceptable. These are given below.

> *Paul rose sleepily.*
> *Paul is very smart.*
> *Paul noticed the window.*

Why are these OK, whereas the earlier sentences are not? The answer is that these clauses carry different kinds of verbs and these verbs require (or allow) different kinds of complements. *Rose* (past tense of *rise*) is intransitive; it cannot take an object, like *the window*; we can say *Paul rose in front of the window*, but not *Paul rose the window*. *Is* (present tense, third person singular of verb *to be*) is copular; its primary role is to link the subject with a word group that establishes its identity or its characteristics and *sleepily* doesn't fit that role; we can say *Paul is sleepy*, but not *Paul is sleepily*. *Noticed* (past tense of *notice*) is transitive; it requires an *object* (something that *was noticed*) and *very smart* doesn't fit that need; we can say *Paul noticed my intelligence*, but not *Paul noticed very smart*. Not all verbs are limited to one class, but some, like the above three, are.

Transitivity describes how meaning is carried across from subject to predicate through the verb. Certain verbs allow certain kinds of complements. Different processes involve different kinds of participants.

Transitivity (from the Latin *trans*, meaning *across*) has to do with the way meaning is carried across from subject to predicate through the verb. It may also help to think about verb phrases as determining kinds of representational processes. In these processes, different kinds of participants are involved. In a rough way, intransitive and transitive clauses describe a world in which things are happening. Copular clauses are about the way things *are* (or *were* or *have been* or *may be*, etc. Transitivity is not effected by tense, modality, or aspect. In any verb phrase, it's the lexical verb that governs transitivity.). That's just a rough understanding to start with. We'll refine our understanding in the sections below. We will need to look at structure closely, but structure alone won't usually tell us how a verb phrase is operating. Once again, we'll need to draw on our deep-rooted understanding of what a clause means. We will need to draw on our own invisible grammar.

6.3   Copular clauses

The prototypical copular verb is the verb *to be*. Not many verbs can be copular. Those that can include *be* and *seem*, which are always copular, *become*, which is almost always copular and various verbs that are sometimes copular, like *appear* and *get* and *grow* and *remain* and *stay* and *turn* and various sensing verbs, like *look* and *taste*.

Copular clauses link a subject with predicate phrase constituents that tell what it is, what it is like, or where it is located in space or time.

The primary function of a copular verb is to link a subject with predicate phrase constituents that tell, not what it does, but what it is and/or what it is like. Typical clause structures are as follows:

NP VP NP, where the second NP identifies or renames the subject.

NP VP AdjP, where the predicate phrase adjective phrase gives characteristics of the subject.

NP VP AdvP, possible with the verb *be* when the AdvP identifies the subject's location in space or in time. Examples follow:

Bill Clinton is becoming an embattled president.
An embattled president is a NP that renames *Bill Clinton*.

Grammar has always been my toughest subject.
my toughest subject is a NP that renames *grammar*.

My youngest son seems very ill.
Very ill is an AdjP that gives characteristics of *my youngest son*.

The tomatoes are too green for picking.
Too green for picking is an AdjP that gives characteristics of *the tomatoes*.

Newark is across the Hudson from New York City.
Across the Hudson from New York City is a PP (adverbial) that gives the location of *Newark*.

Your presentation will be after lunch.
After lunch is a PP (adverbial) that locates *your presentation* in time.

To fully understand copular clauses and relational meaning, it might help to review some of the things we discussed about noun phrases in Chapter 3. Though the popular idea of a noun is that it names a person, place, or thing, this is more true of proper nouns than it is of common nouns, which identify an entity as a member of a group or class. Nouns also name things that are not things at all (at least in a material sense) like *justice*, *peace*, and *wonder*. A lot of noun phrase modification is restrictive, allowing us to identify which member of a class we are talking or writing about.

Identity, though, at least as it's realized through statements, is often heavily dependent on context. If I tell you *Give this to the woman in the third row*, for example, I'm giving you enough identity information to carry out a very discreet task. If you found more than one woman in the third row, you would be surprised and confused. You may find the woman in the third row very interesting and begin to wonder *Who is that woman in the third row?* Being in the third row is suddenly almost irrelevant to her identity. Someone may tell you *she's a sophomore, an English major, a friend of Cathy's. She's a reporter for the student newspaper. She is very smart and very friendly.* All of these are copular statements, ways of identifying, renaming, reclassifying and describing. The point at which you stop identifying and start describing may be hard to pin down. Certainly all these statements about the woman in the third row haven't used her up as a subject.

The names we give entities may help us identify them as distinct from all other entities. It's also true, though, that entities are not limited to single identities. One person's *garbage* is another person's *treasure*.

So, too, I am *Craig Hancock* (a proper noun), but also a father, husband, brother, cousin, nephew, and son-in-law. I remain a son though both my parents are deceased. I am a teacher. I am a writer of a grammar book. I'm a citizen of a village, town, county, state, and country. I am a somewhat lapsed guitar player, a mediocre gardener. I'm someone who loves to fish but rarely gets the time. Clearly, I could go on for pages and not use this subject up, not least of all because *being* shades into *becoming* and *seeming* and *remaining*, into what *was* or *will be* or *appears to be*. I may not be an angry person, but there are times when I am angry. I can be foolish and wise, patient and impatient, caring and careless. At this moment, I am alive and well, but tomorrow I may be ill and someday I will be dead. Renaming and identifying shade easily into describing and the world we name and describe does not stand still.

In a copular clause, relational meaning is the central meaning of the clause.

Naming and describing happen, of course, in all clauses. What makes a clause copular is the fact that these relational meanings are the central purpose of the clause.

In determining whether a clause is copular, I suggest the following advice:

1) If the lexical verb is some form of *be* or *seems*, the clause is copular. (Don't get fooled by the auxiliaries. It's the lexical verb that counts.)

2) If the lexical verb is some form of *become*, it will be copular except in the sense exemplified by the statement *That dress becomes you*.

3) *Get* and *grow* and *turn* are not usually copular, but they are when they can easily be replaced by some form of *become*.

4) Perception verbs – like *appear, taste, look, sound* and *feel* – are probably copular if they can easily be replaced by some form of the verb *seems*. They tend to be copular when the subject is not the perceiver. (*This lunchmeat looks bad*. The lunchmeat is not doing something, but being characterized on the basis of its looks.)

5) *Appear, remain* and *stay* are sometimes copular. You should consider them intransitive if they are immediately followed by adverbials, as in *A ship appeared on the horizon*, or as in *The boy remained in the room*.

If any verb but a form of the verb *to be* is copular, it will pass the structure test described in number 6.

A copular clause requires a copular complement. It cannot be copular without it.

6) A copular clause, by its very nature, requires a copular complement. That's what it's for. The relational process is unfinished without it. With the exception of the verb to be, that complement must be a NP that renames the subject or an AdjP that describes it.

A good test for NP copular complements is whether they can be reversed with the subject.

Albany is the capital of New York State.
The capital of New York State is Albany.

Most NP copular complements will exhibit this reciprocity with the subject. NP's in transitive sentences won't allow this without passive transformation.

The dog bit the man.
The man was bit by the dog.

Copular clauses, in contrast, resist becoming passive. *The capital of New York State is being been by Albany* sounds terribly awkward. If you remember, only transitive clauses can become passive because they require moving the object (receiver) of the action into the grammatical subject role. Since copular clauses have no receiver of the action (no object), they can't be transformed in that way. Certain kinds of transitive clauses will also resist becoming passive, so the test will not always be adequate. If a clause can be made passive, though, we know the clause is transitive and not copular.

For AdjP complements, try combining them into the NP subject to see if they give us a similar meaning. For *The old man appears angry*, move *angry* into the subject NP, giving us *the angry old man*, which seems close in representational meaning to the original (without the qualifying sense that *appears* gives to the clause). *Appears* here seems to act as a link between *the old man* and the characteristic (AdjP) *angry*. The clause is copular. For a word group, like *in good condition*, the result will seem grammatically awkward. *The bike appears in good condition* becomes *the in good condition bike*, but the awkwardness doesn't extend to a feeling that the meaning has been changed or compromised.

Copular complements can be abbreviated as *CC* in our phrase structure diagrams; place the CC in parentheses, as we do with Subj, to show that it's a functional (rather than structural) category. Diagrams for two typical copular sentences would look as follows.

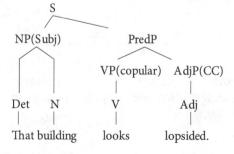

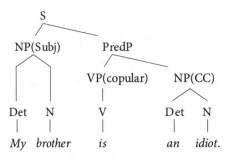

In addition to copular complements, copular clauses often carry adverbial modifiers.

A copular clause requires a copular complement in the predicate phrase. It also allows for other adverbial elements in the predicate phrase that are themselves not part of the copular complement, but modifiers of the verb phrase. An example is diagrammed out below.

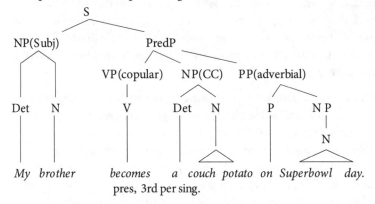

I have also added information to the diagram about the function of the predicate phrase prepositional phrase (adverbial) and about tense and subject verb agreement in the verb phrase. The amount of information we include in a diagram is up to us. The diagram above expresses a rich understanding of both structure and function for all elements in the sentence. If you can read the diagram and understand it, you have gained a complex understanding of grammar.

6.4

Section

exercise

For the following pairs of sentences, one underlined verb phrase is copular and one is not. For each, tell which one is copular and explain how you came to that understanding.

1a) *Paul <u>felt</u> cold.*
1b) *Paul <u>felt</u> the cold.*
2a) *That tomato sauce <u>smells</u> like my mother's.*
2b) *I could <u>smell</u> the sauce cooking.*
3a) *The sandwich <u>turned</u> moldy after three days.*
3b) *He <u>turned</u> the moldy sandwich over with a stick.*
4a) *My opponent <u>proved</u> worthy.*
4b) *My opponent <u>proved</u> a difficult theorem.*
5a) *Through the fourth quarter, our star <u>remained</u> on the bench.*
5b) *Despite a bad game, he <u>remains</u> our star.*

Intransitive and transitive clauses   6.5

From the perspective of traditional grammar, if a verb phrase is not copular, it must be transitive or intransitive.

In a rough way, as stated earlier, transitive and intransitive clauses are not about what is (relational meaning), but about events and happenings. This is easiest to understand through material process clauses, clauses that represent actions and events within the physical world. The term 'actor', introduced in Chapter 4, is also most relevant to these clauses.

The primary structural difference between transitive and intransitive clauses is that a transitive clause contains a direct object, whereas an intransitive clause does not.

The idea of direct object can be hard to pin down, but in a material process clause the direct object is the receiver of the action; it's sometimes described as an affected participant. It's the NP group that gets promoted into grammatical subject position when a clause becomes passive. In the clause *A truck hit our oak tree during last Saturday's blizzard*, *our oak tree* is direct object and the VP *hit* is transitive. *Our oak tree was hit by a truck during last Saturday's blizzard* is the passive version. Both are transitive; only transitive sentences can be made passive, since the passive transformation requires having a direct object (a receiver of the action) to promote.

Direct object
in a material process clause, the direct object is sometimes described as an affected participant.

Intransitive clauses are the only clauses that can have only a VP in the predicate; the only exception to this would be transitive passive clauses with the actor not mentioned (*agentless passives*, like *My car was stolen*). You may recall that copular clauses require a copular complement to be

Transitive clauses require a participant that would normally take on the role of direct object. In passive versions, that participant also functions a grammatical subject.

copular. Transitive clauses require a direct object to be transitive. Some intransitive verbs seem to require adverbial complements; the sentence *We went* seems incomplete (outside of context), whereas *We laughed* does not; and some grammarians use this to classify intransitive verb phrases into two different types, but that is a finer level of distinction than we will concern ourselves with. Unless a verb phrase is passive, we can be sure that a predicate with nothing but a verb phrase is intransitive.

You may have wondered, in the last section, why *A ship appeared on the horizon* is intransitive, whereas *A ship was on the horizon* is copular. One answer to that is that *on the horizon* is not necessary in the first sentence but definitely is necessary in the second. We can say *A ship appeared* and have the sentence feel complete. *A ship was*, on the other hand, strikes us as unfinished. That should clue us in to the understanding that *A ship appeared on the horizon* is a statement about action (what the ship did) and not about relation. A copular verb requires a copular complement.

Using the same logic, why is *The boy stayed in the room* intransitive and not copular?

Intransitive predicates can be as simple as a single verb phrase, but they can also carry a complex array of adverbial modifiers.

Intransitive sentences can be the simplest of sentences – a NP subject and a predicate phrase consisting of just a verb phrase, as in *Our pizza arrived*. But it would be misleading to say that they are or even usually are simple structures. The verb phrase may not have to be elaborated, but it can be and usually is. Consider, for example, the intransitive opening sentence of Louise Erdrich's Love Medicine: *The morning before Easter Sunday, June Kapshaw was walking down the clogged main street of oil boomtown Williston, killing time before the noon bus arrived that would take her home.* All the elements after *Williston* will be confusing to you until we consider them in the next chapter, but the elements before it are very typical adverbial elaborations of the verb. *The morning before Easter Sunday* tells us when she was walking. *Down the clogged main street of oil boomtown Williston* tells us where. Other typical adverb functions are why and how, as in *June Kapshaw was walking quickly for exercise.* They can also tell us the conditions in which something is happening, as in *She walked in the rain.* We call these modifiers rather than complements in part because they show up in all clauses, regardless of type.

Free NP is a Noun Phrase not bound up within another constituent structure.

If a clause is transitive (and not passive), it will generally have a free NP in the predicate phrase. A free NP is a NP not bound up within another constituent structure, like a prepositional phrase. If there is a free NP after the verb phrase, you should eliminate the possibility that the NP is a copular complement and not a direct object by determining whether the free NP renames or identifies the subject. If it does, the clause is copular. If it does not, the clause is almost always transitive. Using that test, which of the following sentences is transitive? Which is copular? Which is intransitive?

1) *The young man was the lake's observer.*
2) *The young man looked across the lake.*
3) *The young man saw the lake.*

Number one is copular because *the lake's observer* renames *The young man*. Number two is intransitive because there is no free NP in the predicate and *across the lake* is an adverbial elaboration of the verb phrase. Number three is transitive because *the lake* is a free NP that does not rename *The young man*.

In using the above test, though, be very careful about NP adverbials. There's an example in the sentence above from Louise Erdrich: *The morning before Easter Sunday* is a NP, but functioning like an adverbial of time. It might help to think of it as a prepositional phrase (*on the morning before Easter Sunday*) from which the preposition has been dropped.

Noun phrases can be adverbials of place or time.

In the following paired sentences, one underlined NP is a direct object and one is a NP adverbial. Which is which? Consider them carefully before you move on.

1a) *We left <u>home</u> on Sunday.*
1b) *We went <u>home</u> on Sunday.*
2a) *We will arrive <u>Thursday morning</u>.*
2b) *I hate <u>Thursday morning</u>.*
3a) *My mother returned <u>Tuesday</u>.*
3b) *My mother returned <u>her birthday present.</u>*

In the first pair, 1a) is transitive and 1b) is intransitive because *home* in 1b) is a NP adverbial. In the second pair, 2a) is intransitive and 2b) is transitive; in sentence 2a), the preposition *on* seems implied and *Thursday morning* is not being arrived, but simply the day on which it is happening. In pair number three, perhaps the clearest example, 3a) is intransitive and 3b) is transitive. In this case, it should be clear that *her birthday present* gets returned but *Tuesday* does not. *Tuesday* just tells us when the returning happened.

You may have noticed in the above sentences that direct objects will answer the question *what* in combination with the verb phrase. What was left? *Home.* What was hated? *Thursday morning.* What was returned? *Her birthday present.* In the above intransitive sentences, *home*, *Thursday morning*, and *Tuesday* tell us where or when, typical adverb functions and not what. Because of that, we can't come up with passive versions of these sentences that maintain the original sense. *Home was went by us. Thursday morning was arrived by us. Tuesday was returned by my mother.*

Failing the passive test gives us another indication that the sentences in question are not transitive.

6.6   Types of transitive clauses

Types of transitive clauses
Mono-transitive sentences have one required complement.

Di-transitive and complex transitive patterns have an additional verb phrase complement in the predicate phrase.

Transitive clauses in the above section can be thought of as regular or base pattern transitives. They are sometimes called mono-transitive sentences because they have only one required complement. Two other very common transitive patterns are di-transitive and complex transitive, each of which gives us an additional verb phrase complement in the predicate phrase.

Typical verbs in di-transitive sentences would include *give* and *tell*. Both giving and telling often include three participants rather than just two. If I give something (direct object, which here means something like *transferred entity*), I will almost always have someone one (or thing) to give it to. We will call this receiver of the gift 'indirect object', in harmony with traditional grammar. In a more general sense, indirect object for this kind of verb would mean something like 'receiver of a transferred entity'. In *I gave my son a new Nintendo system*, *I* is actor (giver), *a new Nintendo system* is direct object (transferred entity), and *my son* is indirect object (receiver of transferred entity).

In most di-transitive sentences, the indirect object can be dropped without distortion of meaning (*I gave a new Nintendo system*), but the direct object cannot (*I gave my son*) because then the indirect object gets shifted into direct object role by the word order rules of the grammar. (It's not *my son* that's being given, but *the new Nintendo system*.) This test isn't foolproof, though, because it will give us misleading results with verbs like *tell* and *show*.

This typical di-transitive sentence can be diagrammed out as follows:

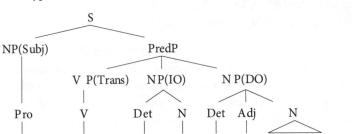

Indirect object and direct object can change position within the predicate phrase, but only by putting the indirect object in a prepositional phrase introduced by *to* or *for*. *I gave a new Nintendo system to my son*. We will follow the recent practice of continuing to call *my son* indirect object despite its being bound up within a prepositional phrase, stressing the fact that its function (as receiver of the transferred entity) remains intact. Shifting the indirect object like this is an excellent test for di-transitivity within a sentence. It should be pointed out that the two sentences retain the same representational meaning, but could be thought of as conveying different messages by shifting the word group that gathers clause ending emphasis. They could be thought of as answers to two different questions: *What did you give your son? I gave him a new Nintendo system. Who did you give a new Nintendo system to? I gave a new Nintendo system to my son.*

> Indirect objects can follow the direct object with the addition of *to* or *for*. The representational meaning remains the same, but the emphasis shifts.

The verb *tell* is frequently di-transitive for parallel reasons. Just as *giving* gives us three participants, a giver, gift, and receiver of the gift, *telling* gives us a teller, message, and receiver of the message, as in *My sister told my mother a big lie*. Dropping the direct object here, though, will give us confusing results: *My sister told my mother*; we can assume that we have a transitive sentence without a direct object or that the person being told (*my mother*) has now shifted into a direct object role. Either way, it seems to be an exception to the general pattern.

Other verbs that are often di-transitive are those related to sending (again, we have three participants – sender, something being sent, and someone or thing doing the receiving), showing, teaching or instructing, and making or preparing, especially when there is a beneficiary for what is being made or prepared. (An indirect object is sometimes called beneficiary).

The chef prepared us a big feast.
I built my wife her dream house.
I cooked the hungry children a nice breakfast.

Again, it's not *us*, *my wife*, or *the hungry children* that are being *prepared*, *built*, or *cooked*. Dropping the direct object (and therefore shifting the indirect object to a direct object role) will give us a fairly comical meaning. (*I cooked the hungry children.*) In all three cases, the indirect object can shift order, though this time with the preposition *for* (rather than *to*).

The chef prepared a huge feast <u>for us</u>.
I built her dream house <u>for my wife</u>.
I cooked a nice breakfast <u>for the hungry children</u>.

One interesting characteristic of di-transitive clauses is that either object can be promoted to subject when the clause becomes passive.

My son was given a new Nintendo (by me).
A new Nintendo system was given my son (by me).

When the indirect object gets promoted to subject, as with the first of the two examples above, the direct object remains a direct object, so we have a strange anomaly – a passive sentence that retains a direct object within the predicate phrase. When the direct object gets promoted to subject, as in the second example above, the indirect object maintains its indirect object role. In this case, it can occur with or without the preposition and with or without an expressly stated actor. *A new Nintendo system was given (to) my son (by me).*

> **Any of the three participants in a di-transitive clause can be made grammatical subject or theme.**

Again, the principal characteristic of di-transitive clauses is that they will have three major participants: an actor (giver, teller, teacher, sender, preparer, etc.), a transferred entity (gift, message, knowledge, created entity, etc.) and a receiver or beneficiary of whatever was transferred (given, told, taught, sent, prepared, etc.). Message structure flexibility allows us to make any of those three participants both grammatical subject and theme.

> **Complex transitive clauses will have two verb complements, but only two participants.**

Like di-transitive clauses, complex transitive clauses will also have two major complements in the predicate phrase. They differ from di-transitive clauses in that they only have two major participants. This is a key difference and a major tool in analysis. Like any transitive sentence, they will always have a direct object. The other element, which will always follow the direct object, is called a predicate complement (abbreviated as PC when we diagram). In some grammars, the PC is called an object complement, which makes some sense, since it seems to complement the direct object as much as the verb. Unlike indirect objects, which are always NP's or their equivalent, a PC can be adjectival or adverbial in function and so can include adjective phrases or prepositional phrases as well noun phrases as common elements.

*The **predicate complement** represents the change in a direct object as a result of the action of the verb.*

Two notions are critical to understanding complex transitivity. One is that the verb in a complex transitive clause is in some way a causative verb. It acts upon the object in such a way that the object is changed by the action and it is that change (new condition or location) that the predicate complement defines or describes.

The other important notion is that the relationship between a direct object and a predicate complement is very much like the relationship between subject and copular complement in a copular clause. This is so true, in fact, that inserting some form of the verb to be between direct object and predicate complement is a very practical test for complex transitivity.

Examples of all three types (NP, AdjP and adverbial predicate complements) are given below.

Unfounded rumors made me the enemy of the whole town.
The teacher's comments left the class very happy.
We raised the flag over the stadium.

The three sentences would be diagrammed as follows.

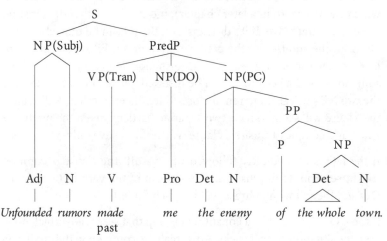

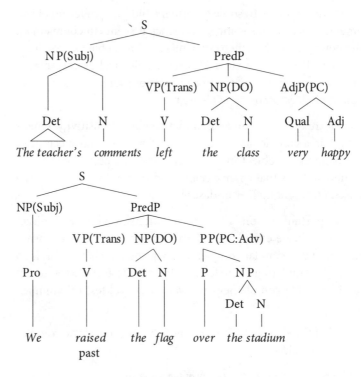

The idea of a predicate complement may elude you for awhile. Luckily, structural tests for two of the three patterns are very straightforward.

Adding some form of the verb *be* between direct object and a possible predicate complement is a useful test. The predicate complement tells us the new identity, new characteristics, or new location (in space or time) of the direct object, very similar to the kind of meaning presented by copular complements in a copular clause. In this case, though, it's a change resulting from the action of the verb.

If a VP is followed by two free NP's (and we don't have a compound direct object as in *He bought magazines and a book* or an appositional phrase, which we will get to in a later chapter), the clause is either di-transitive or complex transitive. If it's di-transitive, the IO can be moved past the DO with the addition of the preposition *to* or *for*. Either object can be promoted to subject in a passive transformation. If it's complex transitive, some form of the verb to be can be inserted between DO and PC and the two NP's will seem to rename or re-identify each other. A di-transitive clause will seem to have two separate participants in the predicate, whereas a complex transitive clause will seem to have only one.

If the DO is immediately followed by an AdjP, the clause is complex transitive. If in doubt, inserting some form of the verb to be between DO and the following phrase will be a helpful test.

If the DO is followed by a constituent group that seems adverbial, however, the situation can get tricky. Adverbials are common in the predicates of all clauses as modifiers of the principal verb. Structural tests won't give you a satisfactory analysis and you will need to draw heavily on your own internal grammar, your own intuitive sense of how the clause means.

PC adverbials are usually the same kinds of adverbials acceptable as copular complements with the verb to be. They are almost always adverbials of time and place, with the notion that it is the action of the verb on the object that has in some way located or relocated that object in time or place. (*They scheduled our talk <u>after lunch</u>. She placed the bush <u>under our front window</u>.*) Other adverbials, like those of purpose or manner (how or why) just don't fit, for the same reasons we won't find them as complements in copular clauses.

He built the shed <u>slowly</u>.
How it was built: manner

He built the shed <u>with leftover materials</u>.
How it was built: instrument

He built the shed <u>for garden tools</u>.
Why it was built: purpose

He moved the shed <u>across the lawn</u>.
Where the shed ended up as a result of his moving it

Though all four of the above sentences contain predicate phrase adverbials, only the fourth contains an adverbial PC.

The concept of complex transitivity may frustrate you for a while; I can still recall my own difficulty with it, though now it seems clear as day. Learning grammar can be like that. You find yourself being told, say, five different things, which seem to add up to an impossible accumulation of detail. In reality, it can be like seeing five different fingers pointing at the same moon. Once you see the moon itself, it will be easy to recognize when you see it again. All those fingers are just pointers, not the moon itself. Of course, there is one way that this metaphor breaks down. You already know what a predicate compliment is because you have been using them all your life. If someone says *We have elected Joe Smith president*, we all know who is president and we know what actors and action brought that about. This pre-knowledge can't be emphasized enough in a natural grammar. We are not adding grammar to the language, but bringing to light the grammar that is already there.

6.7

Section

Exercise

Identify each of the following sentences as copular, intransitive, transitive, di-transitive, or complex transitive.

1) *The teacher gave us a stern lecture.*
2) *This will be a hard lesson.*
3) *The ball rolled into the garden.*
4) *The ball smashed our tulips.*
5) *The team selected Paula team captain.*
6) *We practiced all day.*
7) *The police soon gave up the chase.*
8) *The teachers' jokes put us in the best of moods.*
9) *Your decision made everybody happy.*
10) *She remains the best of my friends.*

6.8   Ergative and non-ergative patterns

If we want a deep and full understanding of the connection between grammar and representational meaning, we cannot ignore the categories of traditional transitivity that opened this chapter, but it would also be misleading to end with them. In some instances, they seem simply not to apply. In other instances, they seem too rough to be useful. Any attempt to understand how grammar helps us map the world has to include these traditional categories, but by themselves, they will not give us a particularly satisfying or full understanding.

When we make statements about transitive, di-transitive, or complex transitive processes, we often leave out elements of the process that are not important to our purposes.

We started out with examples of verb phrases (*is*, *rose*, and *noticed*) pretty much frozen into categories of transitivity: copular, intransitive, and transitive respectively. Most verbs in English are not frozen into a specific category, both transitive and intransitive being the most common variations. We can say *Paul ate the eggs* (transitive) and *Paul ate early* (intransitive) as representations of the same process that has an explicit object (*the eggs*) in one case, but not in the other. We can say *he kicked well* (intransitive), *he kicked the ball* (transitive), and *he kicked the ball through the goal posts* (complex transitive) as different ways of representing the same real world happening. We can simply explain away the differences in transitivity (intransitive, transitive, or complex transitive) by assuming that the writer or speaker may or may not have felt a need to describe all elements or all participants in the process. All this seems in deep harmony with the transitivity system as we have envisioned it. *He* is the actor and what *he* does can be thought of as extending to an object or goal, and the goal can be thought of as having been directed (or changed) by the actor's activity. We know also that English allows us to focus on the eggs or the ball (the direct objects) by taking the same process and making our statements passive. *The eggs were eaten. The ball was kicked. The ball was kicked right through the goal posts. The ball was kicked well.* All this is easily explained by our current understanding of transitivity and how it works. A process in the world, with an actor and a receiver of the action, is being encoded in different message structures.

What may surprise us, though, is that the language also allows us to speak or write about the object as if it were the agent in these processes. *The eggs disappeared. The ball went through the goal posts. The ball flew through the air. The ball sailed into the memory of all football fans, into history*. It's not that these are intransitive so much as non-transitive. It's as if the normal system of transitivity is being displaced or subverted.

Sometimes we can turn the object into active subject without making the sentence passive and without even having to change the verb processes involved. We can say *the wind cracked the window* and *the window was cracked by the wind* (transitive active and transitive passive versions). Or we can simply say *the window cracked*. Or *the window broke. The window shattered. The boulder rolled down the hill. The child woke suddenly.* These are 'ergative processes'; what they have in common is that all approach the process from the perspective of an entity not in itself an agent of its own change. But it treats these entities as if they have brought about their own change. If there are causal connections, they may be simply juxtaposed and not explicitly rendered. *The bomb fell. The hill exploded. The sun shone warm. The fields dried up.* The listener or reader is not being explicitly told that the bomb exploded the hill or the sun dried up the fields, though these are natural connections.

Ergative processes treat a changed entity as if it were the instrument of its own change.

Writers of modern narratives often seem to want to be non-intrusive, to simply juxtapose events or happenings without explicitly making the causal connections. The explicit versions may seem childish to us or overly explanatory. This same juxtapositional approach may be a convenient tool for advertisers as well. They can show happy and successful people using their product without explicitly having to say that the one causes the other. (Buy our beer and you'll go home with the beautiful woman.) But that may be unfair to this meaning-making pattern, unfairly implying that it can't and hasn't been used to powerful and honest effect.

The one indispensable element in an ergative process is the **medium**, the element undergoing change.

One way of thinking about this is that there is one participant in most processes that is absolutely essential to that process. For cooking, for example, we need something to be cooked. For tearing, we need something that can be torn. And so on. English allows us to make a statement about these processes that takes the agent right out of our field of view. *The rice cooked in an hour. The cloth tore in two places.* This absolutely essential participant has been called *the medium* and pairs of statements with the agent expressed or not expressed have been called *ergative* and *non-ergative* pairs.

> *My sister cooked the rice. The rice cooked in an hour.*
> *The sharp edge tore my jacket. My jacket tore in two places.*

Since there can't be cooking without *the rice* or tearing without *my jacket*, these are the medium in the above sentences. *My sister* and *The sharp edge* are optional.

In contrast, *My sister cooked* and *Sharp edges can tear* would be thought of as intransitive versions of transitive / intransitive pairs, with or without an explicit object.

6.9   Process approaches to transitivity

An alternate view of transitivity, one mentioned in the opening of this chapter, is that it has to do with the way a clause represents certain kinds of processes, each of these processes dictated by the nature of the verb. In one sense, each verb governs a certain kind of representational meaning. One clause is about *being*, another about *becoming, staying, remaining, putting, causing, kicking, telling*, and so on, almost forever.

As cumbersome as this kind of analysis might be, it has distinct advantages, one being that it makes clear how the nature of actor and object shift, sometimes remarkably, from clause to clause.

Charlie kicked the dog could be analyzed with *Charlie*, not just as 'actor', but as 'kicker'. The process would be 'kicking'. *The dog* would be, not just direct object, but 'receiver of the kick'. Neither process nor roles would change in the passive version. *The dog* (receiver of kick) *was kicked* (kicking as past passive process), *by Charlie* (kicker).

In *That man is my brother*, it seems strange, though, to think of *That man* as actor. Perhaps a better term would be 'identified element'. *Is* is a 'being' process. *My brother*, as we know, is not object at all, but copular complement. It is also the identifier, the element in the sentence which gives us the identity of *That man*.

The more we closely observe verbs as separate processes, the more it becomes clear that terms like 'actor' and 'direct object' begin to break down. 'Actor' seems too specific (true of just certain kinds of processes, like *kicking*). And 'direct object' seems too general. What are we to do with direct object in a statement like *I admire Mahatma Ghandi*? *I* can reasonably be construed as *actor* (*admirer* would be more precise), but in what sense is *Mahatma Ghandi* an affected participant? Even if he were still alive, it seems obvious that he could be admired from afar and not be at all affected by it. Yet when we think of Ghandi as a receiver of admiration, the analysis is easy and clear.

What are we to make of actor and direct object in *I know grammar*? It certainly seems strange to think of *grammar* as an affected participant. It's even hard to make this clearly transitive clause passive: *Grammar is being known by me*. The clause even seems to resist the present progressive, something we have already described as typical for representing the here and now: *I am knowing grammar* just seems like something a native speaker would never say. Yet if we think of *I* as 'knower', the process as knowing and the direct object (*grammar*) as 'what I know' or 'object of knowing', or even 'content of knowing', many of the problems seem to pass away.

Difficulties in recognizing direct objects will increase in later chapters when we consider structures other than typical noun phrases in both subject and object roles. What are we to do with *I hear what you are saying* where *what you are saying* is direct object? It certainly doesn't seem like an object and certainly doesn't seem like a participant, let alone an affected one. Yet when we consider hearing as a process, all becomes easy. *I* here is *hearer*. The process is *hearing*. *What you are saying* is what was heard. *I like swimming in the ocean on hot summer afternoons* will give us similar problems unless we can consider the sentence to be representing the process of liking. *I* is liker. Liking is process. *Swimming in the ocean on hot summer afternoons* is quite simply *what I like* (what is being liked) and therefore direct object.

It is wonderful, in some ways, to think that each sentence (each separate process) carries with it its own grammar. This is, in fact, a bit of what it's like to learn a new language or to add to the one you already carry. We learn a new verb by learning its grammar as well as its semantic meaning. We are beginning now to stray into the territory of dictionary makers, treating each word as carrying its own nuances of grammar and meaning. The process gets even more complicated when we realize that a good dictionary will rarely give just one meaning for a word. Thus, the process represented by *work* in *I work in the University* is not the same as *work* in *The comedian worked the audience* and both are different from *work* in *My computer still works*. They could be replaced by *am employed*, *manipulated*, and *functions*, though certainly not interchangeably. My own reasonably comprehensive desk dictionary lists, under the term *work*, 14 noun meanings, one adjective meaning, 11 intransitive verb meanings, and 10 transitive verb meanings; it adds four phrasal verb combinations (like *work off*), each with more than one meaning of its own. The dictionary makers would be the first to tell us that they did not get them all, especially any that may have been added to the language since the dictionary went to press. What a wonderful complexity a language is. We swim in a sea of words and the sea is never still.

Analyzing each verb phrase separately, useful as it is, can leave us with the feeling that we have not enough forest and too many trees. Since we are building an understanding of grammar and not a lexicography (a dictionary), we should look for patterns that are a bit more specific than those given us by traditional grammar but more general than considering each verb process as unique. Luckily for us, functional grammar has already beaten us to that. It breaks down representational structures into six major types, each with corresponding patterns in the grammar.

6.9.1 *Material process*

Used for actions in the material (physical) world, where actor, material process, and direct object as affected participant seem fine.

6.9.2 *Behavioral process*

Some processes seem more like behaviors than actions. Behavior as a process implies a 'behaver' rather than an 'actor', an entity that is more organic than physical. These are routinely intransitive, though they can become transitive in structures like *I dreamed a terrible dream* or *I slept a wonderful sleep*, where the objects seem more like extensions of the verb. Verbs like *laughed*, *danced*, *cried*, and *moaned* denote behaviors. Sometimes the same verbs will shift properties in context. *I woke up my brother* seems material process, whereas *I woke up early* seems a behavior.

Sometimes there will seem to be material / behavioral verb pairs, as with
kill and *die*, *collapse* and *faint*.

6.9.3   *Mental process*

Language, of course, is not just about the outside world, about the world
of material processes and behaviors, but about our own internal world
as well, the world of our perceptions, feelings, and thoughts. Functional
grammar makes a wonderful case for seeing these processes as a separate
grammatical category.

> Language does not simply represent the outside world, but often presents our own internal world, our thoughts, sensations, and feelings.

At least one participant in a mental process clause must be a conscious
being (or treated like one). In a material process clause, none of the
participants can be conscious. (That's not to say that people can't appear
in material process clauses, but that they are treated like any other object
when they do.)

There is a fascinating reciprocity between subject and object in a mental
process clause that has no parallel in material processes. This is perhaps
most easily exemplified by clause pairs like *I admire her* and *She impresses
me*, where subject and object can shift roles without the need for passive
constructions. *I fear the prospect of failure. The prospect of failure frightens
me.* The only way to explain this is to say that the object in a mental
process clause is in some way remarkably different from the object in
a material process. Common sense wisdom should help us here; this
concept is deeply ingrained in the way we see the world. If I say *I love
my wife*, that can certainly be seen as an action, but we understand it as
a reaction as well. We often have the feeling that we can't help feeling
what we're feeling. Something about my wife causes me to love her as
well. She is an affecting participant as well as an affected one. This same
reciprocity carries over to our perceptions and our thoughts. *I noticed
the picture. The picture caught my attention. I had an idea. An idea struck
me.* Both members of these pairs can be seen as true statements about the
same process, come at from different directions – what I did and what
I felt compelled or drawn to do. These are not simply active and passive
pairs, since each has its own passive version, as in *My attention was caught
by the picture*. It's as if in a mental process we are subjects and objects
simultaneously. Nothing in material process comes close to this.

> In a mental process, we often seem objects and subjects simultaneously.

The range of participants in a mental process is much wider than the
range of participants in a material process, where they are limited to
objects. A subject or object in a mental process clause for example, can be

One participant in a mental process clause is often a fact or idea.

a fact or idea, as in *I know <u>the way to San Jose</u>, I dislike <u>the fact that you are always late on Mondays</u>*, or *<u>The fact that you are always late on Mondays</u> irritates me.* This will become important in later chapters when we begin to explore subordinate clause structures. Participants in a mental process clause are frequently processes themselves, something that shouldn't surprise us if we think about the nature of sensing (perceiving), feeling, and knowing. Thus, the refrain from a once popular song – *I love what you do when you do what you do to me* – is typical of mental process statements in its clauses within clauses structure. We will unravel that sentence in Chapter 9. Everything after *love* is direct object. Functional grammar uses the term *phenomenon* for a mental clause object; we will stick with more traditional terminology, though *phenomenon* gives us a wonderful way of saying that the object in this kind of clause is very different from a direct object in a material process. What we see, feel and know is not just object, but 'phenomenon'.

A full discussion of this would take us off track, but mental process verbs often act differently in situations that would normally call for the passive or for progressive aspect. We normally wouldn't say *I am seeing ducks by the river* for something happening right now. As mentioned earlier, *I am knowing grammar* and *Grammar is known by me* seem ungrammatical. I mention this here as one more reason for considering mental process verbs a separate grammatical category.

6.9.4   *Verbal process*

Verbal process verbs include the most obvious, like *say* and *tell*, as well as many others, like *report, order, criticize, insult, praise*, and *imply*, verbs that in some way denote the expression of a message.

The role of actor (sayer) in a verbal process clause is not limited to conscious beings, but can include things: *The light on the dashboard told me to add oil; The look on her face suggested that I should be quiet.*

Verbal process clauses often include whole clauses that represent the content of a message.

Verbal process clauses can take typical NP direct objects. *She praised my efforts. We blamed the weather.* Functional grammar distinguishes between these objects (called the target) and objects that represent the actual content of a message (called verbiage).

It should not be surprising that the direct object (verbiage) of a verbal process clause is often a whole clause of its own. Statements are usually whole clauses of their own, and a verbal process clause is a statement about a statement.

I will stay late.
He said 'I will stay late.'
He said he would stay late.

Sentences two and three are verbal process clauses with the underlined portion as direct object. Sentence two is a direct quotation, using the actual words of the statement. Sentence three is an indirect quotation. We will run into these again as we explore subordinate clauses.

As said earlier in the chapter, verbal process clauses are often di-transitive. Quite often, they include a receiver (indirect object) of the message as well as the message itself. *I told you what to do.* In this sentence, *I* is sayer, *told* is verbal process, *you* is receiver (indirect object), and *what to do* is both verbiage and direct object.

Verbal processes are common, of course, in fiction, where dialogue is often a considerable part of the content. They also show up often in news reports. Journalists are constrained from directly presenting their own feelings, judgments, and speculations, but can easily slip in the expressed feelings, judgments, and speculations of others. *A source close to the mayor has told us... It has been alleged that...* They also show up often in scholarly writing as we try to incorporate the expressed views of others in a field.

6.9.5   Relational process

Functional grammar extends the notion of relational process beyond what we have described as copular. For our purposes, we will consider the categories as equivalent.

The two major subcategories are identifying and attributive. *My toughest class is grammar* is an identifying clause. *My toughest class* (identified entity) is being identified by *grammar* (identifier). *Paul is tall* is an attributive clause. *Paul* is carrier. *Tall* is an attribute (that *Paul* carries).

6.9.6   Existential process

I said of copular clauses that a copular clause requires a copular complement. This should be clear once we realize the nature of copular clauses. 'Copular' derives from a Latin verb meaning 'couple'. A copular clause is a way of establishing relationship, of identifying or attributing. You need two elements, including a copular complement, for this to happen.

English does allow, though, for another type of clause, an 'existential' clause, that simply affirms the existence of something.

It is raining.
There are two good reasons to stay home.

In the above examples, *It* and *There* have no representational meaning. They just simply stand in as place markers for the subject. The representational meaning could be expressed as something like the following: *Raining is*; *Two good reasons to stay home exist*. These easily shade toward material process, as with the colloquial (intransitive) *Stuff happens*.

A convenient chart of these processes, from M. A. K. Halliday's *An Introduction to Functional Grammar* (p. 143) appears below.

process type	category meaning	participants
material	doing	Actor, Goal
action	doing	
event	happening	
behavioural	behaving	Behaver
mental	sensing	Senser, Phenomenon
perception	seeing	
affection	feeling	
cognition	thinking	
Verbal	saying	Sayer, Target
relational	being	
attribution	attributing	Carrier, Attribute
identification	identifying	Identified, Identifier; Token, Value
existential	existing	Existent

6.10
Section
Exercise

Identify process types for each of the numbered clauses in the passage below. For your convenience, verb phrases have been underlined. Does this help us understand the kinds of meaning being represented in the passage? Is it a useful aid in interpretation? If this were the opening paragraph of an essay, what would you expect to follow?

> I <u>was kicked and hit</u>[1] quite often when I <u>was</u>[2] a child. I never <u>knew</u>[3] when it <u>would happen</u>[4] or what <u>would bring</u>[5] it about. But I <u>am</u>[6] not alone in this. Child abuse <u>is</u>[7] a terrible problem in our society.

I. The following are from W. S. Merwin's *Asian Figures*, his own versions of translated proverbs and sayings from Asian cultures. Merwin's versions are presented in poem form, often with very short lines. With apologies to Merwin, I have reprinted them here as short sentences to minimize distraction by the line breaks.

For each, underline the verb phrase and tell whether it is copular, intransitive, transitive, di-transitive, or complex transitive.

1) *Even the rich prefer cash.*
2) *Charcoal writes everyone's name black.*
3) *No flower stays a flower.*
4) *Knife can't whittle its own handle.*
5) *How long is a snake in a cave.*
6) *Water follows a water leader.*
7) *Buried diamond is still a diamond.*
8) *Every grave holds a reason.*
9) *Better than the holiday is the day before.*
10) *The labor of the poor makes the hills higher.*
11) *Tomorrow's wind blows tomorrow.*
12) *To the winners the losers were rebels.*
13) *Nobody bothers the bad boys.*
14) *As two clauses: When he draws a tiger, it's a dog.*
15) *As two clauses: When you're poor, no one believes you.*

II. Diagram the following sentences, adding abbreviations for function to each node of the diagram. Be sure to add information about transitivity, tense or modality, aspect and if passive to the verb phrase (Not all categories will apply).

1) *I made her my wife on the twenty-first of June.*
2) *I pledged her my love on the twenty-first of June.*
3) *The United Nations remains our best hope for peace.*
4) *The wind threw open the door.*
5) *Two strangers wandered into town on Thursday.*

III. Identify process types for the verb phrases in the sentences in Part I.

Chapter 7
Section Exercises

Page 120
Identify verb forms; identify their use as as adjective or as part of a finite verb phrase.

Page 121
Identify verb forms; identify their use as adjectives, as nouns, or as part of a finite verb phrase.

Page 132
Sentences from Alex Kotlowitz's book *There Are No Children Here* for study: identify structure and function. Structures include adjective, NP, participial clause, or infinitive clause. Functions include adverbial or adjectival or any of the usual NP functions.

Chapter Practice

Page 135
Sentences from John McPhee's book about Alaska, *Coming Into The Country*. Identify structure and function. Structures include adjective, NP, participial clause, or infinitive clause. Functions include adverbial or adjectival or any of the usual NP functions.

Chapter 7

Verbs as adjectives, nouns, and as heads of non-finite subordinate clauses

The English language can be delightfully flexible or maddeningly flexible, depending on the perspective we bring. As language users, we have a rich and delightful array of options at our disposal, options we mastered long ago and use quite easily without needing to be consciously aware of them. When we analyze those structures, though, that same flexibility can leave us confused.

In this chapter, we will be looking at verb forms in roles other than as the principal verb phrase of a clause: verbs as adjectives, as nouns, and as heads of non-finite clauses that themselves function as adverbial or adjectival modifiers or in roles (like subject or direct object) typically carried out by noun phrases. We will not be adding functions in this chapter, but simply looking at verb derived structures that can fill the function slots we are already aware of.

We will try to understand structures like the underlined structures in the following sentences:

The _shouting_ student rose from his seat.
shouting is adjective

The _defeated_ team slouched toward the bus.
defeated is adjective

Swimming can be excellent exercise.
swimming is noun

I love swimming in the ocean on hot summer afternoons.
swimming heads a participial clause including all the underlined words that follow it. The whole clause is direct object of VP *love*.

I love to swim in the ocean on hot summer afternoons.
to swim heads an infinitive clause including all the underlined elements that follow it. As in sentence four, the whole clause acts as direct object of VP *love*.

You may be asking yourself how it is possible for a verb to be an adjective or a noun? When we say that a word is a verb, we are saying that it belongs to the form class of verbs, one of four principal form classes in the language. (As you no doubt recall from Chapter 3, the other form classes are nouns, adjectives, and adverbs.) You may have learned in grade school that a verb is a word that conveys action or a state of being. Because we have studied representational meaning in the last chapter, you can recognize that as a representational definition, one closely tied to the notions of transitive and intransitive (action) and copular (state of being). It's not a complete definition by any means, but it does seem like a reasonable beginning.

We also explored in Chapter 5 how verbs change form and combine with auxiliaries to express tense and aspect and (sometimes) to agree with the subject in person and/or number. Because action or a state of being can be hard notions to pin down, the structural test is our most reliable indicator that the word in question is a verb. It is true of all verbs; they may be regular (weak) or irregular (strong), but all verbs change form and combine with auxiliaries to carry tense and aspect.

When verbs function as adjectives and nouns, they maintain their verb-like qualities.

When we say that verbs can act like adjectives and nouns, we are talking about how they routinely function when combining with other words within the structures of actual statements. They do not stop being verbs (members of a form class) when they do that.

Words can also be members of more than one form class at a time. *Slow* is a verb as well as an adjective. My own dictionary lists both transitive and intransitive meanings for it. *The car slows as it nears the intersection* (intransitive). *He slowed the car as it neared the intersection* (transitive). *Slow* is a verb as well as an adjective because it passes the tests for verbs that we discussed earlier. It seems to represent an action (material process). Even more importantly, it picks up regular verb inflections (*slows, slowed, slowing*) and combines with auxiliaries to show tense, aspect, and subject / verb agreement – an always reliable test for including a word in the verb form class.

Like most adjectives, *slow* can also function as a noun in statements like *The track coach has no sympathy for the slow.* (Compare to *Only the strong survive*, or *Blessed are the meek*.) In those three sentences, *slow, strong,* and *meek* are adjectives functioning as nouns because they are the head of a structure we have come to recognize as a noun phrase. These are sometimes called a 'fused head' because the head noun is now fused with the adjective. Placing a word within a form class is very important to the makers of dictionaries and it can give us important information about a word. But these words will find their ways into structures and carry out functions that are much wider than the form class alone would imply.

Slow can also function as an adjective using its present participle and past participle verb forms, as in *the slowing car* or *the slowed car*. Why, you might ask, has the language derived these additional forms for the same (adjectival) role? One answer is that most verbs aren't words that also belong to the form class adjectives. Another answer is that the meaning is different. Look at these three sentences and think about the differences in meaning before you move on.

> *The slow car approached the intersection.*
> *The slowing car approached the intersection.*
> *The slowed car approached the intersection.*

My own sense is that *the slow car* (sentence one) conveys a more permanent sense of the car's characteristics. If the statement is true, the car is incapable of being fast. *The slowing car* (sentence two) is more immediate and continuous in its meaning; at the moment in time we are focusing on, the car is in the process of reducing its speed. (It's possible that the car itself is *a fast car*.) *The slowed car* (sentence three) gives a sense that the slowing has already been completed; at the moment we are focusing on, the car carries the characteristic of having already been slowed; *slowed* picks up a sense of the passive – a past action that has happened to the car is now carried as a characteristic into the moment of our attention.

Present participle as adjective tends to denote an ongoing activity. Past participle as adjective often retains a sense of the passive.

Another example might help clarify the meaning sense of present participle and past participle forms as adjectives. Consider the following sentence – *Her remarks wounded her friend* – where *wounded* is past tense and transitive. That might likely be followed by *her wounding remarks* or *her wounded friend* as NP's in a following sentence. In this case, the present participle as adjective (*wounding*) modifies the subject (actor) and the past participle as adjective (*wounded*) modifies the object. In *her wounding remark*, *remark* is still clearly doing something and in *her wounded friend*, the *friend* has clearly had something done to him. Even though they are functioning as adjectives, these verb derived forms still carry a verb-like meaning into their adjectival roles.

7.2

Section

Exercise

Identify verb forms in the following sentences and then tell whether they are being used as adjective or as part of a finite verb phrase.

1) *The cat has broken the vase.*
2) *The breaking vase sprayed glass shards across the room.*
3) *The broken vase had been given to me by my mother.*

7.3   Verb forms as nouns

The present participle form of a verb can function like a noun; when it does so, it has traditionally been called a 'gerund' by grammarians. The past participle cannot move into a noun slot except in the way any adjective can (as fused head) in sentences like those we explored in the last section: *Only the defeated know true humility*. But the present participle can easily act like a noun. Gerunds can show up in any slot typically occupied by a noun, as the following sentence examples show.

1) *My swimming has improved.*
   My swimming as subject

2) *I admire her swimming.*
   her swimming as direct object of VP *admire*

3) *I read a book about swimming.*
   swimming as object of preposition *about*

4) *One excellent exercise is swimming.*
   swimming as copular complement to VP *is*

5) *The Olympics gave swimming a boost in popularity.*
   swimming as indirect object to di-transitive VP *gave*

You should usually consider a present participle in an NP slot to be a noun (gerund) when it is a single word phrase, as in sentences 3 to 5 above. (Though occasionally these single word phrases will be adjectival, the present participle an adjective, as in *Her daughter seemed <u>charming</u>*.) Like other noun heads, these can also be expanded out with determiners and other adjectival modifiers, as in sentences 1 and 2 above, and as in the following: *her strong swimming; his incessant smoking of cheap cigars*. In both these phrases, the determiners and adjectives give us a clear indication that *swimming* and *smoking* are acting like nouns. We will consider a present participle a noun if it is modified by modifiers that are clearly adjectival in nature, as in *I dislike <u>long-distance running</u>*. We will consider it to be the head of a non-finite subordinate clause when it is followed by elements that seem like verb complements, direct objects and adverbial modifiers and copular complements and the like. Sometimes these clause-like structures will pull in pronoun determiners that act like implied subjects. (*<u>His incessantly</u> smoking cheap cigars*, which seems clause-like in carrying an adverbial modifier and a direct object, but also pulls in a possessive determiner.)

A word group headed by present participal form of a verb should be considered a noun phrase if it is modified by adjectives and determiners. It should be thought of as a non-finite subordinate clause if it takes verb-like complements and adverbial modifiers.

7.4

Section

Exercise

Identify verb forms in the following four sentences and then tell whether they are used as adjectives, as nouns (gerunds), or as part of a finite verb phrase. If all or part of a noun phrase, tell what NP function the phrase carries out. If adjective, tell what word or word group it modifies.

1) *They followed the meandering stream through the valley.*
2) *He examined my studying and found it lacking.*
3) *Seeing is believing.*
4) *Don't cry over spilled milk.*

Non-finite subordinate clauses   7.5

What is a non-finite subordinate clause? It is built from a verb phrase, but the verb in this structure is not finite, not carrying either tense or modality. It's subordinate because it cannot stand alone as the principal clause of a sentence; this should make sense if you remember our discussion of exchange function in Chapter 4 – a clause needs both grammatical subject and finite verb to be a recognizable proposition and to fulfill the minimum requirements traditionally called for in a sentence. A subordinate clause, in fact, will have a role within another clause, and in all cases it will be a role we have already identified as being carried out by other word groups (like subject or adverbial modifier).

A **matrix clause** is the core foundation of a sentence. A **subordinate clause** has a role within another clause.

The principal clause in a sentence is often called an 'independent clause', a name that highlights its ability to function independently. Subordinate clauses are often called 'dependent clauses', a name that highlights their dependent (subordinate) status. Some current grammars call these independent clauses 'matrix clauses' to highlight the fact that they are the matrix (foundation or core) around which a more complex structure can be built. We will use the terms 'matrix clause' and 'subordinate clause', though 'independent' and 'dependent' are useful descriptors in their own right. In addition to the non-finite subordinate clauses we will cover in this chapter, there are also finite subordinate clauses (subordinate clauses that do carry a finite verb phrase), which we will cover in Chapter 9.

A sentence is not simply a clause, but a clause complex or clause cluster.

Up to this point, we have been examining primarily single clause sentences. We are now expanding our idea of a sentence to accommodate additional clauses in coordinate (next chapter) and subordinate roles. A sentence is not simply a clause, but a clause complex or clause cluster. A sentence includes a minimum of one (matrix) clause. The maximum number of clauses has practical limits – you run out of paper and time and risk exasperating your poor reader – but theoretically, there is no limit to the number of clauses that can be included in a sentence. (Even a single clause can be expanded indefinitely, something we will explore in the next chapter.)

Non-finite subordinate clauses include participial clauses (built from the present or past participle forms of a verb) and infinitive clauses (built from the infinitive form of a verb and usually introduced by the complementizer *to*). Examples are given below.

I love <u>swimming in the ocean on hot summer afternoons</u>.
present participle clause acting as direct object of mental process VP *love*.

Many beach houses <u>battered by the storm</u> were in immediate need of repair.
past participle clause acting as restrictive adjectival modifier of the NP *many beach houses*.

I want <u>to do well in this grammar class</u>.
infinitive clause acting as direct object of mental process VP *want*.

That these clauses are non-finite is easily tested by changing the tense of the overall sentence. Notice that the tense of the matrix clause VP changes, but the head of the non-finite clause remains unchanged. This is an excellent tool in analysis.

I loved swimming in the ocean on hot summer afternoons.
love changes to *loved*, but *swimming* remains unchanged

Many beach houses battered by the storm are in immediate need of repair.
were changes to *are*, but *battered* remains unchanged

I wanted to do well in this grammar class.
want changes to *wanted*, but *do* remains unchanged

Now you know why these clauses are non-finite and why they are subordinate. But why are they called 'clauses'? To this point, we have defined a clause as 'a structure with both subject and predicate'. Non-finite clauses will always seem like they have predicates (they will often seem like predicate phrases themselves), but sometimes they may seem to carry a subject and sometimes not. That is to say, they float in between seeming like phrases and seeming like clauses. Traditional grammar, in fact, calls these structures 'participle phrases' and 'infinitive phrases' rather than 'participle clauses' and 'infinitive clauses'. (Learning grammar is hard enough without these disagreements.) There are arguments to be made for both sides. We will call them clauses because they seem to do the work of a clause (although in a subordinate role) and because their subjects, when not directly stated, are usually clearly implied.

Below is a sentence with a participial clause as direct object diagramed out.

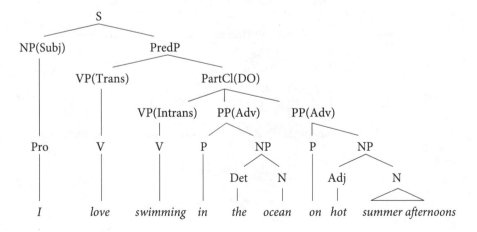

When there is more than one clause in a sentence, each will have independent transitivity.

Swimming as verb phrase and *in the ocean* and *on hot summer afternoons* as adverbial prepositional phrase modifiers should look very familiar. Notice that *love* is transitive but *swimming* is intransitive. Each verb phrase within a sentence will take on its own transitivity. The participial clause takes its place within the matrix clause as direct object, just as a simple NP would do, as in the following:

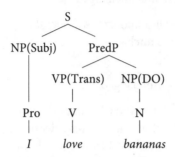

Our doing well in grammar sentence will look a lot like the swimming sentence, with infinitive clause rather than participial clause as object. *To* is a new element. It's a 'complementizer' (Comp), a word whose primary function is to link one constituent group with another without having any role in the clause it introduces.

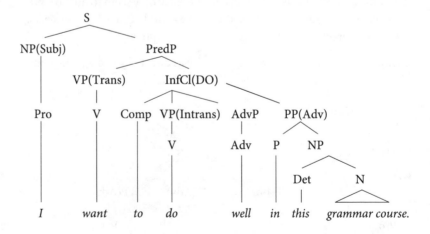

Non-finite clauses built from the present participle form of the verb are common in sentence roles usually filled by noun phrases: as subject, direct object, copular complement, object of preposition, etc.

I enjoy playing golf on Sunday.
playing golf on Sunday is direct object of VP *enjoy*

Eating too much salt is bad for the heart.
Eating too much salt is subject

This is a book about winning elections.
winning elections is object of preposition *about*

Their goal for the season is winning the conference championship.
wining the conference championship is copular complement of VP *is*

7.6.1 *Participial clauses as adverbial*

Participial clauses are almost never adverbial. Occasionally, English speakers or writers will give us verb plus verb combinations that pretty much force us into an adverbial analysis, though these are very rare. *The speaker <u>went rambling on</u> about nothing.* These are rare enough (and certainly more common in speech than in writing) to almost discard this as a category. In the vast majority of cases, if a participial clause is not acting in an NP role, it is adjectival.

7.6.2 *Participial clauses as restrictive and non-restrictive*

Adjectival modifiers

To understand the important categories of restrictive and non-restrictive modification, it helps to remember the nature of nouns and the roles of adjectival modifiers. Nouns are often not just persons, places, and things, but designate something as the member of a category or group (like *cow* or *animal* or *fool* or *car*). Restrictive modification is modification that allows us to narrow down (or restrict) the group or category. Non-restrictive modification tells us attributes or characteristics of something that has already been identified.

Restrictive modification narrows down a group or category and helps establish identity.

Any student cheating on a test should be severely punished.

Cheating on a test is a restrictive adjectival modifier of *Any student* because it helps narrow or restrict the category. It's not true that *any student should be severely punished*. That statement is only intended for *Any student cheating on a test*.

Our starting pitcher, looking tired and defeated, walked slowly off the mound.

Looking tired and defeated is a non-restrictive adjectival modifier of *Our starting pitcher*. *Looking tired and defeated* doesn't help us know who *Our starting pitcher* is. It simply says something additional about him.

Good writers designate adjectival word groups as non-restrictive by setting them off with commas.

Notice that restrictive adjectival modifiers (with word groups that follow a NP) are not set off by commas, but non-restrictive modifiers are. This picks up a pattern of intonation that is natural in speech and can sometimes be very important to the meaning. We'll discuss this again with other postnominal (after the NP) word groups and in our punctuation chapter. In the meantime, when you read the work of a good, careful writer, the presence or absence of these commas can be a reliable tool in analysis and in understanding. A postnominal adjectival modifier not set off by commas is meant to be understood as restrictive. A postnominal adjectival modifier set off by commas is non-restrictive.

When participle clauses are restrictive, they are limited to a position immediately following the NP they modify (where they can be restrictive or non-restrictive). When restrictive, they will also seem to narrow down the meaning of the NP they modify and they will not be set off by commas.

Any student <u>wearing a hat in class</u> should be asked to remove it.
People <u>carrying guns</u> should be prepared to use them.
Travelers <u>looking for a good, inexpensive meal</u> often stop at Harry's Diner.

Non-restrictive adjectival participial clauses can move to a number of sentence positions.

When adjectival participial clauses are non-restrictive, they can move to a number of sentence positions. In that way, they are like adverbial structures in their flexibility of position. The key in determining what NP they modify is to think of them as predicate phrases and look for their implied subject.

Consider the following sentence from Alex Kotlowitz's *There Are No Children Here*. There are five verb phrases, but only one is finite. Which is the matrix clause verb? Which are the heads of non-finite participial clauses? What NP do the non-finite participial clauses modify? Think about these questions before you move on.

> *I spent the summer at Henry Horner, playing basketball with the kids, going to lunch with them, talking with their parents, and just hanging out.*

Spent is the finite VP (and thus the matrix clause VP). It's the only verb phrase that would change if we shifted the sentence to present tense. The rest of the sentence after *Henry Horner* consists of four participial clauses separated by commas and headed by *playing, going, talking,* and *hanging out.* All four clauses modify the NP *I,* their implied subject.

We can hypothesize five source sentences for this sentence. *I spent the summer at Henry Horner. I played basketball with the kids. I went to lunch with them. I talked with their parents.* And *I just hung out.*

One alternative in combining them would have been to keep all five verb phrases finite. *I spent the summer at Henry Horner, played basketball with the kids, went to lunch with them, talked with their parents, and just hung out.* But this would have the effect of making all five predicate phrases equal in status. Making *spent* the matrix clause verb gives its predicate phrase a higher (matrix clause) status and makes the rest of the structures subordinate. This seems nicely appropriate to the meaning, with *spent the summer* as a general (summary) action and the participial clauses elaborating this out in more specific detail, telling us how he spent the summer. (Though they tell how, we need to resist seeing them as adverbial.) These are not just accidental choices, but evidence of a thoughtful and careful writer at work.

Dangling participles

Because of the movability of non-restrictive participial clauses, they can be the source of the notorious error known as a dangling participle. These occur when the NP they modify is left out or when another NP intervenes and introduces another unintended meaning. Here's an example, turned into a joke, from the movie *Mary Poppins:*

Character one: *I once knew a man with a wooden leg named Mr. Smith.*
Character two: *Oh yeah? What does he call his other leg?*

The participial clause *named Mr. Smith,* of course, is intended to modify the NP *a man,* but the listener chooses to interpret it as modifying *a wooden leg,* the NP closest to it. Most listeners would compensate, throwing out the joke meaning as unlikely, perhaps at such speed that the choice never reaches consciousness. The joke calls it back to our attention. It's not unusual for a dangling participle to create comic meanings.

I saw a bear driving through the park.

What the writer means to say, we suppose, is *Driving through the park, I saw a bear.* Moving the participial clause to a place where its true implied subject is the closest NP takes away the comic ambiguity.

A dangling participle occurs when a participial clause seems to modify the wrong noun phrase.

Sometimes a dangling participle will be created when the NP it modifies is simply left out of the sentence. *Riding in a small kayak, the current seemed especially strong. Nearing the corner, the two robbers were seen exiting the bank.* It's not the current that is riding in a small kayak or the bank robbers that are nearing the corner, but a missing subject, probably *I*.

7.7   Infinitive clauses as adverbial

Infinitive clauses are frequently adverbial. When they are, they represent the purpose or intention of an action and they are very easily tested by replacing the *to* with *in order to*. If the structure seems to retain its meaning with *in order to*, the infinitive clause is adverbial:

She went to the store to buy bread.
She went to the store in order to buy bread.
Paul worked two jobs to support his growing family.
Paul worked two jobs in order to support his growing family.
My cousin went to college to please her parents.
My cousin went to college in order to please her parents.

Like adjectival participial clauses, adverbial infinitive clauses are very movable. They show up often as marked themes.

Like most adverbials, these can easily move to sentence opening position for thematic emphasis. *To buy bread, she went to the store. To support his growing family, Paul worked two jobs. To please her parents, my cousin went to college.*

7.7.1   *Infinitive clauses as adjectival*

Adjectival infinitive clauses will almost always be restrictive. A number of very abstract nouns are routinely followed by infinitive clauses that limit (make more concrete) their meaning: *the chance to succeed; the opportunity to advance; the desire to return home; his need to forget his troubled past.* These are relatively easy to analyze because they are frozen in position immediately following the abstract NP they modify. It's not at all unusual for the abstract NP to be an ordinal numeral, as in *the first to attend college*, *the second to enter*, or *the last to escape*. When that happens, there often seems to be a fused head, as in *Of all the members of his family, he was the first (one) to attend college*.

If the NP is already narrowed down to a member of a group of one, the following infinitive clause modifier will be non-restrictive. Given the nature of these structures, it is not as common, but it does happen. *His fondest ambition, to be President of the United States, finally came to pass.*

These infinitive clause modifiers can often also be thought of as appositional (a category we will cover in the next chapter).

7.7.2   *Infinitive clauses in NP roles*

Infinitive clauses as subjects, direct objects, and copular complements are fairly common, often seeming fairly interchangeable with participial clause alternatives.

To err is human.
To err is infinitive clause subject

He wants to visit Paris in the springtime.
to visit Paris in the springtime is direct object of VP *wants*. (Infinitive clauses as direct objects of feeling and desiring verbs are very common, as in: *He loves to… He hates to… He desires to…*)

His fondest desire is to see Paris in the springtime.
to see Paris in the springtime is copular complement of VP *is*

If the matrix clause verb represents a kind of speech act, infinitive clauses in the predicate phrase will often be direct objects, with the matrix clause itself being di-transitive. *He asked us to stay. He told us to stop fooling around.* In both those sentences, the infinitive clause is direct object and *us* is indirect object. The logic here is that the infinitive clause is a summary of the content of what was spoken. *He asked us 'Will you stay?' He told us 'stop fooling around.'*

7.8   Extraposed infinitives

With copular verbs, infinitive clause subjects are often extraposed. This has the effect of placing the subject of the sentence in the position of clause ending emphasis. The pronoun *it* simply stands in for the extraposed subject, as in the sentence *It is easy to love you*. We can hypothesize a source sentence of *To love you is easy*, with *To love you* as subject, *is* as copular VP and *easy* as adjectival copular complement. Generally, *it* is described as expletive and *to love you* is identified as the logical subject or extraposed subject. (We will use the term extraposed subject.)

Infinitive clause subjects and direct objects are often extraposed, with 'it' standing in as grammatical placeholder.

> *It is a shame to waste good food.*
> Again, we can hypothesize a source sentence of *To waste good food is a shame*. *It* is expletive. *Is* is copular VP. *Shame* is adjectival copular complement. *To waste good food* is extraposed subject.

A similar process of extraposition occurs with infinitive clause direct objects in a complex transitive sentence. *I find it easy to love you*. We can hypothesize as source sentence *I find to love you easy*. (If that sounds awkward, that's because extraposing these direct objects has become the normal way these structures are handled.) In the extraposed version, *I* is NP subject, *find* is complex transitive VP, *it* is expletive, *easy* is adjectival predicate complement, and *to love you* is extraposed direct object.

7.9   Perception verbs and causative verbs

Perception verbs will often be followed by non-finite clauses that seem to carry a subject and act like a single direct object, as in the following:

Perception verbs often take subject bearing subordinate clauses as direct object, and causative verbs often take non-finite clauses as predicate complements. These are sometimes difficult to differentiate from each other.

> *I saw the birds landing on the river.*
> *I felt the house collapsing around me.*
> *I watched my father work hard all his life.*
> *I heard the car roar past.*

For each of these sentences, the action in the clause seems to weigh as heavily in importance as the NP. It's not just *the house* that you feel, but *the house collapsing*. *Collapsing* doesn't help us identify which house, but tells us what you feel the house doing. Because they so obviously carry both subject and predicate, these are the best evidence for thinking of these non-finite structures as clauses and not just phrases.

Causative verbs will give us structures that look very similar but need to be analyzed as different (as complex transitive rather than simple transitive, as carrying predicate complements.) If you recall, the category of predicate complement is created by causative verbs, which act upon the object in such a way that a change results, with the predicate complement itself representing the new condition. The following sentences give us non-finite clauses that are clearly predicate complements.

The comic's jokes left us <u>laughing uncontrollably</u>.
The weather forced the team <u>to practice inside</u>.
The teacher made us <u>stay after class</u>.
My room-mate helped me (to) <u>make the dean's list</u>.

The comic's jokes had an effect on *us*, leaving us *laughing uncontrollably*. *The weather* had an effect on *the team*, forcing it *to practice inside*. *The teacher* had an effect on *us*, making us *stay after class*. My room-mate had an effect on *me*, helping me (*to*) *make the dean's list*.

Because transitive and complex transitive sentences may look so similar in structure, this is a very tricky area for analysis. Don't be frustrated if the decision looks fuzzy. Should wanting something or imagining something be thought of as causative? *I imagined my teacher <u>running naked through the streets</u>. I wanted my son <u>to be President</u>.* I would interpret these to be causative in the sense that wanting and imagining are acts that bring about *running naked through the streets* and being *President,* though those states exist only in the mind. The same would be true for statements about thinking and judging or about finding and discovering. (*I found the boy crying in a corner.*) We could spend a long time looking at sentences like this and trying to build a consensus. Without that, don't be afraid to step back and think about the representational meaning as you interpret it. Have faith in your own convictions. If the verb seems to be acting on the NP in such a way as to bring a new condition about, read the non-finite clause as a predicate complement. (*They made us do well.*) If the NP plus non-finite structure seems to act like a single unit, with subject and predicate of equal importance, then the sentence is mono-transitive and the clause is subject bearing. (*With great pride, I watched my son do well.*)

7.10   Infinitive clauses without *to*

The presence of to as complementizer is an aid in recognizing infinitive clauses. Some verbs, though, will routinely take infinitive clauses without the to, especially in predicate complement positions (*He made us stay late. She helped us learn grammar.*) This is also common in subject bearing direct objects following perception verbs. (*I saw the plane land on the water. I felt the floor lean. I heard the horn sound in the driveway.*) When the sentences these appear in are in present tense, it may be hard to recognize these as non-finite. *I see the plane land on the water*. If you change the tense of the sentence, though, the finite and non-finite verb phrases will separate themselves out; only the finite verb phrase will reflect the tense change. *I saw the plane land on the water.*

7.11   Participial clauses as absolutes

Certain adjectival subject bearing participial clauses are called 'absolutes' in traditional grammar. They may or may not come with the preposition *with*: *With his hands tied behind him, Paul was led into the courtroom. His hands tied behind him, Paul was led into the courtroom.* In both cases, *his hands tied behind him* is an absolute. They also occur with present participial clauses: *The ground rising to meet him, he fumbled for the release of his parachute.*

7.12

Section
Exercise

Word groups have been isolated in the following sentences. For each, identify structure and function. Structures include adjective, NP, participial clause, or infinitive clause. Functions include adverbial or adjectival (tell what word groups they modify) or any of the usual NP functions (subject, object of a preposition, direct object, indirect object, copular complement, or predicate complement.) If the object of a preposition, tell which preposition. If complement of a verb phrase, tell what VP it complements. If non-finite clauses are adjectival, tell whether they are restrictive or non-restrictive. Tell whether participial clauses are present participle or past participle. If a participial clause or infinitive clause is subject bearing, say so. The sentences are all from Alex Kotlowitz's book *There Are No Children Here.*

1) [*The book*] *is, instead, about a beginning, the dawning of
   two lives.*
   a)   *a beginning*
   b)   *the dawning of two lives*

2) *I... had been asked by a friend to write the text for a photo essay.*
   a)   *to write the text for a photo essay.*

3) *He... had spent a number of days taking photographs of them at the
   Henry Horner House, a public housing complex.*
   a)   *taking photographs of them at the Henry Horner House, a public
   housing complex.*

4) *This book follows Lafayette and Pharoah over a two year period as they
   struggle with school, attempt to resist the lure of the gangs, and mourn
   the death of friends, all the while searching for some inner peace.*
   a)   *to resist the lure of the gangs*
   b)   *all the while searching for some inner peace.*

5) *The train passed without incident, and soon most of the boys had joined
   James and Lafayette in the boxcar, sitting in the doorway, their rangy legs
   dangling over the side.*
   a)   *sitting in the doorway*
   b)   *their rangy legs dangling over the side.*

6) *They dug hole after hole in the hard soil, determined not to go home
   empty-handed.*
   a)   *determined not to go home empty-handed.*

7) *Williams died a few months later when a friend, fooling around with a
   revolver he thought was unloaded, shot Williams in the back of the head.*
   a)   *fooling around with a revolver he thought was unloaded.*
   b)   *unloaded.*

8) *He didn't want to leave this place, the sweet smell of the wildflowers and
   the diving sparrows.*
   a)   *to leave this place, the sweet smell of the wildflowers and the diving
   sparrows.*
   b)   *diving*

9) *Reluctantly, they gathered the crowbars, slid down the embankment, and,
   as Lafayette took Pharoah's hand to cross the busy street, began the short
   trek home.*
   a)   *to cross the busy street*

10) *Lafayette and his nine year old cousin Dede danced across the worn lawn outside their building, singing the lyrics of an L.L. Cool J. rap, their small hips and spindly legs moving in rhythm.*
   a) *worn*
   b) *singing the lyrics of an L.L. Cool J. rap*
   c) *their small hips and spindly legs moving in rhythm.*

11) *In recent years, she had become more tired as she questioned her ability to raise her children here.*
   a) *to raise her children here.*

12) *She worked as a prostitute from time to time to support her drug habit.*
   a) *to support her drug habit.*

13) *For a photograph taken when he was about four, he shoved a big cigar in his mouth and plopped a blue floppy hat on his head.*
   a) *taken when he was about four*

14) *The past spring, he'd been caught stealing candy from a Walgreen's downtown.*
   a) *stealing candy from a Walgreen's downtown.*

15) *Pharoah clutched his childhood with the vigor of a tiger gripping his meat.*
   a) *a tiger gripping his meat.*
   b) *gripping his meat.*

16) *These forays into distant lands and with other people seemed to help Pharoah fend off the ugliness around him.*
   a) *to help Pharoah fend off the ugliness around him.*
   b) *fend off the ugliness around him.*

17) *He wanted to be recognized, to know that he was wanted.*
   a) *to be recognized*
   b) *to know that he was wanted.*

18) *A thin, warped plank of wood substituted for the unbuilt steps.*
   a) *warped*
   b) *unbuilt*

19) *Even the two unfinished buildings, one to the West and one to the South, their concrete frames still exposed, appeared stately.*
   a) *unfinished*
   b) *their concrete frames still exposed*

20) *They were to be the first family to occupy one of its sixty-five apartments.*
    a) *to occupy one of its sixty-five apartments.*

21) *Lafayette froze, then stabbed at a fly resting on the stove.*
    a) *a fly resting on the stove.*
    b) *resting on the stove.*

22) *Pharoah begged his brother to take him back to the railroad tracks.*
    a) *to take him back to the railroad tracks.*

23) *Lafayette reached out again, this time swatting the back of his brother's hand.*
    a) *this time swatting the back of his brother's hand.*

24) *He wanted to get away from his suffocating home, from Horner, from the Vice Lords, from the summer.*
    a) *to get away from his suffocating home, from Horner, from the Vice Lords, from summer.*
    b) *suffocating*

Word groups have been isolated in the following sentences. For each, identify structure and function. Structures include adjective, NP, participial clause, or infinitive clause. Functions include adverbial or adjectival (tell what word groups they modify) or any of the usual NP functions (subject, object of a preposition, direct object, indirect object, copular complement, or predicate complement). If the object of a preposition, tell which preposition. If complement of a verb phrase, tell what VP it complements. If non-finite clauses are adjectival, tell whether they are restrictive or non-restrictive. Tell whether participial clauses are present participle or past participle. If a participial clause or infinitive clause is subject bearing, say so. The sentences are all from John McPhee's book about Alaska, *Coming Into The Country*.

1) *Paddling on through the light rain, Kauffman now began to fulminate.*
   a) *Paddling on through the light rain*
   b) *to fulminate*

2) *Alaska is the last great opportunity to set aside adequate chunks of natural landscape for a variety of conservation purposes.*
   a) *to set aside great chunks of natural landscape for a variety of conservation purposes*

3) *Toward the bottom of the rip, water collected, becoming heavy and white and two feet deep.*
   a) *becoming heavy and white and two feet deep*

4) *The river then turned right – a bending chute with a cut bank on one side and an apron of gravel on the other.*
   a) *bending*
   b) *cut*

5) *If I wanted to, I could always see disaster running with the river, dancing like a shadow, moving down the forest from tree to tree.*
   a) *running with the river*
   b) *dancing like a shadow*
   c) *moving down the forest from tree to tree*

6) *Coming down a long, deep, green pool, we looked toward the riffle at the lower end and saw an approaching grizzly.*
   a) *Coming down a long, deep, green pool*
   b) *approaching*

7) *Instantly, he was motionless and alert, remaining on his four feet and straining his eyes to see.*
   a) *remaining on his four feet*
   b) *straining his eyes to see*
   c) *to see*

8) *Then we came to another long flat surface, spraying up the light of the sun. The wind gradually subsides through the afternoon, and the low gray sky begins to pull itself apart.*
   a) *to pull itself apart.*

9) *Drawing closer, we can see caribou antlers over doorways – testimony of need and respect.*
   a) *drawing closer*

10) *Protecting the antler takes longer than the dismantling and packing of the kayaks, but there is enough time before the flight to Kotzebue at midday.*
   a) *Protecting the antler*
   b) *the dismantling and packing of the kayaks*
   c) *dismantling*
   d) *packing*

11) *He now has with him a slab of dried salmon, and we share it like candy.*
    a) dried.

12) *The berries were intensely sweet, having grown in the long northern light.*
    a) having grown in the long northern light.

13) *finally, he made a sharp southward turn and began to follow a stream course in the direction of its current, looking for a gravel bar, a man, a canoe.*
    a) to follow a stream course in the direction of its current.
    b) looking for a gravel bar, a man, a canoe.

14) *Confidently, he gave up altitude and searched the bending river.*
    a) bending

15) *It appeared to Parish to be the right one.*
    a) to be the right one.

16) *This time, we flew north, low over the river, upstream, looking for the glint of the canoe.*
    a) looking for the glint of the canoe.

17) *One effect of the pipeline charter has been to siphon off pilots from elsewhere in the Alaskan bush.*
    a) to siphon off pilots from elsewhere in the Alaskan bush.

18) *Looking down to the side, the pilot watched the ground below – trying to identify various drainages and pick his way through the mountains.*
    a) Looking down to the side
    b) trying to identify various drainages and pick his way through the mountains.
    c) to identify various drainages and pick his way through the mountains.

19) *The plane was a single-engine Cessna 207 Skywagon, bumping hard on the wind.*
    a) bumping hard on the wind.

20) *Soon his confidence in his reading of the land seemed to run out altogether.*
    a) his reading of the land
    b) reading
    c) to run out altogether

Chapter 8
Section Exercises

Page 145
For isolated coordinating conjunctions determine which elements are being
joined and the structure and function of the compound structure created.
Sentences are from Martin Luther King, Jr. *I Have a Dream*.

Page 152
Locate appositional phrases in sentences from a range of authors. Tell what word
groups they modify and whether they are restrictive or non-restrictive.

Chapter Practice

Page 155
Identify compound elements in sentences from Cornel West; describe the
structure and function of the compound elements created.

Chapter 8

Coordination and compounding:
appositional phrases

Back in Chapter 3, we explored coordination and compounding in a preliminary way. I said at the time that pretty much any sentence element can be compounded. It was important to introduce that concept early; compounding is so common, that trying to limit examples to sentences that don't include it (especially real world sentences, not just grammar book examples) is very difficult. In this chapter, we will explore compounding within a clause in more careful detail and extend our attention to the compounding of whole clauses as well.

Two linked structures that are equal in rank are said to be coordinate. (Think of this as a contrast to subordinate, used to describe a linked structure of lesser rank.) The resulting structure is a compound structure, a term we have already used to describe, for example, compound NP's or compound predicate phrases. Most often, this occurs with the assistance of a coordinating conjunction. A conjunction is a word with a primarily grammatical function, that of linking together two (or more) structures and establishing a relationship between (or among) them. In the next chapter, we will turn our attention to subordinating conjunctions. Coordinating conjunctions leave the linked elements equal in rank, whereas a subordinating conjunction will introduce an element of lesser rank.

The seven conjunctions traditionally thought of as coordinating are *and*, *but*, *or*, *nor*, *for* (in the meaning sense closest to *because*), *so*, and *yet*. The most primary of these are *and*, *but*, *or*, *nor*. (These can't be preceded by

Coordinate
Two linked structures that are equal in rank are said to be coordinate. The resulting structure is a compound structure.

Conjunction
A word which links together structures and establishes a relationship between them.

Coordinating conjunctions
These leave the linked elements equal in rank.

another conjunction, whereas *for, so, yet* can.) A list of typical subordinating conjunctions would include words like *as, when, while, until, if, because, before, after* – though some of these you will recognize already as having other roles, for example as prepositions.

There are solid reasons for wanting to follow a traditional analysis in this area, since the role of a coordinating conjunction and the punctuation of compound as opposed to subordinate structures are given significant attention in most handbooks and style manuals. In other words, *so* and *for* can be treated like coordinating conjunctions when they introduce a clause if your primary interest is in conforming to conventional practice; the clause they introduce won't be thought of as a sentence fragment by most copy editors. If our primary interest is in an analytical look at the kinds of meaning being generated, it would be better to say that *and, or, nor, but,* and *yet* seem like truly coordinating conjunctions, whereas *for* and *so* take on somewhat differing roles. *For* will tell us the reasons something is done, a role very similar to *because*, generally thought of as a subordinating conjunction. (*He made sure he went when given the chance, for he wasn't sure it would come again.*) *So* is clearly adverbial, even in traditional grammar, when it means something like *so that*. (*He went so I wouldn't have to.*) It also means something like *as a result*, which would make it a *conjunctive adverb*, a category we will explore later, though it doesn't have the flexibility of movement we usually associate with members of those groups. (*The weather turned warm, so we took off our jackets and went on in our shirtsleeves.*) We will continue to follow traditional practice in this chapter, but with the understanding that *for* and *so* are different in significant ways from the other coordinating conjunctions.

When two finite clauses are joined with a coordinating conjunction, the result is a compound sentence. The resulting sentence has two matrix clauses and can be diagrammed accordingly.

A clause introduced by a coordinating conjunction is considered independent in traditional grammar. It can stand alone without being thought of as a fragment.

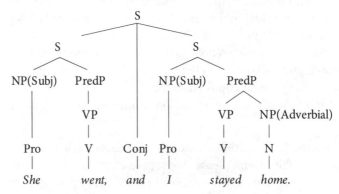

In Chapter 4, we described a typical sentence as an arguable proposition. We can expand that here to include the possibility of two or more arguable propositions conjoined. If you want to transform such a statement into a question, you really need to ask two questions. (Though compound questions are not as common as compound statements, which can make this an awkward test.)

She went, and I stayed home.
statement

Did she go, and did you stay home?
question

The finite verbs move to the front of both matrix clauses in order to frame this statement as a compound question. If one clause is subordinate, clearly only one question is called for.

Because *and, but, or, nor, for, so,* and *yet* are coordinating rather than subordinating conjunctions, it is possible to start a sentence with them, and it is possible for a clause they introduce to stand alone as a sentence. You may have been discouraged from doing this by teachers who pay little attention to what writers actually do when they write, but it is perfectly legitimate and often very effective. We already looked closely at two sentences like this from the Martin Luther King passage in Chapter 4. *But one hundred years later, we must face the tragic fact that the Negro is still not free.* This is a single matrix clause introduced by *but. But* introduces what follows as a contradiction to what comes before, in this case the entire first paragraph, which describes the promise of the emancipation proclamation one hundred years earlier. The last sentence in this paragraph is a single matrix clause sentence introduced by *so: So we have come here today to dramatize an appalling condition. So* here introduces what follows as a result of everything that had been described in three previous sentences. This happens quite frequently in the work of many fine writers. It is certainly not an error, but evidence of thoughtful and careful choice. What it means, in effect, is that grammatical meanings (grammatical connections) can and do extend beyond the boundaries of sentences. *And* can be implied in a series of sentences. And *but* can mark a shift in thought that takes more than a sentence to complete.

Grammatical connections often extend beyond the boundaries of sentences.

A compound sentence can include more than two matrix clauses. There is, in fact, no limit to the number of clauses you can join in this way.

Three matrix clauses do not always form a structure of three equal parts. The following sentence includes three matrix clauses, but seems to divide first into two parts: *It was raining hard and we had no rain gear, so we spent the day inside.* The two clauses to the left of the comma seem to work together to describe the two main reasons why we spent the day inside. A diagram that would do justice to this view of the sentence's structure would look like the following:

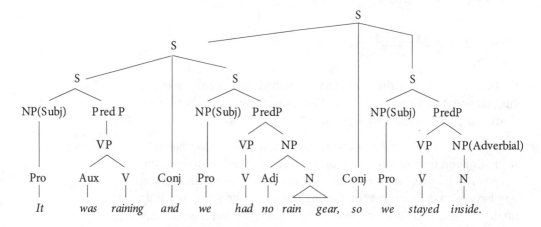

Here is another example, this one from Alice Walker's *The Black Writer and the Southern Experience*:

> *The clothes were in good condition, though well worn, and my mother needed a dress, so she immediately put on one of those from the box and wore it into town.*

Sometimes a writer will place a period before a conjunction simply to slow things down, giving us a chance, in effect, to process or savor a particularly rich or complex meaning. Here are two strong examples from the same Alice Walker essay.

> *A shack with a dozen or so books is an unlikely place to discover a young Keats. <u>But</u> it is narrow thinking, indeed, to believe that a Keats is the only kind of poet one would want to grow up to be.*

> *Perhaps my Northern brothers will not believe me when I say there is a great deal of positive material I can draw from my 'underprivileged' background. But they have never lived, as I have, at the end of a long road in a house that was faced by the edge of the world on one side and nobody for miles on the other.*

8.1.1 *Coordination of longer sequences*

But, so, for, and *yet* are pretty much restricted to linking two constituents or constituent groups together. *And, or, nor,* though, can link an indefinite number of constituents or constituent groups in series. When this happens, the elements are usually divided by commas, with the conjunction itself showing up just before the last linked constituent, but understood retroactively.

> *He put beef, potatoes, carrots, celery, and onions in the stew.*
> *And* is implied between each of the linked elements.

> *You can take French, Spanish, German, Italian, or Chinese to satisfy the foreign language requirement.*
> *Or* is understood between each of the linked elements.

8.1.2 *Shared constituents*

When elements are compounded, they share a role within a larger structure. Sometimes the nature of that role can be hard to pin down. Part of pinning it down involves the recognition of shared elements within the sentence. Two nouns can share a determiner (*my brother and sister*, where *brother and sister* is a compound noun sharing the determiner *my* within the larger NP.). Two determiners can share a noun (*Paul and Mary's courtship*, where *Paul and Mary's* is a compound determiner sharing the noun *courtship* within the larger NP.). A compound NP as subject will share at least one predicate phrase (*My friend and your cousin George went to a movie.*). Or a single subject can be shared by two or more predicate phrases (*Bob went to a movie and stopped for pizza.*). A single preposition can take a compound NP as object or a single NP can be the object of two or more prepositions (*among deep forests and clear rivers. Over, under, and around the fence.*). You can have a compound verb phrase within a single predicate phrase or compound verb within a single verb phrase (*She is studying and will study grammar. She will study and learn grammar.*). It takes patience, concentration, and practice to determine which elements are being combined and which elements are being shared. The above examples are diagrammed below.

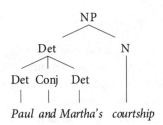

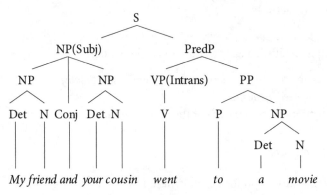

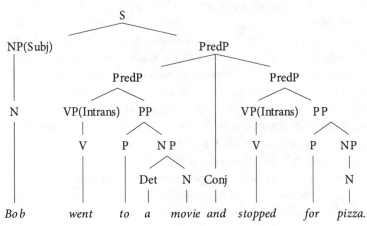

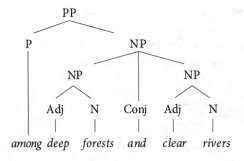

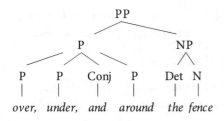

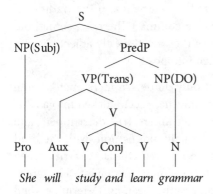

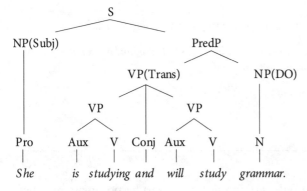

8.2

Section

Exercise

In the following sentences, the coordinating conjunctions have been underlined. For each, determine which elements are being joined and the structure and function of the compound structure created. Where relevant, describe shared elements. The following sentences are from Martin Luther King, Jr. *I Have a Dream*:

1) *One hundred years later, the life of the Negro is still sadly crippled by the manacles of segregation <u>and</u> the chains of discrimination.*

2) *One hundred years later, the Negro is still languishing in the midst of a vast ocean of material prosperity <u>and</u> finds himself an exile in his own land.*

From Tim O'Brien *How to Tell a True War Story*:

3) *It does not instruct, <u>nor</u> encourage virtue, <u>nor</u> suggest models of proper human behavior, <u>nor</u> restrain men from doing the things men have always done.*

4) *you have been made the victim of a very old <u>and</u> terrible lie.*

5) *you can tell a true war story by its absolute <u>and</u> uncompromising allegiance to obscenity <u>and</u> evil.*

6) *Then he spits <u>and</u> stares.*

8.3   Coordinate adjectives

In a noun phrase, only certain adjectives are truly coordinate, and these alone are capable of being separated/joined by *and*. (The traditional punctuation rule calls for an *and* or a comma.) These are sometimes called 'moveable adjectives' because they are the only adjectives in a noun phrase that are not fully frozen into position.

As we discussed in Chapter 3, not only do determiners open a noun phrase, but when more than one occur, these seem locked into a hierarchical structure of their own: predeterminers, true determiners, and postdeterminers. When modifiers (usually nouns) join with the head noun to form a compound noun, these are always the last to arrive; when there are more than one, these too are pretty much frozen into a hierarchy governed by position that helps us process the meaning. Determiners and nouns as modifiers (creating compound nouns) are acting as adjectives, but not moveable or coordinate adjectives.

All my brother's first ignorant attempts.
These phrase structure tree diagrams.

Compare *All my ignorant brother's first attempts*; *All my first brother's ignorant attempts*; *tree structure these phrase diagrams*; *these tree phrase structure diagrams*. In all four cases, meaning gets seriously lost or seriously changed by changing the order of the modifiers. They are not moveable or coordinate.

Are the following noun phrases equivalent in meaning, or do they carry meaning differences as a result of the change in word order? Think about that before you read on.

My brother's first rich wife.
My brother's rich first wife.

My own interpretation of the first sentence is that it conveys the notion that *my brother* has had more than one *rich wife* and the notion that the wife in question may not have been his first. (He may have had one or more poor wives before this rich one.) The second NP conveys the sense that his first wife was rich and that the wife we are now being told about is this first one. (He has probably had more than one wife since, though we don't know that for sure. He has had only one wife, his first, who we are sure is rich.) Because the meaning of the phrase changes when we change the order of these modifiers, these adjectives are not moveable or coordinate and would not normally be connected or separated by a comma or by *and*.

We saw two examples of coordinate (moveable) adjectives in the previous exercise, both by Tim O'Brien: *a very old and terrible lie*; *its absolute and uncompromising allegiance*. O'Brien could have written *very terrible and old lie* or *terrible and very old lie*. Or *its uncompromising and absolute allegiance*. In either phrase, too, the *and* could have been dropped in favor of a comma: *a very old, terrible lie*; *its absolute, uncompromising allegiance*. To me, the phrases sound best in their original form, perhaps a testimony to the quality of Tim O'Brien's ear; but passing these structural tests without distortion of representational meaning shows that these adjectives are truly coordinate.

Moveable adjectives
So called because these adjectives in a noun phrase cannot be moved without loss or distortion of meaning.

8.3.1 *Commas as implied 'and'*

Occasionally, a writer will let a comma stand in for an *and* in situations other than between coordinate adjectives. We saw an example in the last chapter from Alex Kotlowitz: *He wanted to be recognized, to know that he was wanted.* Sometimes a comma will stand in for an *and* when the second coordinate element is some sort of negation. Here is an example from Cornel West's fine book on race in America, *Race Matters*: *Race was the visible catalyst, not the underlying cause.* As said earlier in the chapter, a comma also stands in for *and* or *or* routinely in a series of three or more coordinate elements.

8.3.2   *Two part conjunctions*

Sometimes conjunctions are not single words alone, but pairs, including an anticipatory term that precedes the joined elements and a conjunction in its usual place between them. Here's an example from the opening sentence of Cornel West's *Race Matters*: *What happened in Los Angeles in April of* 1992 *was neither a race riot nor a class rebellion. Neither* begins the connection, creating an anticipation that makes the connection more explicit and emphatic; *nor* stands in the usual conjunction spot between the two linked NP's, *a race riot* and *a class rebellion*. We could diagram the compound NP copular complement as follows:

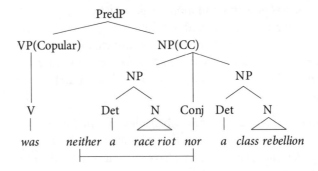

Other word pairs that work this way are: *either/or; both/and; not only /but. Not only/but* has a funny way of adding up to *and*, though often in situations where the coexistence of the two elements seems somewhat extreme or surprising: *He is not only* president of a large corporation, *but a fine family man as well. This is not only a terrible proposal, but an insult to our intelligence.*

8.4   Appositional phrases

An **appositional phrase** will modify by renaming. It asserts an additional identity.

An appositional phrase provides a kind of renaming. They are modifiers rather than compound elements, a way of renaming a constituent group (usually a NP) that is itself of higher rank within a matrix clause. In some ways, they also resemble copular structures, with some form of the verb *to be* sliding easily between a constituent group and its appositional modifier as a reliable test.

This book opens with a sentence that contains an appositional phrase: *You are about to start on a difficult and wondrous exploration, a journey into the heart of your own language.* Your first instinct may to see *a difficult and wondrous exploration* and *a journey into the heart of your own language* as a compound NP, object of the preposition on. But this would imply that you are about to start on two separate ventures. What I intended to represent (I hope successfully) is the idea that you are about to start on a single venture that can be described (named) in two different ways. I remember this sentence more than most in the book (It was my fifth attempt at a good first sentence) and I remember trying to choose between *exploration* and *journey*, then deciding that I could and should include both. The second sentence of the book has an appositional phrase as well: *You may expect that a grammar book will be about someone else's language, a correct or proper language that your own has often failed to measure up to.* Everything after the comma renames *someone else's language* and joins with *someone else's language* in creating a single object of preposition *about*. That is to say, the intention was not to describe two separate subjects that you may be expecting the book to be about, but a single subject that can be named in two different ways.

Perhaps simpler sentences will help make the point clearer. Your room mate is named Gloria. She is also your friend. She is also your favorite tennis partner. She is someone who has always been there when you need her. All these statements are not describing two, three, or four different people, but the same person in different ways. A sentence that might incorporate much of this meaning using appositional phrases would be as follows: *Gloria, my room mate, my friend, and my favorite tennis partner, has always been there for me when I need her.* In this sentence, *my room mate*, *my friend*, and *my favorite tennis partner* are all appositional phrase noun phrases, modifying (renaming) *Gloria*.

Most 'things' that we talk or write about have multiple identities. We can name them in many different ways. Like noun phrase copular complements, appositional phrases assert an additional identity.

There are two very good tests for whether a noun phrase is appositional. If it is, some form of the verb *to be* can easily be slipped between the NP and the word group it follows. *Gloria is my room mate. Gloria is my friend. Gloria is my favorite tennis partner.* The second test is whether the group you think of as appositional can replace the group that it modifies without a distortion of meaning. *My room mate has always been there for me when I need her. My friend has always been there for me when I need her. My favorite tennis partner has always been there for me when I need her.* Meaning gets lost (cut out) in each of those test sentences, but meaning is not distorted. They all seem to carry representational meaning in harmony with our larger sentence.

Appositional phrases can be restrictive as well as non-restrictive. As we have seen with other postnominal modifiers, a good writer will signal the difference through the presence (non-restrictive) or absence (restrictive) of commas.

As with other postnominal modifiers, appositional phrases can be restrictive or non-restrictive. The same comma rules apply.

> *The late Jamaican songwriter Bob Marley merged politics and deep feeling in his songs.*

The late Jamaican songwriter is renamed by *Bob Marley* (the appositional phrase). Commas here would imply that there is only one late Jamaican songwriter. The appositional phrase has the effect of narrowing (restricting) the category down, in this case to a category of one.

> *The Pulitzer Prize winning poet Charles Simic will be on campus this semester.*
> *Charles Simic*, our appositional phrase, narrows down the category of *Pulitzer Prize winning poet*.

If we reversed the order of NP's and their appositional modifiers in the above two sentences, the appositional phrases would be non-restrictive and commas would be routinely called for.

> *Bob Marley, the late Jamaican songwriter, merged politics and deep feeling in his songs.*

> *Charles Simic, the Pulitzer Prize winning poet, will be on campus this semester.*

There may be many people with the names *Bob Marley* and *Charles Simic*, but in English grammar we treat proper names as if they represent a category of one.

Noun phrases may be the most common word group modified appositionally, but adjective phrases and adverbial phrases can have appositional modifiers as well.

> *All day long he became increasingly restless, <u>as unsettled as a dog in heat.</u>*
> *He moved very quickly, <u>an instantaneous lunging that caught us all by surprise.</u>*

The key here, again, is that the phrases being modified are being renamed by the phrases that follow. In the first, he did not become two things, but one thing that is being described in two different ways. In the second sentence, he did not move in two different ways, but in one way that is described in one way and renamed in another. In this second sentence, we have an adverb phrase (*very quickly*) being renamed (modified) by a noun phrase (*an instantaneous lunging that caught us all by surprise*). This notion of a noun modifying an adverb may seem very strange to you, especially if you are used to thinking that adverbs modify verbs and adjectives modify nouns. This common sense understanding does have some central truth to it, but the language turns out to be much more flexible than that in actual practice.

Non-finite clauses as appositional   8.5

Some of the structures we have previously identified as adjectival modifiers can also be understood as appositional. These would include renaming type infinitive and participial clauses like the following:

The movement <u>protesting the war</u> had a large impact.
Our attempt <u>to influence his behavior</u> was a failure.

Both of these structures pass the verb *to be* test. The movement *was* protesting the war. Our attempt *was* to influence his behavior. They will give us uneven results in the interchangeable test, though. *Protesting the war had a large impact* seems fine, but *to influence his behavior was a failure* seems awkward, perhaps because infinitive clauses when left by themselves seem to be about something that always happens or something that has not happened yet. This seems to me to show that the participial clause is truly appositional, but that the infinitive clause is in a fuzzy, in-between category of its own. At any rate, the choice is not an overly important one if our prime concern is to understand the kinds of meaning being generated. Appositional phrases are a kind of modifier and if they modify a noun phrase, they are adjectival. We will run into this again in the next chapter when we look at finite subordinate clauses in pretty much the same role.

His belief <u>that aliens have landed</u> seems absurd. That aliens have landed certainly seems like a restrictive modifier of *His belief.* He probably has many beliefs and this clause tells us which one the speaker is talking about. Is it appositional as well? What happens when you run it through our two tests? We will continue this exploration in the next chapter.

Dashes can replace commas when setting off appositional modifiers. Dashes have the effect of adding emphasis.

Non-restrictive appositional modifiers are usually set off by commas, but some writers seem routinely to use dashes for the same purpose. Here's an example from Judith Ortiz Cofer's *Silent Dancing*:

> *Having come from a house designed for a single family back in Puerto Rico – my mother's extended family home – it was curious to know that strangers lived under our floor and above our heads, and that the heater pipe went through everyone's apartment.*

8.6
Section
Exercise

Locate appositional phrases in the following sentences. Tell what word groups they modify and whether they are restrictive or non-restrictive.

1) *It is a credit to a writer like Ernest J. Gaines, a black writer who writes mainly about the people he grew up with in rural Louisiana, that he can write about blacks and whites exactly as he sees them and knows them, instead of writing of one group as a vast malignant lump and of the others as a conglomerate of perfect virtues.* (Alice Walker)

2) *To engage in a serious discussion of race in America, we must begin not with the problems of black people but with the flaws of American society – flaws rooted in historic inequalities and longstanding cultural stereotypes.* (Cornel West)

3) *We have created rootless, dangling people with little link to the supporting networks – family, friends, school – that sustain some sense of purpose in life.* (Cornel West)

4) *One essential step is some form of large-scale public intervention to ensure access to basic social goods – housing, food, health care, education, child care, and jobs.* (Cornel West)

5) *He... had spent a number of years taking pictures of them at Henry Horner Homes, a public housing complex.* (Alex Kotlowitz)

6) *There was a certain tranquillity here, a peacefulness that extended into the horizon like the straight, silvery rails.* (Alex Kotlowitz)

7) *Ashland Avenue, a six lane boulevard just west of Henry Horner, was named for the estate of Henry Clay.* (Alex Kotlowitz)

8) *If the youngsters had one guidepost in their young lives those few months, it was their mother, Lajoe.* (Alex Kotlowitz)

Ellipsis is the presence of information that is not explicitly stated, but which is recoverable from the context of the writing. It is an especially important concept for the analysis of real world text. For someone not alert to it, many structures will seem to be incomplete (syntactically) and confusing.

Any writer needs to presuppose a good deal of information that is present without being spoken and this goes well beyond what we normally include under ellipsis. This is one of the greatest challenges and frustrations of writing. We can mention Bill Clinton or Jimmy Carter or Abe Lincoln and reasonably suppose in most contexts that our readers understand that these are former presidents of the United States. We can talk about earned run average to a baseball fan and not expect to have to explain it, just as we suspect that all our readers know what a flat tire is, how dangerous or irritating it can be, or why a car shouldn't run with one. My son, on the other hand, just asked me if I know what *picaresque* means because he was reading something in which the author used the phrase *picaresque novel* without explaining it. Sometimes we make the mistake of over-explaining, and sometimes we make the mistake of not explaining enough, and that may differ from reader to reader in the same text. Writing is not easy. Communicating is not easy. At least face to face, the audience has a chance to look bored or confused, to stop your over-explaining or ask for more information. In writing, we don't usually have that opportunity. Honest feedback from thoughtful readers is always worth so much to a writer for this reason alone, that we are not as knowledgeable of our readers as we need to be. If we have a range of readers for a text, we may weaken it for one reader while we strengthen it for another, something writing texts and handbooks rarely talk about.

Ellipsis is generally reserved for a kind of missing meaning that is much more localized to the text. (This is not just a text based phenomenon; we use elliptical structures all the time in speech.) Sometimes, this comes from substitution, the process of using a word or words, like a pronoun or finite auxiliary, to stand in for meanings that have been established close by.

Ellipsis is a missing meaning recoverable from the local text.

> *When my first son was growing up, I did not give him the full attention he needed.*

Him and *he* in the second clause stand in for 'my first son,' for a meaning we can recover from elsewhere in the text, generally understood as the antecedent of the pronoun. (The antecedent is not just a noun, but a whole noun phrase, and that noun phrase will begin to pick up an accretion of meaning as a text evolves. The *he* will begin to mean everything we know about the person the pronoun stands in for.) The next sentence could be something like *If I had done so, we would be closer today*, where *done so* now stands in, not for a noun phrase, but for an entire predicate (If I had given him the full attention he needed, we would be much closer today.) Quite often a finite auxiliary stands in for an entire predicate. *You may not vote in this year's election, but you should. I wanted to be there for your big speech, but I couldn't.* In the above sentences, *should* stands in for *vote in this year's election* and *couldn't* stands in for *be there for your big speech.* Sometimes determiners will stand in for a whole noun phrase, as in *I couldn't stand his music, but he liked mine*, a category we described before as 'fused head'.

From the perspective of a writer, ellipsis will often seem like a tightening of the writing, keeping meaning intact with fewer words. As readers, we will generally provide the missing meanings easily and not be conscious of doing so. If we're alert to its presence, grammatical analysis will often be much easier to carry out; with the missing words added, a baffling sentence suddenly looks very familiar.

One common usage disagreement arises from how to deal with elliptical structures for comparatives, whether to treat them as phrases or as whole clauses (with the missing predicate or predicate elements implied). Should I write *My brother thinks he is smarter than me* or is it better to write *My brother thinks he is smarter than I*? We would certainly use the *I* if the finite auxiliary were included: *My brother thinks he is smarter than I am.* My own sense is that *My brother thinks he is smarter than me* is too common a practice these days, even among literate, educated writers, for it to be the cause for objection in someone else's work. We have more important concerns to attend to than this. If you want to vote against it, don't use it in your own language; we can all influence use in that way. Certainly, *smarter than me* sounds more colloquial and informal and seems at home in those contexts.

Identify compound elements in the following sentences and the conjunctions (occasionally punctuation) that join them. Describe the structure and function of the compound elements created. When appropriate, describe shared elements. The sentences are from Cornel West.

1) *To establish a new framework, we need to begin with a frank acknowledgment of the basic humanness and Americanness of each of us.*

2) *The result is unemployment, hunger, homelessness, and sickness for millions.*

3) *We have created rootless, dangling people with little link to the supporting networks – family, friends, school – that sustain some sense of purpose in life.*

4) *We have witnessed the collapse of the spiritual communities that in the past helped Americans face despair, disease, and death and that transmit through the generations dignity and decency, excellence and elegance.*

5) *Post-modern culture is more and more a market culture dominated by gangster mentalities and self-destructive wantonness.*

6) *Sexual violence against women and homicidal assaults by young black men on one another are only the most obvious signs of this empty quest for pleasure, property, and power.*

7) *First, we must admit that the most valuable sources for help, hope, and power consist of ourselves and our common history.*

8) *As in the ages of Lincoln, Roosevelt, and King, we must look to new frameworks and languages to understand our multilayered crisis and overcome our deep malaise.*

9) *Second, we must focus our attention on the public square – the common good that undergirds our national and global destinies.*

10) *Our ideals of freedom, democracy, and equality must be invoked to invigorate all of us, especially the landless, propertyless, and luckless.*

11) *Let us hope and pray that the vast intelligence, imagination, humor, and courage of Americans will not fail us.*

12) *Either we learn a new language of empathy and compassion, or the fire this time will consume us all.*

Chapter 9
Section Exercises

Page 161
Identify adverbial finite subordinate clauses in given sentences and tell what word group they modify.

Page 165
Identify content clauses in given sentences and explain what typical NP function they are carrying out.

Page 169
Sentences from Judith Ortiz Cofer. For each relative clause, tell what NP it modifies, whether it is restrictive or non-restrictive, and what role the relative pronoun plays in the clause it introduces.

Chapter Practice

Page 171
Sentences from Judith Ortiz Cofer and Alex Kotlowitz. Identify finite subordinate clauses, and tell whether each is a content clause, adverbial clause, or relative clause. If an adverbial clause, tell what word group it modifies. If a content clause, tell what typical NP role it carries out. If a relative clause, tell what word group it modifies and whether it is restrictive or non-restrictive.

Chapter 9

Finite subordinate clauses

To fully understand grammar, it helps to understand it as a system, a unity of interacting elements. It would be wonderful to be able to teach everything at once because everything is there and everything is connected, even in the speech of a fairly young child. Yet so many concepts are so difficult to analyze (as easy as they may be to use in practice) that a grammar study inevitably has to portion out an understanding bit by bit, risking the faulty understanding that the grammar itself is fragmented and the elements under consideration exist in isolation from the rest. Traditional, prescriptive grammar reinforces this idea of grammar by presenting it as a collection of do's and dont's, a collection of somewhat disconnected and often arbitrary mandates, generally disconnected from purpose or actual practice. We are in a wonderful position now, through the final three chapters, to begin pulling all those seemingly disparate elements together, to finally look at the grammar of the language as an interplay of interrelated elements. We are also in a position to put that understanding into robust practice, to look at ways in which a reasonably full understanding of our unconscious grammar can help us as readers and writers.

This chapter will complete our overview of the grammar by looking at finite subordinate clauses. The next chapter will explore key aspects of the grammar of writing, including the punctuation system as an aid in the representation of language in writing. In our final chapter, we will look very closely at longer passages, exploring ways in which grammar and meaning are inextricably linked in the hands of a purposeful writer.

Finite subordinate clauses carry explicit subjects and finite predicates, but have a subordinate role within another clause.

The terms finite, subordinate and clause are not new to us. A finite subordinate clause is a clause and therefore has a subject and predicate structure. (Unlike non-finite clauses, these will always have an explicit subject, not just an implied one.) To say that they are finite is to say that they carry a verb phrase grounded in tense or modality. To say that they are subordinate is to say that they do not themselves act as a principle (matrix) clause in a sentence, but take on a subordinate role within a larger matrix clause. The roles they take on are roles we have already covered. These would include pretty much any role other than as principal VP of the matrix clause.

We will divide finite subordinate clauses into three major categories: adverbial clauses, content clauses, and relative clauses. We will also look briefly at content clauses as appositional modifiers. These three types of clauses differ from each other in both structure and function. Adverbial clauses are adverbial modifiers. Content clauses (sometimes called 'noun clauses') take on roles typical of noun phrases (like subject, direct object, indirect object, copular complement, predicate complement, or object of preposition.) Relative clauses get their name from the special kind of pronoun, relative pronoun, that introduces them; they are always adjectival in function.

9.2   Adverbial subordinate clauses

You already have substantial practice identifying word groups other than finite adverbial clauses as adverbial in function. Adverbial prepositional phrases, especially those related to time, will seem most like the adverbial clauses, almost to the point of being interchangeable. Adverbial clauses can sometimes seem like expanded prepositional phrases; prepositional phrases can sometimes seem like abbreviated clauses.

I study grammar <u>before lunch</u>.
I study grammar <u>before I eat lunch</u>.

In the first sentence, we have a prepositional phrase (preposition plus NP) in the common adverbial role of telling when an action (activity) takes place. In the second sentence, we have a finite subordinate clause carrying out the same role. In this second case, *before* is not a preposition, but a subordinating conjunction. (It not only links the finite clause that follows it to the matrix clause, but establishes a subordinate role for it, in this case as adverbial modifier.) The clause itself is clearly a clause because it carries a subject (NP *I*), a verb phrase (*eat*, which is present tense and transitive), and a direct object complement (NP *lunch*). A diagram that captures all that information would look like the following:

A **subordinating conjunction** links the finite clause that follows it to a matrix clause and establishes a role for the subordinate clause within a matrix clause.

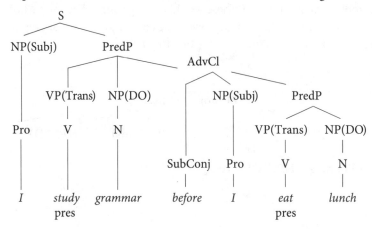

Notice that the subordinate clause has its own sentence like constituency. It has a subject and a predicate, including a finite verb phrase. Without the subordinating conjunction, it could be given its own matrix clause status. (A clause like this is sometimes called a 'downranked' clause to highlight the idea that it has been diminished in rank through subordination.) An alternative version, with *I eat lunch* now given a matrix clause role, would be the following:

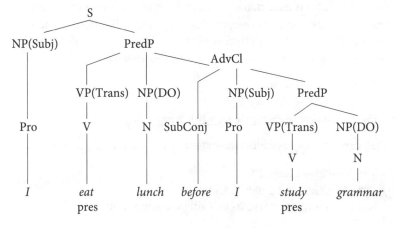

An adverbial clause opening a sentence will act as marked theme.

Like other adverbial structures, adverbial subordinate clauses are highly moveable. The two above examples show matrix clause first and subordinate clause second, but the reverse is very common.

> *Before I eat lunch, I study grammar.*
> *After I study grammar, I eat lunch.*

When this happens, the subordinate clause has become, for the sentence as a whole, a marked theme. These would be diagrammed out as part of the matrix clause predicate, just as we would do for an adverbial prepositional phrase in the same sentence opening position.

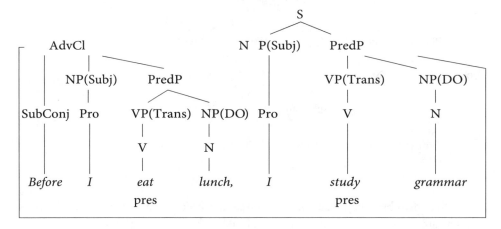

Like adverbial prepositional phrases, adverbial subordinate clauses can convey a number of adverbial meanings. The following list is not intended to overwhelm you with detail to memorize, but is intended to make these purposes familiar and easier to spot.

Adverbial subordinate clauses as adverbials of time are very common. Quite often, as in the above examples, they establish differences in time between two related events (before or after). They can establish two events as happening simultaneously through *when, whenever, while, as.*

> *While I work, I play music.*
> *They grew tired as the day progressed.*
> *The student slept whenever the teacher lectured.*

They can also help establish the extent or duration of an action.

> *He worked until the sun set.*
> *I will stay as long as my money holds out.*
> You can interpret *as long as* as a single conjunction.

Adverbials of place or manner are much more common as prepositional phrases than they are as subordinate clauses. But they do happen.

> He fished <u>where the river deepens out</u>.
> He treated me <u>as if I were a long-lost friend</u>.
> You can treat *as if* and *as though* as compound conjunctions.

Quite common are adverbial subordinate clauses that establish reasons or conditions.

> I went <u>because you wanted me to</u>.
> I will go <u>if I am needed</u>.

It's also common to use adverbial subordinate clauses to give a sense that something happens despite conditions that would lead you to expect otherwise.

> <u>Though it meant certain failure</u>, he did not study for the test.
> <u>Although he needed rest</u>, he could not bring himself to sleep.

As mentioned in Chapter 8, *so* is not always a coordinating conjunction. It can be an adverbial intensifier (as in *It was so cold.*) Even in traditional grammar, a clause it introduces is subordinate rather than coordinate when the clause conveys a sense of purpose (rather than result), often in combination with *that*. (When *that* is not present, it will seem like an optional alternative for these kinds of clauses.) To me, this seems very similar to the *in order to* test for adverbial infinitive clauses.

> My parents worked hard <u>so (that) I wouldn't have to</u>.

So also works with or without *that* to create an adverbial of extent.

> It was <u>so</u> cold <u>(that) the pipes froze</u>.
> I was <u>so</u> hungry <u>(that) I could eat a horse.</u>

In these examples, the adverbial clauses are modifying adjectives (*cold* and *hungry*) rather than the VP.

9.3

Section

Exercise

Identify adverbial finite subordinate clauses in the following sentences and tell what word group (usually a VP) they modify.

1) *When the going gets tough, the tough get going.*
2) *He came into class after it started and left before it ended.*

3)   *We will stay late if we have to.*
4)   *Though the river rose, it did not overflow its banks.*
5)   *He was so sleepy that he could not finish the test.*
6)   *Before he makes dinner, he does the shopping, and after dinner, he does the dishes.*

9.4   Content clauses

*A **content clause** is a finite subordinate clause that fills a slot typically filled by a noun phrase.*

A content clause (often called a 'noun clause') is a finite subordinate clause that acts like a noun phrase by filling one of the slots traditionally filled by a noun phrase: subject, direct object, etc. I discussed these clauses briefly in Chapter 6 while exploring the special nature of mental process and verbal process verbs, which often take whole clauses as direct objects.

I know <u>what I like</u>.
He explained to me <u>why the sky is blue</u>.

The wh-pronouns that introduce a content clause are highly thematic. They also have a pronoun role within the clause they introduce.

In the above examples, the content clauses are being introduced by interrogative pronouns, the same pronouns used to introduce Wh-questions. As with Wh-questions, these pronouns are highly thematic, directing our attention to the part of the clause that the user wants to be the focus of our attention. Content clauses are not really questions; unlike true questions, they do not invert grammatical subject and finite verb. (We don't say *I know why are you going.*) We also don't follow them with question marks. But they are like questions in using these interrogative pronouns to focus our attention thematically.

I know <u>what you are doing</u>.
going to the store

I know <u>where you are going</u>.
to the store

I know <u>why you are going</u>.
to buy bread

I know <u>how you are going</u>.
walking

I know <u>when you are going</u>.
at three o'clock

I know <u>who you are going with</u>.
no one

Unlike subordinating conjunctions, these pronouns have a role in the clause they introduce. To do a full analysis of the clause, we need to account for that role.

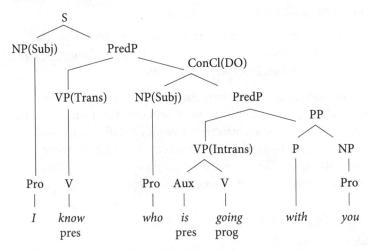

In this sentence, *who* is the subject of the content clause it introduces. The clause itself is direct object. In *I know what you are doing*, *what* is direct object within the content clause. In *I know where you are going*, *where* is an adverbial modifier. In *I know whose car you were riding in*, *whose* is determiner in the NP *whose car*. As you can see, this can make for a tricky analysis.

The above examples are all direct objects, but content clauses are by no means limited to that role.

The decision about <u>who is going with you</u> was badly made.
object of preposition *about*

<u>What you are doing</u> is very important.
content clause as subject

*<u>What you want</u> **is** <u>what you get</u> at McDonald's today.*
content clause as subject and content clause as copular complement

Content clauses
sometimes emulate
yes/no questions.

Content clauses will sometimes emulate yes / no questions as well as Wh-questions. When they do, they are introduced by *if*, *whether*, or *whether or not*.

> Let me know *if you need me*.
> She asked *whether we would return*.
> Please tell me *whether or not I can come over*.

When you see these, though, you cannot assume they are content clauses. Quite often, they will be adverbial. (*If you need me*, I will come. *Whether or not the storm arrives*, I will keep my promise.)

When *that* introduces
a content clause, it is a
complementizer rather
than a pronoun. It has no
role within the clause it
introduces. When the clause
doesn't open a sentence,
the *that* can be thought of
as optional.

Quite often, content clauses are introduced by *that*. When *that* introduces a content clause, most often it is not a pronoun (or a subordinating conjunction), but a complementizer. You may recall that we used the same term to refer to *to* when it introduces an infinitive clause. As a complementizer, *that* has no role in the content clause it introduces. An example, diagrammed out, would be as follows:

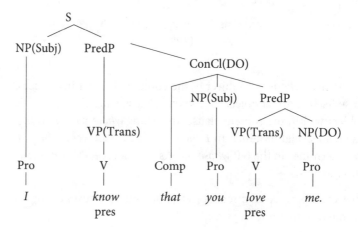

When a content clause introduced by *that* (as complementizer) is direct object, the complementizer can disappear completely: *I know* (that) *you love me*. As with infinitive clauses without an expressed *to*, these can be difficult to spot. We do not drop the *that*, however, when the content clause opens the sentence as subject. *That you love me* is clear. (*You love me is clear* seems ungrammatical.)

Content clause subjects introduced by *that* are frequently extraposed.

That you love me is obvious.

It is obvious that you love me.

extraposed version

This should look familiar to you; it's a pattern similar to extraposition with infinitive clauses. We treat them the same way, with *it* as expletive (standing in for the extraposed subject) and the displaced clause (*that you love me*) as *extraposed subject*.

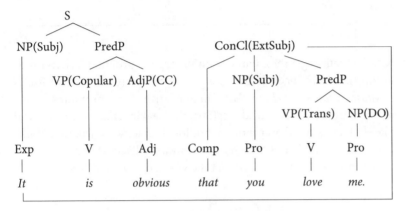

We can imagine a sentence with a content clause and *that* as pronoun rather than complementizer: *I believe that is the best answer*. It seems clear that *that* is the subject of the content clause. We can though, and frequently do, put two *that*'s together in sentences like this: *I believe that that is the best answer*. In this case, the first *that* is complementizer and the second is demonstrative pronoun. The first *that* is optional because the clause is direct object. The second *that* is not optional, because a finite subordinate clause needs an explicit subject.

9.5

Section

Exercise

I. We are now in a position to fully unravel the sentence *I love what you do when you do what you do to me* first mentioned in Chapter 6. We have four finite clauses to explain and some of these clauses are included within other clauses. These clauses are three kinds: matrix, content, and adverbial. Can you identify them? If content clauses or adverbial clauses, what roles do they play within the larger sentence?

II. Identify content clauses in the following sentences and explain what typical NP function they are carrying out.

1) *It is a shame that you came all this way for nothing.*
2) *I agree with what you said, but I don't like how you said it.*
3) *A new car is what I wanted, but an old car is what I could afford.*
4) *I truly believe she will follow through on her promise.*

9.6   Relative clauses

Relative clauses get their name from the kind of pronoun that usually introduces them. They are always adjectival in function.

Relative clauses get their name from the type of pronoun (relative pronoun) that introduces them: almost always *who* (or its variant forms – *whose, whom*), *which*, or *that*. These relative clause pronouns have a role in the clause they introduce. (Strictly speaking, *that* is grammatical placeholder rather than pronoun, but for simplicity, we will treat it like a pronoun.) The clauses themselves are always adjectival and the relative pronoun stands in for the NP that the whole clause modifies.

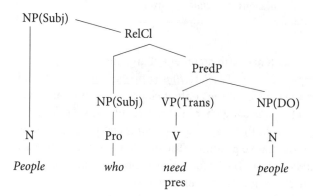

People who need people are the luckiest people in the world.

Who need people is a restrictive adjectival modifier (narrowing down the rather abstract noun *people* to a somewhat smaller group.) *Who* not only stands in for *people* in the relative clause it introduces, but acts as the subject of the relative clause as well. Since the relative clause is restrictive, it is not set off by commas.

> *The study of grammar, which most people do not appreciate or understand, is worth a larger place in the curriculum.*

In this sentence, everything between the commas – *which most people do not appreciate or understand* – is a relative clause, in this case a non–restrictive adjectival modifier of the NP *the study of grammar*. *Which*, as relative pronoun, stands in for the NP *the study of grammar*; in this case, though, it's not subject of the clause it introduces, but direct object. (*Most people do not understand or appreciate <u>the study of grammar</u>. Most people* is relative clause subject, *do not understand or appreciate* is relative clause VP (transitive & present tense) and *which* is direct object.)

Like Wh-pronouns in content clauses, relative pronouns generally open up the clauses that include them, but can take on pretty much any pronoun role in the clauses they introduce. This can include determiners (*whose*) and objects of a preposition.

> Will the person <u>whose keys are lost</u> please report to the office.
> The bag <u>in which I was carrying the groceries</u> broke.

When the relative pronoun is object of preposition (as it is in the second sentence above), the preposition can move to the front of the clause, as it does above, or simply remain in its usual place.

> The bag <u>which I was carrying the groceries in</u> broke.

When the relative pronoun that introduces a relative clause is acting as direct object of the relative clause VP or as object of a preposition within the clause, it can be dropped entirely. Like content clauses without a complementizer, these can be hard to spot.

> The bag <u>I was carrying the groceries in</u> broke.
> Since *which* was object of preposition *in*, it can be dropped from the relative clause without confusion.

Here are some other examples.

> One subject <u>that I like</u> is history.
> Since *that* is direct object of relative clause VP *like*, it can be dropped. *One subject <u>I like</u> is history.*

> The person <u>whom I trust the most</u> is my mother.
> Since *whom* is direct object of relative clause VP *trust*, it can be dropped. *The person <u>I trust the most</u> is my mother.*

> The drawer <u>which I keep my socks in</u> is usually messy.
> Since *which* is object of preposition *in*, it can be dropped. *The drawer <u>I keep my socks in</u> is usually messy.*

The relative pronoun in relative clauses is often an optional element. But it is a required element when the pronoun is acting as subject within the relative clause. Like other finite subordinate clauses, relative clauses require an explicit subject.

Dropping the relative pronoun from the clause, though, can only happen when the relative clause is restrictive. For non-restrictive relative clauses, the lack of a pronoun would create awkwardness and confusion.

My friend Marty, <u>whom I trusted a great deal</u>, disappointed me.
Whom is direct object of relative clause VP *trusted*, but the clause itself is non-restrictive. Dropping *whom* would give us the following ungrammatical sentence: *My friend Marty, <u>I trusted a great deal</u>, disappointed me.* The *whom* is needed for coherence.

My top drawer, <u>in which I keep my socks</u>, is usually messy.
In this sentence, *in which I keep my socks* is no longer a restrictive clause. Even though *which* is object of preposition *in*, it can't be dropped without making the sentence ungrammatical. *My top drawer, <u>I keep my socks in</u>, is usually messy.*

When it's functioning as the subject of the relative clause it introduces, a relative pronoun cannot be dropped. This is true whether the clause is restrictive or non-restrictive. Finite subordinate clauses always carry an explicit subject.

As a general rule, *who* (*whom, whose*) is used for people and *which* is used for things. *That* can be used for both. Many writers limit the use of *that* to restrictive clauses and use *who* and *which* for both restrictive and non-restrictive. (*Cars that I like...; The Lexus, which I like...*)

Who, whose, and *whom* should be thought of as alternative forms of the same pronoun, with use determined by the role of the pronoun in the clause it introduces. If subject or copular complement, *who* is appropriate. If possessive, *whose* is the appropriate form. Traditional grammar has always called for *whom* when the pronoun is in what has traditionally been thought of as an objective case – as direct or indirect object of a VP or as object of a preposition.

He is the man <u>who will marry me</u>.
Who is subject of the relative clause.

He is the man <u>whom I will marry</u>.
Whom is direct object of relative clause VP *will marry*.

He is the man <u>whom I have given my heart</u>.
Whom is indirect object of relative clause VP *have given*.

He is the man <u>whose hand I will take in marriage</u>.
Whose is determiner of relative clause NP *whose hand*.

Whom can sound stuffy in conversation or in informal writing. It can put a writer between a rock and a hard place: do I say something that seems unnatural to me or do I say something that will raise the eyebrows of those who are sticklers for traditional usage? Luckily, it's sometimes easy to avoid. *He is the man I will marry. He is the man I will give my heart to. Whom* drops easily from these clauses because they are restrictive. If the clause is non-restrictive, though, you may find yourself forced into a choice. *Paul Smith, <u>whom I will be marrying in September</u>, is someone* (*<u>whom</u>*) *<u>I have come to know and trust</u>.* The pronoun can't be dropped from the first clause, but it can from the second. It's probably best to make your choices on the basis of the level of formality of the writing occasion. It's your call.

Though relative clauses almost always carry the relative pronouns *who*, *which*, or *that*, other pronouns – like *when*, *where* and *why* – can take on that role. Almost always these take a form like *the time when…, the place where…, the reasons why….*

> *Please come at a time <u>when it's convenient</u>.*
> *I can't remember the street <u>where she lives</u>.*
> *I can't tell you a good reason <u>why I'm here</u>.*

In each of these cases, the relative pronoun takes on an adverbial role in the clause it introduces, standing in for the NP it modifies *It's convenient when. She lives where. I'm here why.*

Here's a nice example from Judith Ortiz Cofer:

> *These were the stores <u>where your face did not turn a clerk to stone, where your money was as good as anyone else's</u>.*

9.7

Relative clauses have been underlined in the following sentences. For each, tell what NP it modifies. Tell whether it is restrictive or non-restrictive. Tell what role the relative pronoun plays in the clause it introduces. (If the relative pronoun has been dropped, tell what role it would play if it was explicitly present and not just implied.)

The sentences are from Judith Ortiz Cofer.

Section
Exercise

1) *It became my father's obsession to get out of the barrio, and thus we were never permitted to form bonds with the place or with the people <u>who lived there</u>.*

2) *Yet El Building was a comfort to my mother, <u>who never got over yearning for</u> la isla.*

3) *Though my father preferred that we do our grocery shopping at the supermarket when he came home on weekend leaves, my mother insisted that she could cook only with products <u>whose labels she could read</u>.*

4) *We always lingered at La Bodega, for it was there that mother breathed best, taking in the familiar aromas of the foods <u>she knew from Mama's kitchen</u>.*

5) *The building <u>we lived in</u> was gray, as were the streets, filled with slush the first few months of my life there.*

9.8   Appositional clauses and adjective complements

In our Chapter 8 discussion of appositional structures, I left you with unanswered questions about the following sentence:

His belief <u>that aliens have landed</u> seems absurd.

At this point in this chapter, our first inclination would be to consider that *aliens have landed* a fairly straightforward relative clause, restrictive, modifying the NP *His belief*. Our problem, though, comes when we try to analyze the role of that in the clause; it has none. It is acting, in fact, like a complementizer, something we have said is only possible with a content clause. Is this a content clause acting like a relative clause? Is it a relative clause that takes a complementizer instead of a relative pronoun? The easiest way out of our dilemma is to call it a content clause but appositional modifier, especially since it passes our two tests for being appositional. His belief is that aliens have landed. That aliens have landed seems absurd. (The verb *to be* slips easily between *His belief* and *that aliens have landed*. *That aliens have landed* can replace *His belief* in a hypothetical sentence.) The same clause might show up as direct object complement of verb *believe*. They are very common with mental process verbs that have a noun equivalent (*hope, wish, desire*, and so on). We can think of them as noun complements since only certain nouns allow them.

These same kinds of structures can also modify adjective phrases appositionally. *I am very happy <u>that you could be here</u>. I am very angry <u>that you came in late</u>*. Again, it seems easiest to call them content clauses because *that* is functioning as a complementizer, not as a pronoun or subordinating conjunction. (Again, by complementizer we mean that it has no role in the clause it introduces; it's not a pronoun and it can be dropped from the sentence, something not true of subordinating conjunctions. *I'm very happy <u>you could be here</u>*.) They seem clearly like content clauses, yet they clearly modify adjectives (*very happy* and *very angry*.) The same role (adjective complement) is filled at times by infinitive clauses. *I am very happy <u>to see you</u>. I am so sad <u>to hear about your loss</u>*.

Identify finite subordinate clauses in the following sentences. For each, tell whether it is a content clause, adverbial clause, or relative clause. If an adverbial clause, tell what word group (usually a VP) it modifies. If a content clause, tell what NP role it carries out in the larger sentence. If a relative clause, tell what NP it modifies and tell whether it is restrictive or non-restrictive. When there is more than one per sentence, the number of finite subordinate clauses is given in parentheses. Remember that clauses can sometimes be included within other clauses.

From Judith Ortiz Cofer:

1) *We lived in Puerto Rico until my brother was born in 1954.*

2) *And as I fall, I can feel the reverberations of her laughter.*

3) *He was assigned to duty in Brooklyn Yard – a place of cement and steel that was to be his home base in the states until his retirement more than twenty years later.*

4) *He left the island first, alone, going to New York City and tracking down his uncle who lived with his family across the Hudson River in Paterson, New Jersey.*

5) *The coat my father had bought for me was similar in color and too big; it sat heavily on my thin frame.*

6) *I do remember the way the heater pipes banged and rattled, startling all of us out of sleep until we got so used to the sound that we automatically shut it out or raised our voices above the racket.* (3 clauses)

7) *The hiss from the valve punctuated my sleep (which has always been fitful) like a non-human presence in the room – a dragon sleeping at the entrance to my childhood.*

8) *Not until years later did I hear how much resistance he had encountered with landlords who were panicking at the influx of Latinos into a neighborhood that had been Jewish for a couple of generations.* (3 clauses)

9) *It made no difference that it was the American phenomenon of ethnic turnover which was changing the urban core of Paterson, and that the human flood could not be held back with an accusing finger.* (3 clauses)

10) *My brother quickly became an avid watcher of Captain Kangaroo and Jungle Jim, while I loved all the series showing families.*

11) *My father's navy check provided us with financial security and a standard of living that the factory workers envied.*

12) *The only thing his money could not buy us was a place to live away from the barrio – his greatest wish, mother's greatest fear.*

13) *Everyone was excited because my mother's brother Herman – a bachelor who could indulge himself with luxuries – had bought a home movie camera, which he would be trying out that night.* (3 clauses)

14) *Even the home movie cannot fill in the sensory details such a gathering left imprinted on a child's brain.*

15) *Sofrito was one of the items that women hoarded, since it was hardly ever in stock at La Bodega.* (2 clauses)

16) *The first time I saw a grown man cry was at a New Year's Eve party; he had been reminded of his mother by the smells in the kitchen.*

17) *There was always a 'trick' pastel – one without stuffing – and whoever got that one was the 'New Years Fool'.*

18) *Mexican recordings were popular, but the songs that brought tears to my mother's eyes were sung by the melancholy Daniel Santos, whose life as a drug addict was the stuff of legend.* (2 clauses)

19) *Felipe Rodriguez was a particular favorite of couples, since he sang about faithless women and broken hearted men.*

20) *As he comes closer I realize that in his features I can see my whole family.*

From Alex Kotlowitz:

21) *When he was four or five, he told LaJoe that he wanted to live on a lake so that he could always feel the wind on his back.* (3 clauses)

22) *At the age of five, he had an imaginary friend Buddy, whom he would talk to and play with in his bedroom.*

23) *He had recently developed a slight stutter, which made him seem even more vulnerable.*

24) *He wanted to be recognized, to know that he was wanted.*

25) *The complex was so new that some of the buildings had yet to be completed.*

26) *Thick patches of mud ran where the sidewalks should have been.*

27) *The clean windows reflected the day's movements with a shimmering quality that gave the building an almost magical quality.*

28) *He thought a lot about the fun they had hunting for snakes, the monumental peace of mind it had given him.* (2 clauses)

29) *Consequently, it is a story that doesn't have a neat and tidy ending.*

Chapter 10
Section Exercise

Page 198
Passages from E.B. White and Richard Rodriguez. Explain the typical or
conventional way in which punctuation is being used.

Chapter Practice

Page 200
Passages from Amy Tan and Annie Dillard. Explain the typical or conventional way
in which punctuation is being used.

Chapter 10

Grammar and writing: punctuation

The most common reason students give for studying grammar or taking a grammar class is to improve the grammar of their writing, which they understand as making fewer errors. They want to know what the 'rules' are so they will know when they are breaking them, a very worthy goal considering the common notion of grammar as a set of rules that should not be broken. Of course, there are different kinds of 'rules' associated with grammar and the old, traditional ways tend to present the prescriptive rules and not the meaning-making system, which is what our main focus has been on in this book. This wider base of understanding will allow us to approach writing in a much more effective way, by looking at connections between grammar and purpose, between grammar and meaning. It will help us write, not just correctly, but effectively. Can it help us write 'correctly' as well?

If your primary interest is in understanding the prescriptive rules of traditional grammar, this class will give you a base of understanding that will make it possible to understand those rules and understand advice about how to apply them. It will – and this is perhaps more important – also allow you to exercise your own critical judgement. Prescriptive rules and standard rules are a shifting ground, much more so than their proponents

Our wide base of understanding will allow us to find connections between grammar and meaning and grammar and purpose. It will also allow us to understand prescriptive rules and make our own judgements about them.

are likely to admit, and it helps to be knowledgeable enough to know when the advice you are being given is harmful and misleading rather than helpful. A deeper base of understanding will help you to distinguish between what Edgar Schuster calls 'mythrules' and more reasonable advice. Schuster points out that teachers tend to teach what they believe they are expected to teach, not what they necessarily believe in:

> What gets taught in school is what feels like school.
> [...] Traditional grammar feels like the right thing to do (teach) in school, and so it is taught. (6)

Some of the rules of 'correct English' seem radically disconnected from actual use and practice.

In Schuster's interesting and helpful book, *Breaking the Rules: Liberating Writers Through Innovative Grammar Instruction* he points out a number of rules routinely taught that do not hold up to close scrutiny, including the scrutiny of what he calls (by way of Joseph M. Williams) the 'favorite writer test (xii).' (These are rules that your favorite writer probably breaks.) These would include the rule against starting a sentence with *and* or *but*, rules against splitting infinitives (*to boldly go*; placing a word or phrase between the complementizer and the infinitive verb), the rule that you should avoid passive voice (a rule that seems woven into all the computer grammar checks), the rule against ending a sentence with a preposition, and so on. The rules of so called 'correct English' seem often to be a loose collection of unexamined attitudes and taboos, quite often radically disconnected from actual use and actual practice.

I always try to have a handbook handy to my writing desk, and I certainly use it to remind myself of certain conventional practices, like whether quotation marks go inside or outside the commas and very much for the conventions built around the citation system. Perhaps the biggest problems with traditional grammar are that it is conservative (stodgy) and it gives advice that is deeply decontextualized. By its very nature, it prefers the old ways over new ways, the formal over the informal, the tried and true over the original and adventurous, the tame over the wild and so on. It pretends that the decisions we are making about revising our sentences have nothing to do with the situation of the writing or the sentences that precede and follow the sentence in question. It treats sentences as thought they are 'complete' and isolated thoughts.

Once we understand that traditional grammar cannot be followed as if it were high dogma set in stone, once we understand that it can and should be skeptically measured against a functional test, we are in a position to learn from it, perhaps in the same way we might learn from a curmudgeonly grandfather we might occasionally go to for old time advice. Think about it. Let it offer you suggestions.

Some of the mixed feelings some of us have toward Standard English have to do with dialect interference problems. That is to say, some spoken versions of English have grammatical patterns different from those in the mainstream, and some of those patterns are looked down upon when they find their way into writing. This has been and continues to be troubling to linguists, who see that there is nothing inherently inferior to these patterns of use and so become uncomfortable in knowing that some people are being penalized (poor grades on papers, denial of employment and so on) because these deeply ingrained patterns can be hard to break.

One example would be dropping the *s* inflection for third person singular present tense (see Chapter 5. *He go to the store. She leave tomorrow.*) Since these are a stock pattern of Black English vernacular, it can be argued that the hostile reaction to these forms is way out of proportion, simply a displaced hostility toward the group itself. (Language patterns of the privileged are never looked on quite so disdainfully, even when they differ from mainstream practice.)

One reason why some teachers would shy away from imposition of prescriptive grammar is that it does often seem to be narrow and discriminatory and hostile in its attitudes. Traditional grammarians often fail to point out how useful these non-standard forms are to writers interested in catching the rhythms and patterns of actual speech. Traditional grammarians often act as if the only legitimate use of language is in formal texts constructed for elitists. Teacher researchers like Rebecca Wheeler have also worked through this problem by encouraging an attention to 'code switching', being able to move back and from one language community to another without the notion that one is better than the other.

It is, of course, only from the perspective of a deep understanding of language that we can make these more mature distinctions. The problem is not a knowledge of grammar but an ignorance of grammar among those who want to insist on how other people should behave.

> Traditional grammarians often act as if the only legitimate use of language is in formal texts constructed for elitists. The problem is not a knowledge of grammar, but ignorance of grammar among those who want to insist on how other people should behave.

10.2   Well-edited prose

You now have the deep understanding of syntax you need to follow conventional practices thoughtfully and creatively.

Another goal for learning grammar and putting that knowledge into practice might usefully be called achieving well-edited prose, in your own writing or for other people. One aspect of this would be efficient and effective use of the punctuation system. We would all like our writing to come through to a reader smoothly and effectively, without the awkwardness that we often run into in the work of unpracticed writers. One difficulty is that the conventions of punctuation, certainly among the most functional of all the language conventions, tend to be based on syntax. A typical college student simply cannot read a typical handbook section on punctuation because following the advice means understanding, for example, the difference between a compound sentence and a compound predicate, the notion of restrictive and non-restrictive modification, the notion of a movable (coordinate) adjective, the difference between a subordinating conjunction and an adverbial modifier and the like. In an age in which public knowledge of grammar is slim at best, this sort of understanding can be a powerful and useful resource. You now have the deep understanding of syntax you need to follow conventional practices and use them thoughtfully and creatively for your own purposes.

10.3   Grammar and process approaches to writing

Why is it that grammar and writing have been at odds in our recent past? The teaching of writing has undergone radical transformation in the last 40 or so years, and to accomplish that shift, it had to separate itself from older ways of doing things, including an over-concern with traditional notions of correctness in writing. Inexperienced writers tend to see writing as linear; you have something to say and sit down to say it, putting it into the best (correct or fancy) words and sentences. Traditionally, at least, a student is led to feel that a sentence is a complete thought and that writers should not repeat themselves. From this inexperienced perspective, writing can be thought of in some ways as cleaning up the sloppiness of speaking, within which form seems less important (less insisted on) than content. Revising writing is then thought of largely as a correcting or proofreading process, each sentence held up to a decontextualized standard of correctness. In the words of Nancy Sommers, who did substantial research on the differing attitudes and practices of experienced and inexperienced writers:

The students [inexperienced writers] decide to stop revising when they decide that they have not violated any of the rules for revising. These rules, such as 'Never begin a sentence with a conjunction' or 'Never end a sentence with a preposition,' are lexically cued and rigidly applied. In general, students will subordinate the demands of the specific problems of their text to the demands of the rules.

Sommers found that experienced writers viewed revision as *holistic* and recursive: the parts needed to be adjusted to how they fit within an evolving sense of the whole, and meaning was never just preexisting and then spilled out on the page, but developed and shaped over the course of the whole writing experience. 'As their ideas change, revision becomes an attempt to make their writing consonant with that changing vision.' If grammar is understood as decontextualized notions of error (the sentence is right or wrong without regard to its place within a text) and writing is thought of as a context-based evolution of meaning, then clearly grammar and writing are at war with each other. From this misleading perspective, grammar has, at best, a place in the final (proofreading) stages of writing, but is thought of as getting in the way of the real work of writing, the making of meaning. Because of insights and partial understandings such as this, the teaching of grammar has been minimized within the curriculum. It might also be safe to say that questions about the use of grammar create mutually hostile camps, those in favor of teaching an outmoded grammar and those in favor of avoiding the teaching of outmoded grammar as much as possible.

> Error-based approaches to grammar render it unimportant, even harmful, in the making of meaning. From a deeper understanding, we see that meaning cannot and does not happen without it. Attention to grammar is attention to the evolving meaning of the text.

We are taking a position different from the above. If in fact grammar is the underlying meaning-making system of the language, then an approach to writing that emphasizes the production of meaning should also acknowledge the enormously important role of grammar in the making of that meaning. We cannot write without grammar any more than we can write without words, and what we hope for is a meaningful arrangement, in harmony with the evolving purposes of a text.

We need, of course, to reaffirm some of the core understandings first presented in Chapter 4. A sentence is not a complete thought, but more like a move in a series of related moves. Sentence boundaries are very flexible, and thoughtful writers certainly play with the way in which content is portioned out. Sentences can vary widely in the amount of content they contain and can vary widely in the way their content is organized. Sentences do not exist in isolation from other sentences.

Sentences do not exist in isolation from larger purposes. Good writers do not avoid repetition, but exploit it in order to build coherence (unity and emphasis) within a text. Grammar and true revision (the evolution of meaning within the process of writing) are mutually inclusive.

10.4   Trust and distrust

Twenty-plus years of teaching writing have led me to believe that many of you do not trust your own language; building that trust has been an important goal of this book. Good writers trust their own language. It's also true that they tend to distrust any particular output of it; they know that good writing is hard work, not easy to come by.

Effective writers make changes in their writing in order to bring their meaning into focus and carry that meaning across effectively to their readers. They never seem to think of rewriting as simply a way to achieve correctness, at least not in superficial ways. Good writers seem to discover their purposes as they write, and then they make changes to bring their discovered purposes into fruition. They cut and add and arrange and rearrange. A good piece of writing is one in which every element is in harmony with the whole, in which the whole text is a harmonious interplay of its parts. That harmony extends to punctuation choices as well. Punctuation choices are not, and should not be, divorced from meaning and purpose.

An effective writing voice comes from trust in your own language as more than adequate for the work of writing.

Writers often speak or write about voice in their writing. They typically speak about voice as something they find rather than something they create. Though they work very hard at their writing, they seem to sound like themselves when they're done. (A writer might tell you that they are often more like themselves in their writing than they are in anything else.) A good, effective writing voice has to somehow feel comfortable and right. It can sometimes be a struggle, harder for some projects than it is for others. You, too, can develop a comfortable writing voice (or voices) through meaningful writing and consistent practice. It is your own language, not someone else's, that you will be working with.

The grammar of writing and the grammar of speech have a great deal in common. It makes no sense, of course, to say that we speak in sentences, just as it makes no sense to say that we talk in letters. But certainly words, phrases, and clauses are to be found in speech as well as in writing. If you listen to the language around you, even casual conversation, you'll hear noun phrases and verb phrases and prepositional phrases, non-finite and finite subordinate clauses, direct objects, indirect objects, copular and predicate complements; you'll hear, in short, all the aspects of grammar that we have been exploring in primarily written form.

Speech tends to be more elliptical than writing. We often leave out parts of statements that are perfectly understood within context. That's not to say that we are being lazy or ungrammatical. It works, and all of us seem to find it perfectly acceptable.

> *How's it going?*
> *Not bad. And you?*
> *Could be better.*

Quite often it's the mood element (grammatical subject and finite verb) that gets bandied about in conversation; the finite verb can stand in for a whole predicate without causing confusion.

> *Will you be going to the party tonight?*
> *I sure will.*

That said, though, it's probably accurate to say that the base-line structure for speech is the clause and clause complex. We can speak in phrases only because the underlying clause constructs are understood. *Not bad* implies *I am not doing badly. Could be better* implies *I could be doing better. I sure will* implies *I sure will be going to the party tonight.*

> The base-line structure for both speech and writing is the clause and clause complex.

It's also true that meanings build in context in writing as well, and writing, too, can be highly elliptical. 'Should progressive educators vote in the next election? If they care about quality education, they must.' Just as in speech, the mood element (*they must*) stands in for a much more complex meaning already given in the preceding sentences: *Progressive educators must vote in the next election.*

The grammar of speech is heavily dependent on intonation. We do not signal meaning in speech primarily through pauses (and certainly not through punctuation), but through the raising and lowering of volume in the voice and the raising and lowering of pitch. A rise in volume creates emphasis. A downward pitch denotes certainty or statement; a rising pitch denotes uncertainty or a question. More often than not, an intonation unit is a clause, and more often than not the emphasis falls on the last lexical element of the clause, which is usually the position of new information. In writing, where the physical voice of the writer isn't there to redirect emphasis, the last element gathers emphasis by default.

> More often than not, an information unit is a clause, and more often than not, emphasis falls on the last lexical element in the clause, which is usually the position for new information.

When we speak, stress quite typically falls on the last lexical element of a clause, but speech gives us the flexibility to alter that, a flexibility we do not have in writing. When you read your writing aloud, you may be tempted to place stresses in places a reader would not. In writing, a clause will sound awkward if the default stressed element is not new information or does not seem highly important. *Give me liberty or give me death* carries a natural stress on both *liberty* and *death* as clause ending elements. *Give me liberty or death is what you should give me* sounds terribly awkward because the content clause copular complement (*what you should give me*) carries absolutely nothing new. If you say it aloud to yourself with an emphasis on *death*, you will be saving the sentence in your own mind but falsely predicting the way it will sound to a reader. It can be very, very helpful to read your writing aloud; it can also be very helpful to hear someone else read it aloud, giving you an accurate feel for how it might sound to someone else.

Let's look at a few ways in which punctuation and the sound system can coincide. The first has to do with what we have identified earlier as a marked theme – any element other than grammatical subject that opens a clause. Consider the sentence *As she walked, the streets grew empty*, where *as she walked* is an adverbial subordinate clause and marked theme. Compare this to *As she walked the streets, they grew empty*, noting the changed position of the comma. A diagram of intonation patterns would be as follows. It should be emphasized that the rise in the wave is not a rise in pitch (which, in fact, goes down), but a rise in the volume of the voice and, with it, a rise in attention or emphasis.

As she walked, the streets grew empty.

As she walked the streets, they grew empty.

In the first sentence, stress falls on *walked* and *empty*. In the second sentence, it falls on *streets* and *empty*. The placement of commas helps reflect that pattern. The first sentence in particular would be problematical without the comma because *the streets* is potentially direct object in the subordinate clause. Because it's needed as subject of the second clause, a reader will compensate and reconfigure the sentence with a stress on *walked*; however, it's better if your reader doesn't have to make that adjustment. Appropriate placement of the comma makes the reading smooth and effortless. Good punctuation is invisible, unnoticed. Only the meaning shines through.

In effective writing, punctuation is invisible, unnoticed. Only the meaning shines through.

Similar patterns occur with restrictive and non-restrictive modification, sometimes with profound effect on the meaning of a statement. Consider the following sentences that differ only by a comma. Read them aloud. Is there a difference in intonation pattern? Is there a corresponding difference in meaning? Think about that before you read on.

Non-restrictive modification is signaled in speech through an additional intonation unit. In writing, that pattern is reinforced by setting off the word group with commas.

> *She grew tired of men who only care about themselves.*
> *She grew tired of men, who only care about themselves.*

My own sense of the difference in intonation patterns is the following:

She grew tired of men who only care about themselves.

She grew tired of men, who only care about themselves.

To me, the first sentence says that she has grown tired of some men, those who only care about themselves, the implication being that there are men who don't fall into this category. The second sentence implies that she has grown tired of all men because all men fall into the category of only caring about themselves. The first relative clause is restrictive and the second is not. Using the comma appropriately helps the writer convey this important nuance of meaning, a nuance that would be signaled in speech by a single intonation unit (the first sentence) or two (the second).

Say the following sentence aloud. How would you diagram its intonation? Where would you place commas to create a smooth reading?

> *Students from other schools not our own caused the trouble.*

If your ear is like mine, you placed voice stress on *other schools, our own,* and *the trouble.* Commas after *schools* and *own* would orchestrate a smooth reading. *Students from other schools, not our own, caused the trouble.*

Each of these comma uses will be discussed again in the comma section later in the chapter.

Stress is often gathered by a number of marked theme openings, including those that tell us how a statement is to be understood or how it is to fit into the text.

To be frank, I don't think we should have hired the man.

By way of example, consider the opening stanza of the poem.

Another stress grabbing feature of both speech and writing would be certain attitude marking modifiers (modal adjuncts) like *never, usually* and *always.*

I will never change my position. I will always be by your side.

These are different from the other examples (above) in that they aren't generally marked by punctuation.

10.6   Lexical density

Speech tends to be grammatically complex (lots of clauses and complex relationships between them). Writing tends to be lexically dense (fewer clauses, but more information packed into each clause). Take, for example, *A good writer sets off non-restrictive relative clauses with commas,* which is far more typical of writing than it is of speech, with seven lexical terms (*good, writer, sets off, non-restrictive, relative, clauses,* and *commas*) within a single clause. Lexical density also increases when the lexical terms are unusual or unfamiliar. Someone who hasn't studied grammar would find our comma sentence very intimidating and confusing. Since we now share a complex understanding of grammar, we can read the sentence with relative ease.

Here is an example of part of a sentence from Stephen W. Hawking's *A Brief History of Time*, taken almost at random, the kind of sentence you would almost never find in unrehearsed speech:

> *The quantum hypothesis explained the observed rate of emission from hot bodies very well...*

Grammatically, it is a very simple transitive clause, with much of the complexity built into the NP direct object. In defense of Mr. Hawking, whose book is famous for its ability to bring the most complex ideas of modern science across to the non-scientific world, the sentence is not that hard to follow in context. Certainly one of the differences between writing and speech is that a writer gets a chance to build meanings over time, creating a context of joint understanding between writer and reader that makes this kind of lexically dense structure possible. This same sort of building of meaning happens within a technical discipline; learning the field is in essence a learning of the language of the field and complex meanings can then be conveyed in a very concise (lexically dense) fashion.

Michael Halliday presents this building of technical language within a field as a movement toward nominalization (the complexity being built into the noun phrases) and away from a more natural way of seeing and saying things, representing the world as a place of processes. If people can be impaired by alcohol (a process, with agent and victim), this can be rendered in subsequent sentences as *alcohol impairment* (not a process, but a thing). Since it is difficult from the word group itself to tell whether alcohol is agent or victim, these sorts of statements tend to create a large gap between the elite and the uninitiated. This may be a necessary step in the evolution of a technical discipline – we can't have chemistry and physics and so on without it – but excess nominalization also wends its way into places where it is not at all necessary, serving as 'largely a ritual feature, engendering only prestige and bureaucratic power. (*Writing Science*,15)'. If our primary goal is to communicate and to extend the reach of human community, then we should avoid lexical density when it serves largely to exclude.

The readability of a lexically dense text will deeply depend on shared understanding between writer and audience. To a baseball fan, certainly, a statement like *He has a 3.0 ERA despite a tendency toward blown saves* will not seem difficult to follow. The writer presupposes that you know what an earned run average is, that you know a 3.0 earned run average is very good, that you know what a save is and that you know that a blown save is very disastrous for a team.

This notion of a shared understanding involves a great deal of presupposition and it's an easy way for any writer to get into serious trouble with a reader. In conversation, there's a give and take that takes away some of the fear and the guesswork. No matter how experienced you become as a writer, you will probably never outgrow the need for honest feedback from a variety of readers. You sometimes have to bore one reader in order to keep contact with another. These are tough choices.

Lexically dense writing can be very powerful and very rich in non-technical discourse because it packs so much meaning into a short space. It's a compression of energy. But be careful. The power of the writing depends upon an effortless or almost effortless understanding on the part of your reader. If the reader has to expend great energy to find your meaning, the power is lost. Complexity has to be built and earned. It is a careful interweaving of the familiar and the not so familiar, of the given and the new. Consider the following from Annie Dillard, especially the last of the three matrix clauses:

> *Night is rising in the valley; the creek has been extinguished for an hour, and now only the naked tips of trees fire tapers into the sky like trails of sparks.*

To me, the writing carries a great, rich power, a marvelous balance between readability and compressed meaning. The clause subjects – *night*, *the creek*, and *the naked tips of trees* – are wonderfully concrete. As rich as the sentence is, it doesn't seem manufactured. Read aloud, it has such a wonderful rhythm and flow.

10.7   Arbitrary elements and conventional practice

It's undoubtedly true, as all serious linguistic studies have shown us, that learning a language is inevitable and natural for any member of the human species not isolated from a speech community and not in some way biologically damaged. We seem innately programmed to be language learners, learners of a sound system, vocabulary and grammar, much of it well before we attend school. What we do not learn, before school, is how to represent our language in writing. We do not know the alphabet and we do not know how to use it to represent our words. We have never spoken in capital letters. We have never spoken periods and commas and quotation marks.

There is no inherent reason why a dot on the page (a period) should represent the notion of a declarative sentence. There is no inherent reason why a small curved line (a comma) between words should be used within sentences to represent the many things that it does. There is no inherent reason why a question mark should end a sentence rather than begin one. There is no inherent reason why we use quotation marks to represent exact, quoted speech but not indirect speech (no matter how close to the original). Much of the same could be said about colons, semicolons, dashes, parentheses, and brackets. If everyone agreed to it, they could be replaced tomorrow by smiling faces and little moons. This is, of course, not likely. These tools are deeply woven into current practice. Part of becoming adept at written language is to accept and embrace the inevitably arbitrary aspects of its form. Once you do so, though, I think you'll see that there is a great deal of room for creativity and playfulness in their use. These are tools for the representation of your language. There is no need to be intimidated by them.

> Part of becoming adept at written language involves accepting and embracing the inevitably arbitrary aspects of its form. We can use them playfully and creatively, as tools for the representation of our own language.

Sentences and disparaged types   10.8

The idea of a sentence has been touched on a number of times in earlier chapters. Perhaps more importantly, you have formed a working knowledge of a range of possibilities in English sentences and, I presume, a deep respect for the immense variety of possibility.

The notion of a sentence you will find in a typical handbook and the notion of a sentence that has been insisted on by English teachers for decades relies very heavily on the notion of an arguable proposition. A traditionally correct sentence requires at a minimum at least one matrix clause (generally called an independent clause in traditional grammar). As you recall, a matrix clause requires a grammatical subject and a finite verb and it cannot, by virtue, for example, of being introduced by a subordinating conjunction, be itself an element in some other matrix clause. In other words, *She is my friend* is permissible as a sentence because it has a grammatical subject (*she*) and a finite verb (*is*). But *While she is my friend* is not a sentence by traditional standards because the subordinating conjunction *while* gives the constituent group a subordinate status, probably as adverbial modifier, in another matrix clause. (*I can't say anything bad about her while she is my friend.*)

A word group presented
as a sentence that does
not include a matrix
clause is called a **sentence
fragment** in traditional
grammar.

Any word group followed by a period that does not satisfy these mini-mum requirements for a sentence has traditionally been disparaged as a sentence fragment in traditional grammar. What complicates this somewhat is the use of sentence fragments, often quite effectively, in the work of many fine writers. (Current practice and traditional rules give us different advice.) This may be because the logical meaning highlighted by traditional grammar is not the only kind of meaning conveyed in writing. A sentence fragment may be a meaningful unit within the message structure of a text.

Consider the following sequence.

I was hurt badly when my father left. Very badly.

From a traditional (and logical) perspective, *very badly* shouldn't stand as a sentence. It's an adverb phrase modifying VP *was hurt* in the preceding sentence and shouldn't be separated from the word group it modifies by a period. Yet the sentence can easily be defended as a message structure. Placing *very badly* alone gives it a heightened emphasis and this is done, it seems to me, with no real danger of confusion.

Writers who use sentence fragments seem to do so sparingly. With care.

Two or more matrix
clauses connected without
conjunction, semicolon, or
colon is called a **run-on
sentence** in traditional
grammar. Connecting them
with just a comma is called
a **comma splice**.

There is no legal limit to the number of matrix clauses a writer can combine together into what is classified as a compound sentence, though traditional grammar has rules about how matrix clauses can be linked without producing what is called a run-on sentence. The idea seems to be that a sentence can have more than one arguable proposition, but the presence of more than one should be made very clear and explicit. The most common way to link them would be a comma plus conjunction (*and, but, or, nor, for, so,* or *yet*). *Everything seemed right for the journey, but Paul hesitated.* Simply linking matrix clauses with a comma is a practice disparaged in traditional grammar as a particular kind of run-on sentence, called a comma splice. *Everything seemed right for the journey, Paul hesitated.* Some writers will routinely give the conjunction, but not the comma; Hemingway is a famous example.

Another common way to link matrix clauses is with a semicolon. One of the semicolon's two primary functions is to link closely related matrix clauses. *His room was a mess; it seemed to mirror the current mess of his life.* I will cover semicolons in more detail later. Some writers use a full colon in this way as well, though it is not as typical (see next section).

The primary use of a colon (:) is to introduce a quotation or a list, especially when the quotation or list is appositional.

> *I'll never forget my father's encouraging words: 'You got yourself into this mess; you can get yourself out of it.'*

> *He pocketed everything he needed for the trip: his car keys, his toothbrush, and a credit card.*

> *This is a book about ways to succeed in college: managing your time, studying efficiently, managing your finances, and choosing the right friends.*

A colon introduces a quotation or list, especially when the quotation or list seems appositional. Conventional practice calls for a fully independent clause to the left of the colon.

Conventional practice calls for a fully independent clause to the left of the colon. In other words, don't use a colon if the quotation or list is direct object or copular complement of a matrix clause verb or object of a matrix clause preposition. For that reason, the following sentences contain no punctuation or commas rather than colons before the quotation or list.

> *My father told me, 'You got yourself into this mess; you can get yourself out of it.'*
> *For the trip, he pocketed car keys, a toothbrush, and a credit card.*
> *This is a book about succeeding in college through managing your time, studying efficiently, managing your finances, and choosing the right friends.*

Because of its role in introducing quotations, the colon is a handy tool when incorporating source material from reading. It shows up frequently in academic and scholarly writing.

Edward Sapir, in *Language*, seems to say that thought arises as a latent content of speech:

> It is, indeed, in the highest degree likely that language is an instrument originally put to uses lower than the conceptual plane and that thought arises as a refined interpretation of its content. The product grows, in other words, with the instrument...(15)

In conventional practice, quotations of over four typed lines are indented.

Some writers use colons between fully independent matrix clauses. The reasons for doing so (and not using the semicolon) seem to differ from writer to writer. Here's an example from Annie Dillard in which the material after the colon seems an extension of the first clause; it would almost be possible to describe it as an appositional clause.

The literature of illumination reveals this above all: although it comes to those who wait for it, it is always, even to the most practiced and adept, a gift and a total surprise.

10.10   Semicolons

A semicolon links elements of equal rank, the most common being closely related matrix clauses.

Whereas a colon generally links sentence elements of unequal rank, a semicolon (;) is used to link elements of equal rank. The most common of these would be closely related independent clauses. They can be a very effective choice when two matrix clauses seem like part of a single statement, but the coordinating conjunctions would add nothing or be misleading. Quite often, these are juxtaposed statements or two ways of saying the same thing.

> *My father was a patient man; I could always count on him to listen when I talked and give advice only when it was clear that I was still searching for an answer.*

The only coordinating conjunction that might fit between these two major clauses is *and*, but *and* would imply that the writer is saying two different things, not saying the same thing in two different ways.

> *In New England, they call it 'tonic'; in many places, they call it 'pop'; most of us know it as 'soda'.*

This sentence about the different names for carbonated soft drinks simply juxtaposes three ways of naming them in three independent clauses. An alternative would be to put *and* between the first two clauses and *but* before the third one, but that would subtly change the meaning, perhaps implying that soda is a better term for it and the other two uses are trivial. It's hard to conjecture outside of context. The semicolon version seems to give all three clauses (and therefore all three meanings) an equal weight.

Most handbooks fairly routinely advocate using semicolons before matrix clauses that begin with conjunctive adverbs, though Edgar Schuster tells me that his as yet unpublished research in this area show that this does not carry over into the practice of successful writers. (In *The Best American Essays of* 2003, he found not a single instance.) To some extent, the handbooks are trying to get us to understand the difference between a subordinating conjunction and a conjunctive adverb.

Subordinating conjunctions (words like *when, while, as, because*) have the effect of fully subordinating the clause they introduce and giving it a role (usually adverbial) in another matrix clause. Other adverbs, though, as you have seen throughout the book, simply have a role within a matrix clause. These would include common terms like *then, now, often, always, only*. Though adverbs have a high degree of movability and can occur in a number of places within a clause, there are some adverbs that more routinely open a clause and take on roles similar to conjunctions (without actually being conjunctions). Those would include words like *however, consequently, nevertheless, nonetheless*, and *therefore* as well as phrases like *as a result*. Though these quite often begin a clause, they are not (like subordinating conjunctions) limited to that position. And unlike subordinating conjunctions, they do not make the clause they introduce subordinate. For that reason, handbooks seem to advocate the semicolon as a way to connecting them. A semicolon is certainly not necessary in that role; a clause introduced by a conjunctive adverb is a fully independent matrix clause, fully capable of standing on its own. Linking the two clauses with just a comma, however, would be considered a comma splice.

Conjunctive adverbs often open a clause, but don't subordinate the clause when they do so. A clause they begin remains fully independent.

> *He was a very consistent pitcher; however, he tended to tire in the late innings.*
> *It rained all day before the big game; therefore, the field was slick in places, and there was a large puddle in left field.*

A good test for whether a word is a subordinating conjunction rather than a conjunctive adverb is movability. In the above sentences, *however* and *therefore* can easily be moved.

> *He was a very consistent pitcher; he tended to tire, however, in late innings.*
> *It rained all day before the big game; the field, therefore, was slick in places, and there was a large puddle in left field.*

Notice that the semicolon remains between the matrix clauses. It's real role is to link the independent clauses, not to precede the conjunctive adverb. In all four sentences, a period between the clauses would be perfectly standard.

Compound elements in a series of three or more are routinely separated by commas (see next section), but semicolons are often used to fill that role when the linked elements themselves include commas of their own. The semicolon is considered a larger pause; it separates elements of higher rank. It gets called into play because constituent groups including commas separated by commas can create a confusion of meaning.

Semicolons are useful for separating compound elements when the linked elements include internal commas. The semicolon establishes a larger break and helps avoid awkwardness or confusion.

We had several kinds of sandwiches at the picnic: tuna and onion, bacon, lettuce, and tomato, ham and Swiss cheese, and salami, provolone cheese, ham and mustard on rye.

As you can see, with commas between the elements of the appositional series, it's hard work to follow. Semicolons smooth out the reading.

We had several kinds of sandwiches at the picnic: tuna and onion; bacon, lettuce, and tomato; ham and Swiss cheese; and salami, provolone cheese, ham, and mustard on rye.

This version makes it clear that there were four types of sandwiches and it is now much clearer what each type contained.

10.11   Commas

Commas may be the most difficult punctuation form to master because they are used for a number of different purposes. Most have been touched on in one way or another in various places in the book.

Commas routinely follow marked themes, marking the end of the first intonation unit and the beginning of the second.

Commas are often used after an introductory word group (after marked themes). Any time a constituent group other than grammatical subject of a matrix clause opens a sentence, the comma signals an end to the initial intonation unit and the beginning of the core of the main clause. As we saw earlier in this chapter, lack of a comma in this position can sometimes create awkwardness in constituency. *As she ate her cat watched.* Without the comma, it sounds at first as though she was eating her cat. *As she ate, her cat watched.* Many writers seem to regard this comma as optional, putting it in when the introductory word group is substantial or there is a potential for awkwardness in meaning. Using it routinely, however, seems a better practice to me, more congruent with the opening word group's status as marked theme. Exception can be made for single word adverbials like *often, then, now, usually, always,* as in the following: *He was once a terrible student. Now he is serious and disciplined.* Even with these, though, the comma can highlight the thematic effect. *Once, he was a terrible student. Now, he is serious and disciplined.* These are very much contrasting statements about *once* and *now*. This is highlighted through the choice of *once* and *now* as marked themes, with the commas playing an important role in establishing that message structure emphasis.

Sometimes more than one marked theme will open a clause; if so, a writer will usually set both (or more) off with commas. Here's an example from E. B. White:

> *On an afternoon in the spring of 1938, foreseeing a change in my life, I rode the subway down to Cortland Street, visited Peter Henderson's seed store, and came away with a mixed order of flower and vegetable seeds.*

In a compound sentence, either or both matrix clauses can have marked themes.

> *As a child, he was shy, but as an adult, he was at ease with people.*

Commas are usually used to separate compound elements in a series of three or more. As you know, pretty much any element of a clause can be compounded and the number of elements linked can continue indefinitely. Coordinating conjunctions *and, or,* and *nor* occur before the final element, but are understood retroactively. If there are only two elements linked, the conjunction is a clear and sufficient connector. When three or more elements are linked, commas between each element help keep constituency clear and anticipate the final conjunction.

Commas typically separate elements in a compound series of three or more.

> *In our household, spring is a time for lawn work, gardening, fishing, and baseball.*

Some writers seem to routinely leave out the comma before the final conjunction, but be careful about that; sometimes that leaves the impression that the final two elements are one element combined.

> *He likes children, old friends and dogs.*

Does he like *old dogs* or just *dogs*? Just *dogs* seems the more likely, but an additional comma would keep a reader from wondering. *He likes children, old friends, and dogs.*

At times, writers will leave out the conjunction before the final element in the series, though this can only happen with *and*.

> *He missed his house, his wife, his children.*

Most writers place commas before a coordinating conjunction linking matrix (independent) clauses. Conjunctions considered coordinating – *and, but, or, nor, for, so, yet* – have been listed before. With whole clauses, traditional practice calls for commas even when only two ele-

Commas typically precede a conjunction linking independent clauses.

ments are being linked, in keeping with the idea that the compound nature of a proposition should be made explicit.

Our bags were packed, and we were ready to go.

When three or more clauses are being connected, *and, or* and *nor* can work retroactively, just as they do in other series of compound elements. *Our bags were packed, our good-byes were all said, and we were ready to go.* One exception to this rule might be when two of the clauses in a three (or more) clause sentence seem to go together as one unit.

> *It was raining hard and the wind was howling, but no mere hurricane would keep us from going.*

Though three clauses are being combined here, a single comma between *howling* and *but* helps emphasize the two part meaning of the sentence; the first part describes the negative conditions and the second part expresses a determination to carry on despite them.

Commas typically occur between movable, coordinate adjectives (unless there's an *and*).

Conventional practice calls for commas between coordinate (movable) adjectives unless there's an *and*. A good test for whether adjectives are truly coordinate is moveability. As you no doubt recall, determiners and nouns as modifiers will be frozen in position; if you can move them at all, it will probably change the meaning of the noun phrase.

> *Some of the first commercial aircraft were an adventure to ride.*

Since none of the adjectives in *some of the first commercial aircraft* are movable, no commas are called for. Another good test is whether *and* can be placed between them.

> *The tired and discouraged team mates climbed onto the bus.*
> *The tired, discouraged team mates climbed onto the bus.*

In general, you have a choice between a comma or *and* in these slots, though a series of three or more with *and* between the final two adjectives would typically carry commas between each.

> *The red, white, and blue flag flew high over the stadium.*

Commas routinely set off postnominal word groups to establish them as non-restrictive.

The presence or absence of commas, in harmony with the intonation grammar of speech, is used to signal whether postnominal adjectival word groups are restrictive (no commas) or non-restrictive (with commas). This would include prepositional phrases, appositional phrases, relative clauses, participial clauses and infinitive clauses. This has been explored elsewhere in the book. It's a very important way in which a writer uses punctuation to establish important differences in meaning.

> *I don't like college students who are into wild parties as neighbors.*
> *I don't like college students, who are into wild parties, as neighbors.*

The first of these sentences singles out certain college students, those who are into wild parties, as undesirable neighbors. The second says that all college students are undesirable neighbors because all are into wild parties. Technically, either is standard (correct), but only one choice will correctly convey your meanings to a reader.

Commas are routinely used to set off mildly parenthetical expressions.

> *This is, as you know, the tenth chapter of the book.*
> *President Clinton, it turned out, remained popular despite his many brushes with scandal.*

These tend to interrupt the normal flow of a sentence. Commas before and after keep that normal flow clear. These parenthetical interruptions are usually highly movable. They tend to modify a whole clause rather than a single part of it. For parenthetical interruptions of greater length and importance, you can use dashes and parentheses (see below).

Use commas to set off contradicting elements.

> *It was my mother, not my father, who taught me how to be tough.*

These, too, follow the natural intonation patterns of speech.

Subordinate clauses that open a clause are usually followed by commas, whereas subordinate clauses that follow the main subject and verb are not preceded by one; the one exception to this would be when the second (subordinate) clause constitutes a contradiction of the first.

> *They went to sea every day when the weather was nice.* (*no comma*)
> *They went to sea every day, though not when threatened by storm.*

Subordinate clauses not only precede or follow matrix clauses, but sometimes interrupt the normal flow of a matrix clause; when they do, they are routinely set off by commas:

> *He began, as he had promised, the long trip home.*

Use commas to set off tag questions and direct address:

Commas typically set off parenthetical interruptions, generally sentence modifiers, as a separate intonation unit. They also routinely follow opening subordinate clauses and precede subordinate clauses that establish a contradiction. These, too, follow and highlight patterns of intonation.

This is a difficult but useful chapter, don't you think?
tag question

It is time, my brothers and sisters, to put your commitment to the test.
direct address

If you say these sentences aloud, you should be able to hear the way these commas help orchestrate the natural intonations of speech.

Many writers use a comma to introduce a direct quotation (*He said, 'I have nothing to wear.'*) or to follow one when the words identifying the speaker follow or interrupt the quote. (*'I have nothing to wear,' he said. 'I have,' he said, 'nothing to wear.'*) Commas generally aren't used when introducing an indirect quotation (a summary or paraphrase of the original words). *He said that he has nothing to wear.*

10.12   Dashes

Parentheses, dashes and commas are all capable of setting off material from the rest of a sentence or text. With parentheses, you need both a beginning and ending, both a before and after. With commas or dashes, you can set off material that ends a sentence, thus effectively beginning with a dash or comma and ending with a period, question mark, or exclamation point. Material enclosed in parentheses can include a period; there's no limit, in effect, to how long a parenthetical interruption can last, though your reader may very well forget where it started if you go on too long. Commas and dashes are limited to setting off material within a single sentence. In general, dashes are a more pronounced break than breaks signaled by a comma, so using them will imply a bigger pause and greater emphasis on the set off material. One wonderfully handy way to use dashes is in setting off appositional material that includes commas within it. The dashes, in effect, help the reader understand where the larger break begins and ends:

> Dashes signal a larger break than commas would, often establishing greater attention or emphasis on the set off elements. They are a good way to set off appositional modifiers with internal commas.

He pocketed everything he needed for the trip – his car keys, his toothbrush, and a credit card – before saying a glad good-bye and hitting the road.

If material is placed in parentheses, the writer is saying that it's an interesting sidenote, perhaps explanatory, perhaps more essential and useful for some readers than for others, but not necessary to the primary purpose and primary movement of the text. Dashes, on the other hand, tend to signal a heightened emphasis or heightened importance. They may set off a grammatical digression, but the meaning is to be attended to very carefully. For that reason, it's probably best to use them for special occasions and not diminish their effect through overuse.

He came to college from a fancy prep school, made sure we knew how smart he is – and flunked out.

The dash here, in place of the normally called for comma, draws attention to the abrupt shift in meaning.

Brackets   10.13

Brackets ([]) are used to add your own information to a quotation. A sentence taken out of context will quite often contain references (often pronouns) that will not be clear without explanation.

He said, 'she [his mother] still treats me like a child.'

Ellipses   10.14

Ellipses (three consecutive periods or four consecutive periods when the omitted material includes at least one period) are used for material left out of a quotation. These are useful when the material you are interested in from a source is mingled with material that seems irrelevant to your purpose. You need to be careful, of course, to do this honestly and not simply leave out material that contradicts what you would like to say. People who quote movie or book reviews might be tempted to this kind of dishonesty, quoting the part of a review that's the most positive and leaving the qualifiers out.

This is a not very satisfying movie.
This is a ... very satisfying movie.

The ellipses in the second sentence is fundamentally and blatantly dishonest. You obligation is not just to copy words, but to accurately represent the meaning.

10.15

Punctuation has been numbered in the following sentences. For each, explain the typical or conventional way in which the punctuation is being used.

From E. B. White:

1) *Weapons are worrisome and expensive;[1] they make everyone edgy.*

2) *That is why we may profitably talk about stopping nuclear tests:[1] national self-interest happens in this case to coincide with universal interest,[2] and the whole business is a simple matter of human survival on a shaky planet.*

3) *A copy-desk man would get a double hernia trying to clean up that sentence for the management,[1] but the sentence needs no fixing,[2] for it perfectly captures the meaning of the writer and the quality of the ramble.*

4) *One of the things commonly said about humorists is that they are really very sad people–[1]clowns with a breaking heart. There is some truth in it,[2] but it is badly stated.*

5) *On the whole,[1] humorists who give pleasure to a wide audience are the ones who create characters and tell tales,[2] the ones who are storytellers at heart.*

From Richard Rodriguez:

6) *In public,[1] my parents spoke a hesitant,[2] accented,[3] and not always grammatical English.*

7) *Conveyed through those sounds was the pleasing,[1] soothing,[2] consoling reminder that one was at home.*

8) *During those years when I first learned to speak,[1] my mother and father addressed me only in Spanish;[2] in Spanish I learned to reply.*

9) *My own sounds I was unable to hear,[1] but I knew that I spoke English poorly.*

10) *Walking toward our house,[1] climbing the steps from the sidewalk,[2] in summer when the front door was open,[3] I'd hear voices beyond the screen door talking in Spanish.*

11) *It was still then ingles,[1] a language foreign to us,[2] so we felt drawn to it as strangers.*

12) *As we children learned more and more English,[1] we shared fewer and fewer words with our parents.*

13) *Especially when talking to other men,[1] his voice would spark,[2] flicker,[3] flare alive with varied sounds.*

14) *The silence at home,[1] however,[2] was not simply the result of fewer words passing between parents and children.*

15) *It is true that my public society today is impersonal;[1] in fact,[2] my public society is usually mass society.*

Ernest Hemingway is famous for his minimalist use of punctuation. The following is the opening paragraph from *The Old Man and the Sea*. Read it carefully, trying to pick out the places where a more conventional writer would add punctuation. There are only four commas in the paragraph; do you feel these commas are especially important? Do you find this style effective?

He was an old man who fished alone in a skiff in the Gulf Stream and he had gone eighty-four days now without taking a fish. In the first forty days a boy had been with him. But after forty days without a fish the boy's parents had told him that the old man was now definitely and finally salao, which is the worst form of unlucky, and the boy had gone at their orders in another boat which caught three good fish the first week. It made the boy sad to see the old man come in each day with his skiff empty and he always went down to help him carry either the coiled lines or the gaff and harpoon and the sail that was furled around the mast. The sail was patched with flour sacks and, furled, it looked like the flag of permanent defeat.

Punctuation has been numbered in the following passages. For each, explain the typical or conventional way in which the punctuation is being used.

From Amy Tan:

> *Fortunately,[1] for reasons I won't get into today,[2] I later decided I should envision a reader for the stories I would write. And the reader I decided upon was my mother,[3] because these were stories about mothers. So with this reader in mind – [4] and in fact she did read my early drafts – [5] I began to write stories using all the Englishes I grew up with:[6] The English I spoke to my mother,[7] which for lack of a better term might be described as 'simple';[8] the English she used with me,[9] which for lack of a better term might be described as 'broken';[10] my translation of her Chinese,[11] which could certainly be described as 'watered down';[12] and what I imagine to be her translation of her Chinese if she could speak in perfect English,[13] her internal language,[14] and for that I sought to preserve the essence,[15] but neither an English nor a Chinese structure. I wanted to capture what language ability tests can never reveal:[16] her intent,[17] her passion,[18] her imagery,[19] the rhythms of her speech and the nature of her thoughts.*

From Annie Dillard:

1) *It is[2] winter proper;[3] the cold weather, such as it is, has come to stay. I bloom indoors in the winter like a forced forsythia;[4] I come in to come out. At night I read and write,[5] and things I have never understood become clear;[6] I reap the harvest of the rest of the year's planting.*

   Outside,[7] everything has opened up. Winter clear-cuts and reseeds the easy way. Everywhere paths unclog;[8] in late fall and winter,[9] and only then,[10] can I scale the cliffs to the Lucas orchard,[11] circle the forested quarry pond,[12] or follow the left-hand bank of Tinker Creek downstream.

2) *The cloud ceiling took on a warm tone,[1] deepened,[2] and departed as if drawn on a leash.*

3) *Night is rising in the valley;[1] the creek has been extinguished for an hour,[2] and now only the naked tips of trees fire tapers into the sky like trails of sparks.*

4) *In the great meteor shower of August,[1] the Perseid,[2] I wait all day for the shooting stars I miss. They're out there showering down,[3] committing hari-kari in a flame of fatal attraction,[4] and hissing perhaps at last into the ocean.*

5) *We have really only that one light,[1] one source for all power,[2] and yet we must turn away from it by universal decree. Nobody here on this planet seems aware of this strange,[3] powerful taboo,[4] that we all walk about carefully averting our faces,[5] this way and that,[6] lest our eyes be blasted forever.*

6) *A crayfish jerks,[1] but by the time I absorb what has happened,[2] he's gone in a billowing smokescreen of silt.*

7) *I look at the lighted creekbottom:[1] snail tracks tunnel the mud in quavering curves.*

8) *Until,[1] one by one,[2] by the darkest of leaps,[3] we light on the road to these places,[4] we must stumble in darkness and hunger.*

9) *I'm blind as a bat,[1] seeing only from every direction the echo of my own thin cries.*

10) *I breathed an air like light;[1] I saw a light like water. I was the lip of a fountain the creek filled forever;[2] I was ether,[3] the leaf in the zephyr;[4] I was flesh-flake,[5] feather,[6] bone.*

11) *The literature of illumination reveals this above all:[1] although it comes to those who wait for it,[2] it is always,[3] even to the most practiced and adept,[4] a gift and a total surprise.*

12) *Some unwonted,[1] taught pride diverts us from our original intent,[2] which is to explore the neighborhood,[3] view the landscape,[4] to discover at least where it is that we have been so startlingly set down,[5] if we can't learn why.*

Chapter 11

Chapter Practice

Page 215
Study the opening paragraphs to *I Have a Dream* by Martin Luther King Jr. to explain all grammatical elements and look at ways in which meaning and form work harmoniously.

Chapter 11

Grammar and meaning in longer texts

We understand clearly by now that words in sentences do not simply add up their individual meanings, but establish grammatical relations with each other. The same is true of sentences in a paragraph and paragraphs within a text. The meaning of an individual sentence has everything in the world to do with the meaning of the sentences that precede and follow it. It also has everything in the world to do with the context of its creation: the intentions of the writer, the effects on its reader or readers, and the world it may be trying to change or describe.

Every writer comes to know very quickly that sentence boundaries are highly flexible. Under the pressure of composition, a single sentence may be broken into several sentences or several sentences may be combined into one. The notion of a sentence as *a complete thought*, as helpful as it may or may not be for beginning writers with very little conscious knowledge of grammar, is ultimately more harmful than helpful. It certainly wouldn't be unusual for a writer to describe a whole essay or even a whole book as an attempt to convey a single idea. It's probably safe to say that a complete thought will more often than not require more than a single sentence and even then may leave a writer feeling that the words were somehow inadequate to the task.

It has been very important, very necessary, for us to isolate individual sentences as we developed a complex understanding of grammar. It is very important also to understand that a fully integrated understanding of grammar does not and should not end there. In this chapter, we will further explore ways in which grammar participates in the making of a more extended meaning.

Painstaking description of the formal structure of a text may help lay a groundwork for an analysis of meaning, but form alone will never carry us all the way home. For that reason, it may make more sense to begin with meaning and look for ways in which that meaning is being carried out, fully open to the possibility of changing our minds about the meaning of a text as our exploration unfolds. We can always examine sentences in isolation, as we have throughout this book; but our main task here is to explore how these same sentences work in harmony with others toward purposes more essential than the mere creation of form.

I will start with a short poem by Robert Hayden, *Those Winter Sundays*. It has the advantage of being a short text meant to be read as a unified whole. In the interest of efficiency and brevity, I will for the most part ignore poetic structure (lines and stanzas) and focus on syntax and meaning. I will then look closely at a passage from a longer non-fiction work by Richard Rodriguez. The chapter will end with a few more passages for your own exploration and discussion.

The Hayden poem is as follows. You should spend some time reading it and thinking about it before you read on.

Those Winter Sundays

Sundays too my father got up early
and put his clothes on in the blueblack cold,
then with cracked hands that ached
from labor in the weekday weather made
banked fires blaze. No one ever thanked him.
I'd wake and hear the cold splintering, breaking.
When the rooms were warm, he'd call,
and slowly I would rise and dress,
fearing the chronic angers of that house,
Speaking indifferently to him,
who had driven out the cold
and polished my good shoes as well.
What did I know, what did I know
of love's austere and lonely offices?

The poem, as I see it, is a love poem and a poem about love. It is a poem about his father's love and about his own love for his father. It is about the nature of parental love and the belated way we come to appreciate it. The word *love* doesn't show up until the last line of the poem, but has a retroactive effect on the whole poem when it does.

Like many past tense narratives, the meaning of the poem exists in the tension between past and present attitudes. Though there is only one *I* (speaker), that *I* has two different incarnations, the old *I* being looked back on and the new *I* doing the looking. Much of this comes into clearest focus with the last two lines of the poem.

The long first sentence begins with *Sundays too*, an adverbial marked theme. The writer presupposes that his audience thinks of Sunday as the proverbial day of rest. It is news, therefore, that his father gets up *early* on *Sundays too*. *Early* ends the first (of three) predicate phrases, in a position of tonic prominence. *My father* is grammatical subject and actor. All three matrix clause VPs (*got up*, *put on*, and *made*) are material process and active – intransitive, transitive, and complex transitive, in that order. They help convey a portrait of the father as an active and competent man. The second predicate phrase ends with the adverbial PP *in the blueblack cold* in position of emphasis. *Blueblack* is a rather unusual adjective, conveying a rich sense of the earliness of the hour and the harshness of the cold. *With cracked hands that ached from labor in the weekday weather* is an adverbial marked theme for the second predicate phrase, coming as it does before the VP. Though the focus of the poem is on Sunday, this gives us a strong physical sense of the harshness of the father's life the rest of the week and the way that harshness carries over. *Cracked* lets us see the hands and *ached* helps us feel them as the father would. It's interesting that *ached* is downranked into the subordinate clause, thus giving the father's suffering a minor status, something overcome rather than something that might defeat him. *Made* is causative verb, with *banked fires* as direct object and *blaze* as infinitive predicate compliment. *Banked fires* may be lost on a generation unfamiliar with older heating systems; if you heat with wood or coal, a fire needs to be banked in the evening, diminishing its output for night hours when heat is not as needed and also insuring that there will be some fire still burning in the morning; bringing a banked fire to life is much easier and quicker than starting a new one. This, in particular, shows the father as not only active, but competent. The thirty-two word first sentence is then followed by a marvelously succinct (five word) sentence. Message emphasis falls on *No one* and *thanked*. (*Him* is a grammatical term and given, so prominence moves backward by default.) *Ever* is an adverbial intensifier, combining with *No one* to give a sense of completeness to the absence of thanks. The two sentences aren't explicitly connected, but juxtaposed. The reader is left to create the connection – that the father very much deserves the thanks that never came. The word *lonely* (last line) is anticipated here. It's not simply the son that failed to thank him, but everyone, always, who benefited from his effort and sacrifice.

The second stanza shifts the subject from *my father* to *I*, though the *my* in effect put *I* present all along. *I* is theme (unmarked), grammatical subject, and actor. The matrix clause VPs are now behavioral process (*wake*) and mental process perceptual (*hear*). What *I* hears is the result of his father's actions. *The cold splintering, breaking* seems to me a subject bearing participial clause. A sensitive reader is placed within the recurrent moment through hearing the sound of a house being warmed. The second sentence shifts back to *he* as subject. *When the rooms were warm* is an adverbial subordinate clause as marked theme. He has, of course, made the rooms warm for a purpose. *He'd call* presents the father once again as active, this time through verbal process verb. *And* connects a new matrix clause, itself a response to the house's warming and the father's subsequent call. *Slowly* is an adverbial marked theme, perhaps a contrasting emphasis on the son's lack of purpose, responsibility, and discipline (a luxury that the father's actions make possible). *Rise* and *dress* are material process, but intransitive, actions without much implication beyond the self. Two participial clause modifiers follow. *Fearing the chronic angers of that house* is particularly interesting in the use of *chronic*, more often used in context with disease, as a modifier of *angers*. *Angers* are attributed to *that house*, rather than the father, perhaps as a way of minimizing blame. *Chronic*, too, gives the sense of inevitability; a disease, after all, is something we don't usually think of an individual as being responsible for. A *chronic* condition is incurable and subject to flaring up at any time, thus the reference to *fearing*. We have enough detail already to fill in some reasons for it; in the midst of so harsh a life, we are not surprised by a *chronic* anger. *Fearing* is mental process (emotion), with the usual reciprocity of subject/object. (Anger causes the fear; the fear does not make the anger. In meaning terms, the verb is virtually passive.) *Speaking indifferently* picks up the *No one ever thanked him* theme, bringing it home to the *I*. *Indifferently* carries much weight; again, the writer presumes that we should understand that the father deserves more, but here the point is driven home through a more explicit (same sentence) juxtaposition. The man he speaks to indifferently *has driven out the cold and polished my good shoes as well. Driven out the cold* reinforces a meaning already established and reinforces our view of the father as a productive and powerful presence. *Polished my good shoes as well* adds an additional duty to the others, this one a duty the son should certainly have been able to accomplish on his own. I can't help supposing that they are headed for church and that the father cares more than the son about how he looks when he arrives there. The VPs in the relative clause are material process, transitive, and active, again helping build a portrait of the father as a man of competence and action.

The last sentence brings in a more explicit attention to time. The whole poem has been past tense, more specifically a past tense of repeated or habitual action. *Would* does not become explicit as a modal auxiliary until the second stanza, but the plural on *Sundays* in the first sentence and the title and *ever* in the second sentence make clear that this is not a one time occurrence. As in many past tense narratives, a tension is being built between the *I* of past time and the *I* of the telling. He is remembering the thoughts, feelings, and experiences of his own childhood, but juxtaposing them with a portrait of the father both loving and admiring. *What did I know* brings this tension to the surface. That it is said twice seems to force a different emphasis on the second telling. I would read it as *What did I **know**, what **did** I know....* Quite clearly what he does know now (at the time of the telling) is very different, summed up in the concluding prepositional phrase *of love's austere and lonely offices.* Much of the brilliance here is in compactness and word choice. *Austere* gives a sense of harshness and also of making do with very little. *Lonely* is a fitting summation to the material about the father never being thanked. *Offices* gives a sense of both duties (a role) and place where they are to be carried out. The final line may have the effect of surprising us and not surprising us; it simply brings into clearer focus the meaning that has been being built all along.

The poem is an expression of love and appreciation for his father. If it's an excellent poem (I think it is) it is because it is not simply a poem about his experience, but about ours as well. It is ours to do with as we wish; I can't help but read it as a son who never fully appreciated his father until he became a father of his own and as a father who needs to remember that his children need parents they can somewhat take for granted.

Our next passage is a somewhat longer non-fiction excerpt from Richard Rodriguez's autobiography, *Hunger of Memory*. The frequently anthologized longer essay it's taken from is generally described as an argument against bilingual education. In teaching it, though, I have found that it appeals to opponents and proponents of bilingual education alike because it succeeds so well in capturing the experience of an immigrant child. An immigrant child, as Rodriguez describes him through a focus on his own experience, is caught, not just between two languages, but between two worlds. The words *public* and *private* show up frequently within the larger essay as ways to name these two worlds – the private world of the home (in his case, Spanish speaking) and the English speaking public world beyond that. Though this passage is taken from a much longer work, it seems to have its own internal consistency and unity. It's given below, with the sentences numbered for convenience. If you feel particularly ambitious, take some time with it before you read on. As with much real world writing, some of the grammar is difficult to characterize. Give yourself a few hours with it and be prepared to scratch your head a few times along the way. Don't be intimidated by language that seems to resist easy characterization; language has a life of its own, apart from our attempts to understand how it works. As with the Hayden poem, our goal should be to explore ways in which the grammar and the meaning work together.

From Richard Rodriguez, *Hunger of Memory*:

1) *At the age of six, well past the time when most middle class children no longer notice the difference between sounds uttered at home and words spoken in public, I had a different experience. 2) I lived in a world compounded of sounds. 3) I was a child longer than most. 4) I lived in a magical world, surrounded by sounds both pleasing and fearful. 5) I shared with my family a language enchantingly private – different from that used in the city around us.*

6) *Just opening or closing the screen door behind me was an important experience. 7) I'd rarely leave home all alone or without feeling reluctance. 8) Walking down the sidewalk, under the canopy of tall trees, I'd warily notice the (suddenly) silent neighborhood kids who stood warily watching me. 9) Nervously, I'd arrive at the grocery store to hear the sounds of the gringo, reminding me that in this so-big world I was a foreigner. 10) But if leaving home was never routine, neither was coming back. 11) Walking toward our house, climbing the steps from the sidewalk, in summer when the front door was open, I'd hear voices beyond the screen door talking in Spanish. 12) For a*

second or two I'd stay, linger there listening. 13) *Smiling, I'd hear my mother call out, saying in Spanish, 'Is that you, Richard?'* 14) *Those were her words, but all the while her sounds would assure me*: You are home now. 15) Come closer inside. 16) With us. 17) '*Si', I'd reply.*

18) *Once more inside the house, I would resume my place with the family.* 19) *The sounds would grow harder to hear.* 20) *Once more at home, I would grow less conscious of them.* 21) *It required, however, no more than the blurt of the doorbell to alert me all over again to listen to sounds.* 22) *The house would turn instantly quiet while my mother went to the door.* 23) *I'd hear her hard English sounds.* 24) *I'd wait for her voice to turn to soft-sounding Spanish, which assured me, as surely as did the clicking tongue of the lock on the door, that the stranger was gone.*

What struck me first about the first sentence in the passage is the way the core matrix clause (*I had a different experience*) is postponed. Much of the meaning of the sentence is built into its adverbial marked theme(s), the second of which, the material between the two commas, is particularly complex. *At the age of six* sets an important time frame; the essay as a whole focuses on the transition from home to school. *Well past the time when most middle class children no longer notice the difference between sounds uttered at home and words spoken in public* can be read as a second marked theme or as an appositional modifier (non-restrictive) of the opening prepositional phrase. At its core, it's a prepositional phrase. (Think of <u>*well past noon*</u>, *we finally ate lunch* as a parallel.) *When most middle class children no longer notice...public* is a restrictive relative clause modifying *the time*, all that together making up the object of the preposition *past*. *Most middle class children* is relative clause subject, *notice* is its present tense transitive VP, and *the difference between sounds uttered at home and words spoken in public* is direct object of *notice*. *Between sounds uttered at home and words spoken in public* is a prepositional phrase modifier of *the difference*. It includes a compound NP as object. *Uttered at home* and *spoken in public* are participle clause modifiers of *sounds* and *words* respectively. The compound NP is nicely parallel.

The position of *I had a different experience* at the end of the first sentence gives it a nice backward and forward contribution to the meaning. Like most comparisons, it is highly elliptical; what he is saying by implication is that at the age of six he <u>did</u> *notice the difference between sounds uttered at home and words spoken in public*. The adverbial *no longer* carries large weight because it implies that *most middle class children* had/have an experience that differs from his own more in duration than in kind. By *the age of six*, they are somewhat comfortable in public.

The next four sentences (sentences two through five) simply extend this notion of *a different experience*. *I* in all four sentences is grammatical subject, actor, given information, and highly unmarked theme. Tonic emphasis in sentence two falls on *compounded of sounds*, with *sounds* a lexical repetition from the first sentence. *Compounded of* seems to imply not just *composed of*, but *complicated by*. The copular *I was a child longer than most* simply brings more explicitly to our attention a meaning already established in sentence one. (*Most middle class children* notice the difference in sounds, but stop doing so well before age six.) The word *magical* jumps out among the first six words in sentence four as the only new information in that group. *Surrounded by sounds both pleasing and fearful* is a past participle clause modifying *I*. (His world is *compounded of sounds* (sentence two), but he is *surrounded by* them.) *Pleasing and fearful* gain tonic emphasis, with *pleasing* reinforcing *magical* and *fearful* somewhat contradicting it, though the two terms together certainly give a sense of heightened intensity. *Lived*, *world*, and *sounds* are lexical repetitions.

The VP in sentence five (*shared*) frames a focus on the home language as *enchantingly private*, with *enchantingly* echoing *magical* and *private* a contrasting echo of *public* (in sentence one). *Different from that used in the city around us* seems to me an appositional expansion of *private* – together, at any rate, they describe the language *shared with my family*. *That used in the city around us* is grammatically interesting; at first glance, it looks like a content clause, but *that* would then be content clause subject, acting like a pronoun in a relative clause. It's probably best to read *that* as a pronoun (standing in for *language*) and *used in the city around us* as a restrictive participle clause modifier of *that*. *Around* echoes *surrounded* in both sound and meaning. A key lexical repetition is *sounds* (three times) coupled with related words like *uttered*, *spoken*, and *language*. *Lived* and *world* both show up twice. *I* is grammatical subject in all five sentences. The verbs are consistently past tense (except for the relative clause verb *notice*) in keeping with the notion of past time retrospective. The one present tense verb (*notice*) helps establish a pattern for middle class children that is still true.

The syntax in sentence six poses an interesting problem. At first glance, we have a participial clause subject with a compound VP (*opening or closing*) sharing *the screen door* as participial clause direct object and *behind me* as adverbial predicate complement. When I think of the representational meaning, though, this analysis is jarring – you can close a screen door behind you, but you can't open one that way. (Compare *just opening the screen door or closing it behind me* as a less problematic version.) The metaphor, however, is brilliant. *An important experience,* the matrix clause copular complement, like *a different experience* in paragraph one, seems highly thematic, setting up the expectation of explanation. How can opening or closing a screen door be important? The answer, of course, is that it is quite literally the doorway in and out of radically different worlds.

Sentences seven through nine take us away from home and sentences 10 through 17 bring us back. The modal *would* (contracted) shows up for the first time in sentence seven and carries through for the rest of the passage. Perhaps the writer felt a need, with the focus shifted to more particular detail, to make more explicit the understanding that this was a pattern of past experience, not just a one-time occurrence. The compound adverbial phrase (*all alone or without feeling reluctance*) carries much of the meaning weight, with *rarely* an important adverbial VP auxiliary. The focus is on fearfulness.

Sentence eight opens with two marked themes – the participial clause *walking down the sidewalk* and the PP *under the canopy of tall trees.* *Under the canopy of tall trees* could be seen as modifying *walking* or modifying the matrix verb '*d warily notice.* (Perhaps it modifies both.) It's interesting that *warily* shows up twice – as modifier of his noticing and the neighborhood kids' watching. There are suspicions on both sides. Why is *suddenly* in parentheses? It seems to me to give the term more emphasis rather than less. They are not normally silent kids, but made (*suddenly*) silent by his presence. *Who stood warily watching me* is restrictive relative clause modifier of *the (suddenly) silent neighborhood kids.* *Stood warily watching* seems almost a compound verb; the more standard alternative would be to see *watching* as participial clause VP with *me* as its direct object. It's interesting that the matrix clause begins with *I* and ends with *me*.

Nervously, in sentence nine, is an adverbial marked theme, extending a meaning pattern begun with *reluctance* and *warily*. *To hear the sounds of the gringo, reminding me that in this so-big world I was a foreigner* is an adverbial infinitive clause, but what happens when we use the *in order to* test? It hardly seems possible that this was a purpose for his going there; it seems more like an undesired, but inescapable result. *Gringo* and *foreigner* are in positions of tonic emphasis and nicely juxtaposed. We are back to a focus on sounds again (and away from a focus on silence). In the participial clause that begins with *reminding*, *me* is indirect object *and that in this so-big world I was a foreigner* is content clause direct object. *In this so-big world* acts like a marked theme in its content clause by virtue of its position (ahead of the content clause subject). This structure also allows the sentence to end with emphasis on the copular complement *a foreigner*. *So-big* is an interesting adjective; it seems to me very much a child's word, helping to frame a childhood perspective. He may not know the words, but the sounds carry a definite message. They establish his identity (as *a foreigner*). The *gringo* may be alien to him, but it is the gringo's world.

The *but* opening sentence 10 links the three sentences before it with the rest of the paragraph. It's a truly transitional sentence, reminding us that the focus has been on the *never routine* nature of *leaving home* and anticipating the shift in focus to the *never routine* nature of *coming back*. *Coming back* is participial clause and matrix clause subject. *Never routine*, its copular complement, is elliptically implied in the second clause.

Sentence 11 opens with three marked themes, two adjectival participial clauses (*Walking toward our house* and *climbing the steps from the sidewalk*) and an adverbial prepositional phrase (*in summer when the front door was open*). *When the front door was open* is a restrictive relative clause modifying *summer*. I read *voices beyond the screen door talking in Spanish* as a subject bearing participial clause, direct object of '*d hear*. *Walking* and *climbing* are material process, '*d hear* is mental process (perceptual), and *talking* is verbal process. *In Spanish* gathers tonic prominence, as it should. He returns from the fearful world of English to the pleasing world of Spanish. The screen door has re-entered the paragraph as a porous boundary between the two worlds.

For a second or two opens sentence 12 as an adverbial marked theme. I read the comma between *stay* and *linger* as conjunctive, though *linger there listening* has an appositional feel. The movement is from material process (*stay*) to behavioral process (*linger*) to mental process (*listening*).

Smiling opens sentence 13 as a participial clause (adjectival) marked theme. Once again, *I* is subject and actor. *Hear* is, of course, mental process (perceptual), a natural extension of *listening* in the previous sentence. *My mother call out, saying in Spanish, 'Is that you, Richard?'* is subject bearing infinitive clause as direct object of the perception verb. *Saying in Spanish, 'Is that you, Richard?'* is a participial clause modifier of *my mother*. *'Is that you, Richard'* could be direct object of either VP, though its proximity to *saying* makes that the more natural choice; like many quoted statements, it is a clause in its own right, in this case, of course, a question. It's interesting that the mother seems concerned about establishing his identity. It reassures him, and perhaps her as well? She speaks his name.

In sentence 14, he makes a distinction again between *words* and *sounds*, between what is explicitly said and the deeper message implied. *Those were her words* is a straightforward copular clause. *But* establishes a meaning contrary to that surface. *All the while* is marked theme adverbial. *Would assure* is di-transitive and verbal process (though it shades toward the emotional as a message). *Me* is indirect object (receiver of assurance). *You are home now* is direct object, though a good case could be made for sentences 15 and 16 as extensions of the direct object (the message of assurance).

Come closer inside is imperative in mood (*you* as understood subject), but certainly more an invitation than a command. *With us* is technically a sentence fragment, an adverbial modifier of the previous sentence's VP. The period has the effect of slowing the message down, allowing us to savor the comfort of the moment. Though it is an imagined statement, not spoken aloud, the period perhaps gives us a feel for the rhythm in which it is imagined as spoken (closer to the patterns of actual speech). It's more than just a house, of course, that makes a *home*. Though the conversation seems imagined, he presents *sí* (marked theme direct object) as if it were explicitly stated. It is, of course, in Spanish. He accepts the invitation, and the shared language is an integral part of that.

Once more inside the house opens the third paragraph as a marked theme, not just for its sentence, but for the paragraph as a whole, which has an inside the house focus. *Once more* reiterates that this is a return. The VP *resumes* reinforces that familiarity as well. *My place with the family* is direct object, though the meaning hardly seems transitive. (Requiring no effort on his part.) *The sounds* is both grammatical subject and theme in sentence 19. *Harder to hear* is copular complement, with *to hear* as a restrictive infinitive clause modifier of *harder*. *Once more at home* echoes the sentence 18 marked theme, with a telling shift from *house* to *home*.

Would grow is repeated as copular VP, this time with *I* as subject. *Them* stands in for sounds. The whole sentence seems to reinforce established meanings rather than add new ones.

Sentence 21 has an extraposed infinitive clause subject – *to alert me all over again to listen to sounds*. Once again, we have verbal process verbs – *blurt* and *alert* – and a mental/perceptual VP (*listen*). *Blurt* and *alert* give us a nice internal rhyme; together, they establish the sound as harsh and foreboding. *All over again* establishes this as a pattern. The infinitive clause VP *alert* is complex transitive (causative), with *me* as direct object and *to listen to sounds* as infinitive clause predicate compliment.

The house is grammatical subject and theme in 22, though the statement is obviously more about the inhabitants than about the house itself. *Instantly quiet* is an adjective phrase copular complement. *While* establishes the subordinate clause as adverbial of duration. *The door* is once again important as the border between the worlds, and it shows up here in sentence ending emphasis. The VP in 23 is once again '*d hear*. *Her hard English sounds* is direct object. *Sounds* appears explicitly for the eighth time (excluding similar words and pronoun substitutes). *Hard* is a particularly important adjective in establishing tone. It parallels (and contrasts with) *soft-sounding* in the next sentence.

The syntax in sentence 24 is complex. Everything after *for* is object of preposition. I read *her voice to turn...was gone* as a subject bearing infinitive clause. *Turn to* is a verb plus particle verb phrase and copular, with everything after it as copular complement. Everything from *which* on is a non-restrictive relative clause modifying *soft-sounding Spanish*. *As surely as did the clicking tongue of the lock on the door* is an adverbial subordinate clause modifying the relative clause VP *assured*. *Assured* is verbal process di-transitive, with *me* as indirect object (receiver of assurance). *That the stranger was gone* is content clause and direct object of *assured*. *Clicking tongue* is a masterful play on all the sound imagery. *Assure me* is elliptically understood within the subordinate clause. (The clicking tongue of the lock on the door assured him as surely as his mother's voice turning to soft-sounding Spanish assured him.) *Stranger* is nicely chosen, meaning, not just someone unknown, but someone strange, inexplicable, different.

It's remarkable how easy it would be to reduce this passage to a one or two sentence summary of its ideas. My own sense is that a great deal would be lost in that process, not least of which is the being there feeling. Regardless of how you feel about Rodriquez's views about bilingual education as expressed in the larger essay, he does a wonderful job of describing the dilemma of a child whose home language is different from the language in the world outside the home. There is considerable repetition, not just of individual words, but of word patterns – thus *different* and *difference* work in harmony with words like *gringo, foreigner,* and *stranger. Language* anticipates *English* and *Spanish* and all the verbal process and mental process verbs, the verbs of saying, listening, and hearing. The second and third paragraphs are particularly rich in concrete detail as Rodriguez shows (not just tells) us his world of extended childhood. It does seem *a magical world...compounded of sounds...pleasing and fearful.* He is out of place and fearful in the outside, English-speaking world, but very much at home in the comforting, Spanish-speaking world of his family. To me, the meaning seems beautifully realized through the form.

11.2
Chapter Practice

For chapter practice, look closely at the passage from Martin Luther King Jr.'s *I Have a Dream* speech that you first looked at in Chapter 4, reprinted below. This time through, you should be able to explain all grammatical elements, but the prime purpose for looking at it as a passage is to look at ways in which meaning and form work harmoniously.

1) *Five score years ago, a great American, in whose symbolic shadow we stand, signed the Emancipation Proclamation.* 2) *His momentous decree came as a great beacon light of hope to millions of Negro slaves who had been seared in the flames of withering injustice.* 3) *It came as a joyous daybreak to end the long night of captivity.*

4) *But one hundred years later, we must face the tragic fact that the Negro is still not free.* 5) *One hundred years later, the life of the Negro is still sadly crippled by the manacles of segregation and the chains of discrimination.* 6) *One hundred years later, the Negro lives on a lonely island of poverty in the midst of a vast ocean of material prosperity.* 7) *One hundred years later, the Negro is still languishing in the corners of American society and finds himself an exile in his own land.* 8) *So we have come here today to dramatize an appalling condition.*

Answers to Section Exercises

The number given to each section below is the corresponding number of each Section Exercise in the main text.

1) *on my foot* is adverbial because it tells where the standing takes place.

2) *in the moon* is adjectival, modifying *the man. of our imagination* is adjectival, modifying *a product.*

3) *under the tree* is adjectival, modifying *that idiot.*

4) *under the tree* is adverbial, modifying the verb phrase *is sleeping.*

5) *of my dreams* is an adjectival modifier of *the meal. with grace* is an adverbial modifier of *served.*

6) *in the hand* is an adjectival modifier of *A bird.* I have added my own word (in brackets) to this familiar quotation. *Birds* seems to me an implied part of the sentence.

7) This one is tricky: *in the chair by the window* is an adverbial modifier of *reads. by the window* is an adjectival modifier of *the chair.*

In the chair by the window is given first as one prepositional phrase because *by the window* is part of the noun phrase headed by *the chair*. This is a prepositional phrase within a noun phrase which is itself part of another prepositional phrase. This exemplifies one important aspect of constituency, that it builds in levels. If that is a difficult concept to grasp, don't worry about it yet. Most grammatical concepts won't come to you on the basis of one example. We will return to this concept again and you will have a much better chance to see it when we do phrase structure tree diagrams in Chapter 3.

2.5

1) The man <u>with a suitcase</u> / hit the big dog. *with a suitcase* is an adjectival modifier of *The man*.

2) The man / hit the big dog <u>with a suitcase</u>. *with a suitcase* is an adverbial modifier of *hit*.

3) You / are standing <u>on my foot</u>. *on my foot* is an adverbial modifier of *are standing*.

4) The bruise <u>on my foot</u> / is very sore. *on my foot* is an adjectival modifier of *The bruise*.

5) Two very small children / were playing <u>near a busy street</u>. *near a busy street* is an adverbial modifier of *were playing*.

6) A boy <u>with little money</u> / became a man <u>of great wealth</u>. *with little money* is an adjectival modifier of *A boy*. *of great wealth* is an adjectival modifier of *a man*.

7) Sarah / kept her diary <u>in a locked box</u>. *in a locked box* is an adverbial modifier of kept. (It's also a predicate complement, which we will explore in Chapter 6.)

8) Two very important friends / helped me <u>in college</u>. *in college* is an adverbial modifier of *helped*.

9) The diary <u>in the locked box</u> / is Sarah's (diary). *in the locked box* is an adjectival modifier of *The diary*.

10) The locked box <u>with the diary</u> / is Sarah's (box). *with the diary* is an adjectival modifier of *The locked box*.

3.7

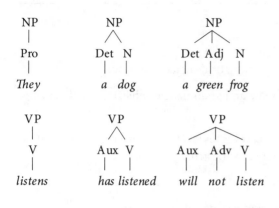

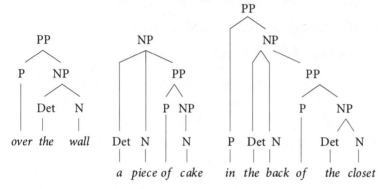

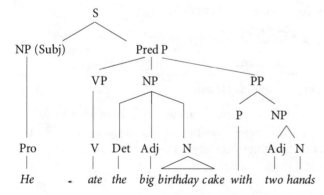

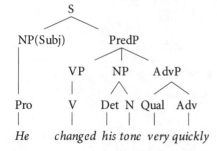

4.5

I.

1) *A truck* is theme, grammatical subject and actor.

2) *Our oak tree* is theme and grammatical subject. *A truck* remains the actor.

3) *During the big blizzard* is theme. *Our oak tree* is grammatical subject. *A truck* remains the actor.

II.

1) *The store on the corner is owned by Paul.*

2) *My deepest feelings are echoed by that song.*

3) *Three mice were caught by our cat in one day.*

4.8

I.

1) The baby (slept) quietly in her crib.

2) The baby can (sleep) through a great deal of noise.

3) She was (sleeping) through a great deal of noise.

4) She should be (sleeping) already.

In number 4. you may have been confused about what to do with *be*. We will cover its function in Chapter 5. For now, keep in mind that the finite auxiliary comes first and the lexical verb comes last.)

II.

1) Did the baby sleep quietly in her crib?

2) Can the baby sleep through a great deal of noise?

3) Was she sleeping through a great deal of noise?

4) Should she be sleeping already?

5.7

I.

1) *sought* irregular verb

2) *knew* irregular verb

3) *wrapped* regular verb

4) *stirred* regular verb

5) *explored* regular verb

II.

1) *lost* past; *submitted* past

2) *provides* present, third person singular; *provides* present, third person singular

3) *was advised* past, singular, passive; *would be* modal (*cunning* I'm interpreting as an adjective rather than part of the verb phrase, something we'll explore in more detail in Chapter 7)

4) *is* present, third person singular

5) *had not been* past, perfect (negative polarity); *would be* modal

6.4

1a) is copular. *Felt* could be replaced by *is* or *seems. Cold* is an AdjP that describes *Paul. The cold* in the second sentence is something Paul felt, but not necessarily something that he *is.* The second sentence can be made passive, whereas the first seems very awkward in that form.

2a) is copular. *Smells* here can easily be replaced by *is* or *seems.* If this sentence was not copular, it would seem like the sauce is doing the smelling. The second sentence can easily be made passive.

3a) is copular. *Turned* here can easily be replaced by *became*. *Moldy* is an AdjP modifying the sandwich. The second sentence can be made passive.

4a) is copular. *Proved* can be easily replaced by *is* and is an AdjP modifying *my opponent*. The second sentence can be made passive.

5b) is copular. *Remains* can easily be replaced by *is* and *our star* is a NP that gives an identity to *he*. In the first sentence, *remained* is followed by an adverbial PP, so the clause fails the structure test that says a NP or AdjP is required as copular complement for any verb but the verb *to be*. The first sentence can't be made passive, but that doesn't automatically make it copular. It is, as you will come to understand in the section below, neither copular nor transitive, but intransitive.

6.7

1) di-transitive.

2) copular.

3) intransitive.

4) transitive.

5) complex transitive.

6) intransitive. (*all day* is a NP adverbial)

7) transitive. (*gave up* is a particle verb)

8) complex transitive.

9) complex transitive.

10) copular.

6.10

1) Material process. The verb phrase is also passive, which high-lights *I* as victim (receiver of *kick* and *hit* as grammatical subject and theme).

2) Relational process: identifying. This is in a subordinate clause, identifying the *I* of the earlier clause in time. *A child* is given clause ending and sentence ending emphasis, which further highlights the vulnerability of *I*. Past tense is important here. The writer is no longer a child.

3) Mental process: cognitive. *Never* is a highly intensifying adverbial modifier. (Compare *didn't always know* or even *didn't know*.) Past tense is important here. It frames the perception of the child. The adult writer may very well know now, but the child never did. Past tense narratives often give us this dual perspective..

4 & 5) *Would happen* and *would bring* are both material process and both are in subordinate clause roles. *Would* emphasizes past pattern (recurring). These clauses are both phenomena (objects) of the mental process verb *knew*. They could be paraphrased as *when* or *why*.

6) Relational: attributive, with *alone* as an attribute of the carrier *I*. *Alone*, though, shades the clause toward mental: affection (feeling) in its effect. The echo here is of *lonely*. You get the feeling that there is some comfort in not being alone in having gone through this. Present tense is very important. It's the adult, not the child, who sees him or her self as *not alone*.

7) Relational: identifying. *Child abuse* (identified) is being renamed as *a terrible problem in our society* (identifier). It could also be thought of as attributive, since child abuse is already recognized as a problem, but what's being added is the notion of extent. By itself, this would be a mediocre sentence, but here it serves to complete a movement within the passage from happening to knowing to being.

If this were the opening (thematic) paragraph in an essay, the writer has a number of natural follow-up moves. The essay has already begun to explore the material circumstances of child abuse (for a particular child), the feelings and thoughts of the abused, both as child and as adult, and the pattern of experience shared by others. Ground has also been prepared for a discussion of social implications.

My own judgment is that an exploration of these process types gives us a rich understanding of a complex field of meaning.

7.2

1) *has broken* is the finite verb phrase.

2) *breaking* is the adjective, *sprayed* the finite verb phrase.

3) *broken* is the adjective; *had been given* the finite verb phrase.

7.4

1) *followed* is the finite verb phrase; *meandering* the adjective (modifying the noun *stream*).

2) *examined* is the finite verb phrase; *my studying* the NP (gerund), direct object of VP *examined*; *found* is the finite verb phrase; *lacking* is the adjective (modifying *it*; predicate complement of VP *found*).

3) *Seeing* is the NP (gerund, subject); *is* as the finite verb phrase; *believing* as NP (gerund, copular complement of VP *is*).

4) *Do...cry* as finite verb phrase; *spilled* as adjective (modifies *milk*).

1a) NP (gerund). object of preposition *about*.

  b) NP (gerund). calling this object of preposition *about* would be a very good, logical answer. It actually renames *a beginning* and is therefore an appositional modifier, something we will explore in the next chapter.

2a) infinitive clause. DO of VP *had been asked*. This one is made tricky by the fact that the matrix clause is passive. The active version would be *A friend had asked me to write the text for a photo essay*. The sentence is di-transitive, with the IO promoted to grammatical subject.

3a) participial clause. present participial. non-restrictive adjectival modifier of NP *He*. (You may have been tempted to interpret this as adverbial, a frequent error with participial clauses, which are almost never adverbial but often seem to be.) It modifies *He* rather than *days* because *He* is the implied subject. (It's not the days that took photographs, but he.)

4a) infinitive clause. DO of VP attempt. (*attempt* may look like a noun to you here, but it's a VP with subject *they*.)

  b) participle clause. present. non-restrictive adjectival modifier of *they* (which stands in for *Lafayette and Pharoah*.) *all the while* may have confused you. Just like finite VP's, participial clauses can take adverbial modifiers to the left.

5a) participial clause. present. non-restrictive adjectival modifier of NP *most of the boys*. By implication, *James and Lafayette* are also being modified.)

  b) subject bearing present participial clause (absolute). non-restrictive adjectival modifier of NP *most of the boys*.

6a) participle clause. past. non-restrictive adjectival modifier of NP *They*.

7a) present participle clause. non-restrictive adjectival modifier of NP *a friend*.

  b) this is either part of a finite verb phrase (*was unloaded*) or a past participial adjectival copular complement of VP *was*. The verb *to be* sometimes gives us these fuzzy choices. In my own thinking, *unloaded* is adjectival, a characteristic rather than something that was done to the gun.

8a) infinitive clause. DO of VP *didn't want.*

 b) present participle as adjective, modifying N *sparrows.*

9a) infinitive clause. adverbial modifier of VP *took.*

10a) past participle as adjective. modifies N *lawn.*

 b) participial clause. present. non-restrictive adjectival modifier of NP *Lafayette and his nine year old cousin Dede.*

 c) subject bearing participial clause (absolute). non-restrictive adjectival modifier of *Lafayette and his nine year old cousin Dede.*

11) infinitive clause. restrictive adjectival modifier of NP *her ability.*

12) infinitive clause. adverbial modifier of VP *worked.*

13) participial clause. past. restrictive adjectival modifier of NP *a photograph.*

14) participial clause. present. non-restrictive adjectival modifier of NP *he.* (It might help to recognize *had been caught* as passive. An active version would be *The past spring, someone had caught him stealing candy from a Walgreen's downtown.*)

15a) Two choices seem reasonable here. This is a NP as object of a preposition *of* or a subject bearing participial clause as object of preposition *of.*

 b) Depending on your answer for *a*, this is a present participle clause, restrictive adjectival modifier of NP *a tiger* or the predicate phrase of a subject bearing present participle clause, with *a tiger* as subject.

16a) infinitive clause. copular complement of VP *seemed.* (It helps to remember that *seem* is always copular.)

 b) infinitive clause. predicate complement of infinitive clause VP *help*. *Help* often takes predicate complement infinitive clauses without the complementizer *to.*

17a) infinitive clause. DO of VP *wanted.*

  b) infinitive clause. DO of VP *wanted.* (To me, the comma here stands in for an *and* and what he wanted are two different things.)

18a) past participle as adjective. modifies N *plank.*

  b) past participle as adjective. modifies N *steps.*

19a) past participal as adjectival modifier of N *buildings.*

  b) subject bearing past participle clause (absolute). non-restrictive adjectival modifier of NP *the two unfinished buildings.*

20a) infinitive clause. restrictive adjectival modifier of NP *the first family.*

21a) Two choices seem reasonable. This is either a NP as object of preposition *at* or a subject bearing present participle clause as object of preposition *at.*

  b) Depending on your answer for 21a) this is either a present participle clause as restrictive adjectival modifier of NP *a fly* or the predicate phrase of a subject bearing present participial clause with *a fly* as subject.

22a) infinitive clause. DO of VP *begged.* A key here is to recognize *begged* as a speech act verb. *his brother* is indirect object. The infinitive clause summarizes the content of what was said.

23a) present participal clause, non-restrictive adjectival modifier of NP *Lafayette. this time* is not a subject for the participial clause, despite its position in front of *swatting.* It's an adverbial modifier. *Lafayette* is the implied subject because he is doing the swatting.

24a) infinitive clause. DO of VP *wanted.*

  b) present participle adjective modifying N *home.*

8.2

1) *and* links *the manacles of segregation* and *the chains of discrimination.* A compound NP is created as object of preposition *by.* (This is also a compound actor in this transitive passive sentence.)

2) *and* links *is still languishing in the midst of a vast ocean of material prosperity* with *finds himself an exile in his own land.* This creates a compound predicate phrase sharing *The Negro* as subject.

3) The three *nor*s in this sentence serve to connect a series of four partial predicate phrases. The term *partial predicate* is appropriate because they all share *does* (*not*) as finite verb. They also share *it* as subject.

4) *and* links *old* and *terrible*, creating a compound adjective sharing *very* as qualifier and modifying the noun *lie.* (It is possible to interpret *very* as intensifying *old*, but not *terrible.*)

5) The first *and* links *absolute* and *uncompromising*, creating a compound adjective modifying the noun *allegiance.* The second *and* links *obscenity* and *evil*, a compound noun phrase acting as object of preposition *to.*

6) *and* links *spits* and *stares*. It's possible to see the structure created as a compound VP within a single predicate or as a compound predicate phrase. (Each predicate phrase would include a single finite VP. *He spits. He stares.*) In either case, they share the subject *he.*

8.6

1) *A black writer who writes mainly about the people he grew up with in rural Louisiana.* non-restrictive modifier of NP *Ernest J. Gaines.*

2) *flaws rooted in historic inequalities and longstanding cultural stereotypes.* non-restrictive adjectival modifier of NP *the flaws of American society.*

3) *family, friends, school.* non-restrictive adjectival modifier of NP *the supporting networks.*

4) *housing, food, health care, education, child care, and jobs*. non-restrictive adjectival modifier of NP *basic social goods*.

5) *a public housing complex*. non-restrictive adjectival modifier of NP *Henry Horner Homes*.

6) *a peacefulness that extended into the horizon like the straight, silvery rails*. non-restrictive adjective modifier of NP *a certain tranquillity*.

7) *a six lane boulevard just west of Henry Horner*. non-restrictive adjectival modifier of NP *Ashland Avenue*.

8) *Lajoe*. non-restrictive adjectival modifier of NP *their mother*.

9.3

1) *When the going gets tough*; modifies VP *get*.

2) *After it started*; modifies VP *came*. *before it ended*; modifies VP *left*.

3) *if we have to*; modifies VP *will stay*.

4) *Though the river rose*; modifies VP *did not overflow*.

5) *so... that he could not finish the test*; modifies Adj *sleepy*.

6) *Before he makes dinner*; modifies VP *does*. (*After dinner* is an adverbial modifier, but it's a prepositional phrase.)

9.5

I.

1) *I love what you do when you do what you do to me*. Full matrix clause, with *I* as NP subject, *love* as transitive VP and the rest of the sentence as direct object.

2) *what you do when you do what you do to me.* Content clause. DO of VP *love.*

3) *when you do what you do to me.* Adverbial subordinate clause modifying the first VP *do.*

4) *what you do to me.* Content clause. Direct object of second VP *do.*

II.

1) *that you came all this way for nothing.* extraposed subject.

2) *what you said*; object of preposition *with*. *how you said it.* DO of VP *don't like.*

3) *what I wanted.* Copular complement of first VP *is. what I could afford.* copular complement of second VP *is.*

4) *she will follow through on her promise.* DO of VP *believe*

9.7

1) modifies *the people*; restrictive; *who* is subject of the relative clause.

2) modifies *my mother*; non-restrictive; *who* is subject of the relative clause.

3) modifies *products*; restrictive; *whose* is determiner in the NP *whose labels.*

4) modifies *the foods*; restrictive; the implied relative pronoun is direct object of relative clause VP *knew.*

5) modifies *the building*; restrictive; the implied pronoun is object of relative clause preposition *in.*

1) ¹ The semicolon connects two matrix clauses.

2) ¹ The colon follows a fully independent clause and introduces two matrix clauses that seem explanatory of the first. Though there are three major clauses, the colon helps set up the two part meaning structure.

   ² The comma precedes a conjunction (*and*) linking two matrix clauses.

3) ¹ and ² These commas precede conjunctions (*but* and *for*) linking a series of three matrix clauses.

4) ¹ The dash sets off a non-restrictive appositional phrase; it gives more emphasis than a simple comma would.

   ² Comma before a conjunction (*but*) linking matrix clauses.

5) ¹ Comma after introductory prepositional phrase (marked theme).

   ² Comma sets off a non-restrictive appositional phrase.

6) ¹ Comma after introductory prepositional phrase (marked theme).

   ² and ³ These two commas separate a series of three coordinate adjectives. Notice that the third has modifiers of its own.

7) ¹ and ² These two commas separate a series of three coordinate adjectives.

8) ¹ Comma after an introductory prepositional phrase (marked theme).

   ² The semicolon links two closely related matrix clauses.

9) ¹ Comma before a conjunction (*but*) linking two matrix clauses.

10) ¹ After an introductory participal clause (marked theme).

   ² After a second introductory participal clause (marked theme).

   ³ After an introductory prepositional phrase (the third in a series of marked themes).

11) [1] and [2] These two commas set off a non-restrictive appositional phrase.

12) [1] After an introductory subordinate clause (marked theme).

13) [1] After an introductory subordinate clause (marked theme).

[2] and [3] These two commas come between the three compound verbs.

14) [1] and [2] These two commas set off the adverb however, which interrupts the normal flow of the clause (between subject and verb phrase).

15) [1] The semicolon links two matrix clauses.

[2] Comma follows an introductory transitional expression.

My own version of the Hemingway paragraph, with added punctuation, is as follows:

He was an old man who fished alone in a skiff in the Gulf Stream,[1] and he had gone eighty-four days now without taking a fish. In the first forty days,[2] a boy had been with him. But after forty days without a fish,[3] the boy's parents had told him that the old man was now definitely and finally salao, which is the worst form of unlucky, and the boy had gone at their orders in another boat,[4] which caught three good fish the first week. It made the boy sad to see the old man come in each day with his skiff empty,[5] and he always went down to help him carry either the coiled lines or the gaff,[6] and harpoon,[7] and the sail that was furled around the mast. The sail was patched with flour sacks and, furled, it looked like the flag of permanent defeat.

[1] This comma comes before a conjunction (*and*) linking two matrix clauses.

[2] This comma follows an introductory word group (marked theme).

[3] after an introductory word group (marked theme).

[4] This is somewhat marginal. It seems to me that *another boat* is already identified and the relative clause gives us additional information. It's a writer's option.

[5] Comma before a conjunction (and) linking matrix clauses.

[6] and [7] The explicit *and*s make these commas less necessary. It seems to me that he's saying the boy carried either one thing (the coiled lines) or three things (*gaff*, *harpoon* and *sail*). More conventionally, it would be *the gaff, harpoon, and sail that was furled around the mast*.

The four commas Hemingway does use seem to me very important. The first two set off the relative clause *which is the worst form of unlucky* as a non-restrictive modifier of *salao*. The second pair set off *furled*, which has the potential to be mistaken for a verb without the commas. (As in *They furled it around the mast*.) The commas make it clearly readable as non-restrictive modifier.

Whatever you think of Hemingway's style, it's important to consider that it is a carefully constructed and consistent approach, not a careless or unthinking one. To me, it works very well, though I'm not tempted to imitate it.

Glossary

Actor

A person or entity that carries out an active process. Depending on the process type, the role of the actor can vary widely. If the process is *seeing*, then the actor will be doing the seeing, and so on.

Agentless passive

A PASSIVE clause in which the actor or agent is not explicitly present. '*The dinner was ruined.*' '*Two college students were attacked.*'

Adjective

One of the four form classes that make up the bulk of words in the language. The most typical role of an adjective is to modify a NOUN. Most can be made comparative or superlative by adding *–er* and *–est* or by being preceded by *more* and *most*. Most can be qualified by words like *so* and *very*.

Adjective phrase

A phrase that has an ADJECTIVE as its head. 'He bought a *very ripe* tomato.'

Adjectival

functioning like an ADJECTIVE normally would, in a noun modifying role. In 'The guitar with the black top sounded tinny,' *with the black top* is a PREPOSITIONAL PHRASE acting in an adjectival role by telling us which guitar is being talked about. *The* (DETERMINER), *black* (ADJECTIVE), and *tinny* (COPULAR COMPLEMENT) are also adjectival in function.

Adverb

One of the four form classes that make up the bulk of words in the language. The most typical role of an adverb is to modify a **VERB**. Many are derived from **ADJECTIVES** by adding -*ly*. Most can be qualified with words like *so* and *very*.

Adverbial

Acting like an **ADVERB** normally would, in a **VERB** modifying role. In 'We leave next Tuesday,' *next Tuesday* is a noun phrase acting as an adverbial modifier of VP *left*.

Adverbial clause

A **FINITE SUBORDINATE CLAUSE** acting in an **ADVERBIAL** role. '*As the day went on*, we became increasingly bored.' These are introduced by **SUBORDINATING CONJUNCTIONS**.

Adverb phrase

A phrase with an **ADVERB** as head. 'They left *rather quickly*.'

Appositional

When a structure, usually a **NOUN PHRASE**, modifies another word group (usually a noun phrase) by renaming or restating it. The renaming is not made explicit, as it would be in a **RELATIVE CLAUSE** or **COPULAR CLAUSE**, but simply juxtaposed.

'Pedro Martinez, *the ace of the Mets staff*, will be pitching the home opener.' Appositional modifiers can be **RESTRICTIVE** or **NON-RESTRICTIVE**. Occasionally, whole clauses can be appositional. 'His greatest fear, *that he would outlive his children*, eventually came to pass'.

Aspect

An optional feature of verb phrases that designates an action as **PERFECT** (*have* auxiliary plus **PAST PARTICIPLE**) and/or **PROGRESSIVE** (*be* auxiliary plus **PRESENT PARTICIPLE**).

Aspect functions independently of **TENSE** (or **MODALITY**.) Generally speaking, **PERFECT ASPECT** gives a sense of an action completed ('She *has eaten* the chicken') and **PROGRESSIVE ASPECT** gives a sense of an action in progress, ongoing ('She is eating the chicken').

Auxiliary verb

An important **STRUCTURE CLASS** word that helps verb phrases convey tense, aspect, modality, and voice. These include forms of *have*, *be*, *do*, and the **MODAL AUXILIARIES**.

Being processes

See **COPULAR CLAUSE**.

Causative verb

A **VERB** in a **COMPLEX TRANSITIVE** clause, one that acts on the **DIRECT OBJECT** in such a way as to cause a new identity, new characteristics, or a new location. 'We *elected* Paul captain.' 'Her departure *made* us sad.' 'He *put* the car in the garage.'

Cohesion

Meaningful connections that extend beyond the boundaries of an individual sentence.

Common nouns

Nouns that designate an entity as a member of a category or group. (*cow, tree, car, road, illusion*, and so on.) These are distinguished from **PROPER NOUNS**, which name a particular person, place, or thing.

Complement

Typically a word group, often a necessary element, that completes the representational meaning of a **VERB**.

The elements of a predicate include the **VERB PHRASE**, its **MODIFIERS**, and its complements. These include **COPULAR COMPLEMENTS**, **DIRECT OBJECTS**, **INDIRECT OBJECTS**, and **PREDICATE COMPLEMENTS**. Some adjectives and nouns can take complements as well, word groups that seem essential to a completion of their meaning. 'I was happy *to see her healthy*.' 'I was fearful *that she would fail*.' 'His fear *that she would fail* proved unwarranted.'

Complementizer

That before a **CONTENT CLAUSE** and *to* before an **INFINITIVE CLAUSE**. 'I saw *that* she was angry.' 'He felt a need *to* check on his children.' These introductory words have no grammatical or semantic role within the clause they introduce, but help subordinate (complementize) it.

Complex transitive

A clause that includes **DIRECT OBJECT** and **PREDICATE COMPLEMENT**. Typically, the **VERB PHRASE** is causative, and the transformation of the direct object is made explicit through the predicate complement, which establishes a new identity, new characteristics, or new location. 'She made me angry.' 'She put me in my place.' 'We elected the wrong man President.'

Compound

A constituent group containing two or more joined elements of equal rank that acts as a single unit.

'My brother and your sister ate the cheese' includes *My brother* and *your sister* as a compound noun phrase acting as a single subject. Almost any element of any sentence can be compounded.

Conflated

Two or more grammatical functions carried out by the same CONSTITUENT GROUP are said to be *conflated*.

Conjunction

A structure class word that has as its primary role the joining of two structures.

COORDINATING CONJUNCTIONS link elements of equal rank in the formation of compound structures, including compound sentences. SUBORDINATING CONJUNCTIONS downrank the clause they introduce into a subordinate (adverbial) status.

Constituency

Constituency involves the membership of a word within a word group and the relationship of a word group to other phrases, clauses, and sentences. This involves a recognition that some words may be more important within a phrase (the HEAD WORD of the phrase) and that word grouping will happen at different levels.

In the sentence '*My little brother eats all the time*,' *brother* is head noun in the NOUN PHRASE *My little brother* and *My little brother* is noun phrase subject in the CLAUSE '*My little brother eats all the time*.' Those are a few of many observations about constituent relations that could be made about even this simple a sentence.

Constituent group

A group of words that acts like a group, combining to perform a distinct grammatical function within its context.

Content clause

A FINITE SUBORDINATE CLAUSE functioning in a typical NOUN PHRASE role, such as SUBJECT or DIRECT OBJECT or COPULAR COMPLEMENT. '*What she got* is not *what she deserves*.' *What she got* is content clause subject and *what she deserves* is content clause copular complement to VP *is*.

Coordinate adjectives

Adjectives in a **NOUN PHRASE** that can switch position and be separated by *and*. 'We entered the *dank, dark* wine cellar.' *Dank* and *dark* are coordinate and reversible, whereas *the* (**DETERMINER**) and *wine* (**NOUN MODIFIER**) are not coordinate and are frozen in position.

Coordinating conjunction

A **STRUCTURE CLASS** word that links elements of equal rank into a **COMPOUND** structure. In traditional grammar, these include *and, or, nor, but, for, so,* and *yet.*

Copular complement

The principal **COMPLEMENT** in a copular predicate. Typically, it renames, identifies, locates, or characterizes the subject. 'I was *your friend*.' 'She was once *very thin*.' 'My session will be *after lunch*.'

Copular clause

A clause whose primary representational meaning is renaming, identifying, characterizing, or locating the subject. The most prototypical copular verb is the verb to *be.*

Other commonly copular verbs are *seem* and *become*. 'This is your last chance.' 'She soon became a trusted friend.' 'The night seemed quite peaceful.'

Correct grammar

A **GRAMMATICAL** construct is considered correct when it conforms to explicit decontextualized standards, such as those of traditional grammar. The construct can be both grammatical and **EFFECTIVE**, but still incorrect.

Count nouns

Nouns that can be made plural and modified by numbers. 'Two *dogs*'. 'Seven *cows*'.

Determiners

STRUCTURE CLASS WORDS that function as modifiers in **A NOUN PHRASE**, helping us differentiate which member or members of a group are being represented. These include articles (*a, the*), demonstrative pronouns (*this, that, these, and those*), possessive pronouns (like *my, his, our*), possessive nouns (like *Sally's*).

The determiner system also includes predeterminers, such as *many, all, several,* and postdeterminers, the ordinal (*first, next , second, last,* and so on) and cardinal numbers (*one, two…seven,* and so on.)

Direct object

The most important complement in a TRANSITIVE clause. It often seems a goal of the process or element changed by the process, though that is certainly not always the case, particularly with perception verbs or mental process verbs. 'I ate *two hot dogs*.' 'I saw *a very strange sight*.' 'I admire *what you have done*.' Typically, it can move into grammatical subject role when the clause becomes PASSIVE.

Di-transitive clause

A clause that includes both INDIRECT OBJECT and DIRECT OBJECT as COMPLEMENTS. Giving, telling, showing, making, and their variants are processes that are often expressed in this way.

Effective

A construct can be considered effective to the extent that it helps carry out the rhetorical purposes of the speaker or writer. Unlike GRAMMATICAL or CORRECT, it is a judgement that can only be made within context.

Ellipsis

Leaving out grammatically important information recoverable within the context of the sentence. 'She doesn't watch what she eats, but she should [*watch what she eats*]'. 'I don't like most landscape paintings, but I like Paul's [*landscape paintings*]'.

Ergative

A clause that presents the potential receiver of an action (what would typically be a DIRECT OBJECT in a TRANSITIVE clause) as non-PASSIVE subject. 'The window shattered.' 'The fields dried up.' 'His shirt tore on the fence wire.'

Existential process

A clause that presents an entity as existing without predicating anything additional about it. 'It is raining.' 'It seems a lovely day.' English requires *it* as EXPLETIVE (stand in) for the EXTRAPOSED subject.

Expletive

A structure that stands in as a grammatical place marker for a structure that has been moved to an unusual position for purposes of emphasis (EXTRAPOSED) or to represent an EXISTENTIAL PROCESS. In 'It is easy to love you', the expletive *it* simply stands in for *to love you*, which is the true subject of the sentence, but has been moved to clause ending position.

Extraposed subject or object

A structure that has been moved from its normal sentence position with the help of an EXPLETIVE (grammatical place holder.) 'It is easy to love you' includes an extraposed subject. 'I find it easy to love you' includes an extraposed object.

Finite verb phrase

A VERB PHRASE that carries TENSE (present or past) or a MODAL auxiliary. It's a very important part of the MOOD ELEMENT (see below). 'The children *cried*.' 'You *should buy* that picture.'

Finite clause

A clause that carries a FINITE VERB PHRASE. This would include MATRIX (independent) CLAUSES, RELATIVE CLAUSES, CONTENT CLAUSES, and ADVERBIAL CLAUSES.

Form class words

These include NOUNS, VERBS, ADJECTIVES, and ADVERBS, the four largest and most open classes of words in the language. Words from all four of these groups are capable of functioning as the HEAD of a PHRASE, and these phrases (NOUN PHRASE, VERB PHRASE, ADJECTIVE PHRASE, and ADVERB PHRASE) are routinely expanded.

Function words

Words, like verb auxiliaries and articles, that have a role more grammatical than lexical in the making of meaning. See GRAMMATICAL WORDS and STRUCTURE CLASS.

Given and new

A division of material in a clause between a carry over of meaning (the given) and content being introduced for the first time. Typically, *given* comes first and *new* material is last, though a careful writer can vary that for rhetorical purposes. This concerns the way meaning is portioned out in longer passages and is very important to COHESION within a text.

Grammar

The natural, inherent, meaning making system of the language, a system that governs the way words come together to form meanings; GRAMMAR is also the study of that system, the various theories or perspectives that attempt to understand and describe it.

Grammatical

A construct is grammatical if it conforms to the internal, inherent grammar of a body of speakers of the language. 'It ain't no good' is grammatical, though considered **INCORRECT** by traditional grammarians.

Grammatical ambiguity

A construct for which two or more meanings are possible, depending on alternative processing of the grammar. 'She hit the man with big fists.' Did the man have big fists? Were big fists used to hit him? *With big fists* is ambiguous.

Grammatical subject

A word group isolated as the focus of a proposition, question, offer, request, order, and so on. One of two major constituents within a clause, the **PREDICATE** being the other. In **SUBORDINATE CLAUSES**, the grammatical subject may lose its propositional role, but maintains an identity distinct from the predicate.

Grammatical words

Members of one of the **STRUCTURE CLASS**es of words. These are relatively closed classes, and the words have a function more grammatical than **LEXICAL** (though their lexical meaning is certainly not unimportant). This would include all words not members of one of the form classes (nouns, verbs, adjectives, and adverbs) and includes **PRONOUNS, PREPOSITIONS, AUXILIARY VERBS, CONJUNCTIONS, QUALIFIERS, EXPLETIVES, COMPLEMENTIZERS,** and **DETERMINERS.**

Head

The head word in a **PHRASE** is the most important element in that phrase (usually semantically and always grammatically). Typically, other elements within the phrase contribute a modifying role. In 'Two very small children were playing,' *small* is the head of the **ADJECTIVE PHRASE** *very small* and *children* is the head of the **NOUN PHRASE** *Two very small children.*

Independent clause

See **MATRIX CLAUSE.**

Indirect object

The **COMPLEMENT** in a di-**TRANSITIVE** sentence that acts as receiver or beneficiary of the action. 'I gave *my mom* a hug.' 'I sent *my mom* a card.' 'I cooked *my mom* a cake.' Typically, these can occur after the **DIRECT OBJECT** with the help of *to* or *for*. 'I sent a card to *my mom*.' 'I baked a cake for *my mom*.'

Infinitive clause

A NON-FINITE SUBORDINATE CLAUSE built from the infinitive (base form) of the verb and most often introduced by the COMPLEMENTIZER to. '*To see the valley at sunset*, he climbed the eastern hills.' In traditional grammar, these are classified as phrases. They are very predicate like in structure, but sometimes carry explicit subjects. 'We saw *the plane fall into the water.*'

Inflections

Changes in the form of a word for grammatical purposes. This would include an *s* on the end of a noun to make it plural (*dog* becomes *dogs*), *-ed* endings on the end of regular verbs to form past TENSE (*walk* becomes *walked*), and so on. Even when deeply unpredictable (*be* and *is*, *buy* and *bought*), we recognize inflected forms as grammatically variant forms of the same word.

Intransitive clause

A clause that is neither TRANSITIVE nor COPULAR without DIRECT OBJECT or COPULAR COMPLEMENT.

Irregular verbs

A verb, sometimes called a *strong verb*, which forms its PAST tense and PAST PARTICIPLE through some way other than the pattern of REGULAR VERBS, which is the ending *–ed* (or *d* or *t*). *Walk*, with its past form *walked*, is regular. *Sing* and *buy* are irregular, since their past tense forms (*sang* and *bought*) don't follow regular verb patterns.

Lexical

Having to do with the meaning of a word apart from its grammatical function. Also used to designate membership in one of the FORM CLASSES (noun, verb, adjective, or adverb), words that carry a heavy burden of representational meaning.

Lexical ambiguity

Two or more meanings are possible, depending on which meaning(s) of a word are called into play. 'The goat keeper played with his kids.'

Lexical repetition

Repetition of a word or variations of a word. 'Now, I do not know what white Americans would *sound* like if there had never been any black people in the United States, but they would not *sound* the way they *sound*' (James Baldwin).

Marked theme

When the opening constituent group in a clause is something other than GRAMMATICAL SUBJECT, the THEME is marked (and more emphatic).

Material process

A clause in which all the participants are treated as entities within the material (physical) world. 'The stone rolled down the hill.' 'A tree fell on my house.'

Matrix clause

A finite clause that does not have a grammatical role within another clause. It is often called an INDEPENDENT CLAUSE within traditional grammar. It is a matrix around which more complex structures can be built.

Mental process

A clause which presents the world as perceived (sensed), felt (in its emotional sense), or known. 'I saw the bird.' 'I admired the picture.' 'I understood what she was saying.'

Modal auxiliaries

Principal auxiliaries within a FINITE VERB PHRASE that convey attitudes of possibility, probability, desirability, and obligation.

The pure modals are *will*, *shall*, *should*, *may*, *might*, *can*, *could*, and *must*. Though they carry the form of TENSE and do convey notions of time, it is best to understand them as having floated free of normal tense.

Other PERIPHRASTIC MODALS would include *have to*, *ought to*, *supposed to*, *is able to*, and *is certain to*. Unlike the other PRIMARY VERB AUXILIARIES (*is*, *have*, and *do*), they cannot stand as the lexical verb in a verb phrase, but have a purely auxiliary role.

Modifiers

These are words that alter (modify) our understanding of another word or word group, generally by restricting or narrowing its referents (for NOUNS or NOUN PHRASEs) or by providing additional information. Words or word groups modifying a noun or noun phrase are thought of as ADJECTIVAL, and words or word groups modifying a VERB or VERB PHRASE are thought of as ADVERBIAL.

Mood element

GRAMMATICAL SUBJECT and **FINITE VERB**. Very important in establishing the kind of interaction being rendered. For example, whether the speaker is making a statement or asking a question. 'She is home.' 'Is she home?'

Non-finite clauses

PARTICIPIAL CLAUSES (built from present participal or past participal forms of the verb) and **INFINITIVE CLAUSES**, which are downranked into subordinate status largely through the loss of a finite auxiliary. Since these often have subjects that are not explicitly stated, traditional grammar refers to them as phrases. They sometimes carry explicit subjects ('I saw the tree *falling on the house*') and sometimes seem more like predicate phrases in structure ('Streets *flooded in the storm* were dry by afternoon').

Noun

One of the four form classes (along with **VERBS**, **ADJECTIVES**, and **ADVERBS**) that account for the bulk of words in the language. The class includes **PROPER NOUNS**, which name a particular person, place, or thing, and **COMMON NOUNS**, which classify an entity as part of a group.

The class includes **COUNT NOUNS**, words that can be made plural by adding *s* and can be preceded by **DETERMINER** *a*. (*cats. a cat.*) It also includes abstract words like *peace* and *justice* and other **NON-COUNT** nouns (like *rice* and *salt*) that won't pass that test. These are words that typically head a **NOUN PHRASE**.

Noun phrase

A word group that has a **NOUN** or **PRONOUN** as its head.

Participial clause

NON-FINITE CLAUSES headed by the **PRESENT PARTICIPLE** or **PAST PARTICIPLE** forms of the **VERB**. Both can be *adjectival*. 'The bus *leaving the station* is the one you wanted.' 'Many houses *burnt in that fire* were never rebuilt.'

Present participial clauses can also act in typical noun phrase roles, like subject or direct object. '*Eating those cheap meals* is not going to help you lose weight.' Though the subjects of these clauses are not generally explicit, they can be subject bearing. 'I saw *the plane crashing into the mountain*.' '*His face lined from exposure to harsh weather*, he seemed a natural part of the mountain landscape.'

Particle

A word that combines with a lexical VERB to create a multi-word verb. (See PHRASAL VERB, below.)

Passive voice

A feature of TRANSITIVE clauses in which the DIRECT OBJECT has been moved into GRAMMATICAL SUBJECT role and the VERB PHRASE includes some form of the verb to *be* (or informally, *get*) plus past participle. 'The house was destroyed by the fire'. *The house* remains the changed element in this process, but has been made the focus of the proposition.

Past

One of two major tenses in the English verb system, generally formed by adding –ed to the base form of the VERB, through less predictable changes to IRREGULAR VERBS, or through changes in the finite auxiliary. It generally denotes a process as occuring prior to the time of the writing or telling. 'I *was* a happy man'. 'I *finished* two books last year'.

Past participal

A form of a VERB, identical to PAST TENSE for REGULAR VERBS but different for some IRREGULAR VERBS (*broken, sung*), used with auxiliaries to create passive voice or perfect aspect. 'The window was *broken*'. 'The singer has *sung*'. It can also function as adjective (the *broken* window) or as the head of a participial clause (the window *broken by the storm*.)

Perfect aspect

An optional feature of VERB PHRASES built from a *have* AUXILIARY, plus PAST PARTICIPLE form of the verb. It typically gives a sense of completion, but with current relevance. 'I *have eaten* twice today'. 'She *had succeeded* once before'.

Phrase

A group of one or more words that acts like a group, the first level of constituency in grammatical structure. Within a phrase structure grammar, all words participate within phrases. We are using *phrase* to refer to all constituent word groups that do not rise to CLAUSE (subject and predicate) stature.

Phrasal verb

A VERB that consists of two or more words that act as a single meaning unit. 'Their pitcher *shut out* our team'. 'I forgot to *look up* those references'.

Predicate complement

In a **COMPLEX TRANSITIVE** clause, the predicate complement makes explicit the changed nature of the **DIRECT OBJECT** by renaming, describing, or locating it. 'The disease left him *a shell of his old self.*' 'The fumes made me *dizzy.*' 'We placed a beautiful bouquet of flowers *on the grave.*'

Preposition

A structure class word that combines with a word group, usually a noun phrase, to form a prepositional phrase. In 'I want the book on the table', *on* is a preposition, combining with *the table* to form a prepositional phrase, adjectival modifier of *the book.*

Prepositional phrase

A phrase with **PREPOSITION** as **HEAD** and as first element, generally in combination with a **NOUN PHRASE**. With very few exceptions, prepositional phrases are **ADJECTIVAL** or **ADVERBIAL**. 'A tip of his hat was given with a flourish.' *Of his hat* is adjectival modifier of *a tip*, and *with a flourish* is adverbial modifier of *was given.*

Present

One of two major tenses in the English verb system. It can designate a process as happening, but more often denotes ongoing or habitual processes. 'I *drive* to work on back roads.' 'The President *is* an important person.'

Present participle

The –ing form of a **VERB**, used in **PROGRESSIVE ASPECT**, in verbs acting as **ADJECTIVES**, in verbs heading **NOUN PHRASES**, and in verbs heading non-finite **PARTICIPIAL CLAUSES**.

Progressive aspect

A structure built from the **VERB** *be* (as **AUXILIARY**) and the progressive form of the following **VERB**. It generally denotes an ongoing, but not necessarily lasting process. 'She *is studying* grammar.' 'He *was waiting* for a bus.'

Pronoun

Typically, a word that stands in for a **NOUN PHRASE** and its accumulated meaning. Some (indefinite pronouns, like *anyone* or *someone*) have indefinite referents, but most stand in for a meaning recoverable within context. The category includes demonstrative pronouns (*this, that, these, those*), indefinite pronouns, reflexive pronouns (like *himself, myself*), possessive pronouns (like *his, my*), interrogative pronouns (like *where, why*), and relative pronouns (most often *who, which*, and *that.*)

Proper nouns
Words that name a particular person, place, or thing. *Yankee Stadium. George Jones. Central Park.*

Qualifier
A word that diminishes or intensifies an **ADJECTIVE** or **ADVERB**, like *so* in *so small* or *very* in *very quickly.*

Regular verb
A **VERB**, sometimes called a *weak verb*, which forms its **PAST** tense and **PAST PARTICIPLE** by adding *–ed* (sometimes *d* or *t*) to the base form of the verb.

Relative clause
A relative clause gets its name from the pronouns (**RELATIVE PRONOUNS**) that usually introduce them. They are **ADJECTIVAL** in function and can be **RESTRICTIVE** or **NON-RESTRICTIVE**. 'Everyone *who studies hard* seems to do well.'

Relative pronoun
A pronoun that introduces a **RELATIVE CLAUSE** and has a grammatical role within that clause. These include *who* (*whom, whose*), *which, that,* and occasionally *where, when,* and *why.* Depending on the grammatical role of the relative pronoun within its clause, dropping it may or may not be an option. Relative clauses do require explicit subjects.

Restrictive modifier
A postnominal modifying phrase or clause that restricts or narrows down the meaning of a **NOUN PHRASE**. Often this will help us identify which members of a group are being referenced. 'People *who talk a lot* find it easy to make friends.' In that sentence, *who talk a lot* is a **RELATIVE CLAUSE** restrictively modifying *people.* A conscientious writer will signal the group as restrictive through the absence of commas.

Rheme
The message structure of a clause is divided between **THEME** (see below) and rheme, which is the remainder of the clause. In 'On Tuesdays, the restaurant is rarely crowded' *On Tuesdays* is (marked) theme and *the restaurant is rarely crowded* is the rheme.

Run-on sentence

Structures disparaged in traditional grammar, these are two or more matrix clauses not linked in standard ways. Standard ways would include a comma plus coordinating conjunction, a semi-colon, or a colon. 'It rained we stopped playing.' Linking matrix clauses with just a comma is a type of run-on sentence known as a 'comma splice.' 'It rained, we stopped playing.'

Sentence fragment

A group of words presented as a sentence that lacks a matrix clause. Though disparaged in traditional grammar, they can be effective and clear in context. 'I worked hard for that degree. *Amazingly hard.*'

Structure class

This would include all words not members of one of the form classes (nouns, verbs, adjectives, and adverbs) and includes PRONOUNS, PREPOSITIONS, AUXILIARY VERBS, CONJUNCTIONS, QUALIFIERS, EXPLETIVES, COMPLEMENTIZERS, and DETERMINERS.

Subject

When not otherwise specified, 'subject' refers to GRAMMATICAL SUBJECT. (See above.) Other subject functions include ACTOR and THEME.

Subject/verb agreement

A change in the form of a verb or its finite auxiliary to agree with the GRAMMATICAL SUBJECT in person and/or number. Other than the verb to BE, this is limited in English to third person singular, PRESENT tense. 'She *walks* the dog.' 'Harry *has* walked the dog.'

In these two examples, *walks* and *has* are present tense forms specifically called for by their third person, singular subjects. The verb *be* also has the forms *am* and *was*; *am* is used with first person present tense subjects, and *was* with singular past tense subjects (other than you). This is an important topic in prescriptive grammar, since some dialects of English don't require these 'agreements,' which are vestiges of a far more comprehensive, older practice.

Subordinate clause

A clause that has a grammatical role within another clause. These include finite subordinate clauses (ADVERBIAL CLAUSES, RELATIVE CLAUSES, and CONTENT clauses) as well as non-finite subordinate clauses (PRESENT PARTICIPIAL CLAUSES, PAST PARTICIPIAL CLAUSES, and INFINITIVE CLAUSES.)

Subordinating conjunction

A conjunction that subordinates a FINITE CLAUSE and establishes its subordinate relationship (generally adverbial) with a MATRIX CLAUSE. '*When* it rains, it pours.' '*After* you finish a hearty meal, you should pass up desert.'

Tag question

A question that gets 'tagged' on to a statement, essentially asking for the reader or listener to confirm the truth of the statement. 'It was you I saw last night, *wasn't it*?' Since they are a natural part of our internal grammar, they can be a handy way to identify GRAMMATICAL SUBJECT.

Tense

A feature of FINITE VERB PHRASES, established through INFLECTIONS or AUXILIARIES, which establishes important notions of time. English has two tenses, PRESENT and PAST.

Theme

The first constituent group within a CLAUSE. It has important status as a point of departure for the message structure of the clause. When something other than GRAMMATICAL SUBJECT is theme, it functions as MARKED THEME.

Tonic prominence

The final constituent group within a CLAUSE, typically a position filled by new information. This can be varied through intonation in speech, but generally falls on the final clause element in written language through natural default. (See GIVEN/NEW above.) It gathers message structure emphasis. Sentences can seem awkward when the material so presented seems unimportant.

Transitive clause

A clause that includes DIRECT OBJECT as verb phrase COMPLEMENT, either in the predicate or as grammatical subject in a passive version. 'The storm tore down a hundred trees.' 'A hundred trees were torn down by the storm.'

Verbal process

A clause that represents a message conveying process, typically DI-TRANSITIVE, typically including a speaker or conveyor of the message, listener or hearer of the message (indirect object), and the message itself (direct object), though sometimes these roles are not explicitly stated. 'I told my mom a lie.' 'I told my mom. I told a lie.'

Verbs

One of the four principal form classes that make up the bulk of words in the language. All members of this class change form and combine with auxiliaries to create TENSE and ASPECT.

Wh-questions

Questions which ask for specific information in response. Typically, the kind of information requested is thematically targeted through opening interrogative pronouns. '*Where* are you going?' '*When* will you arrive?' '*Why* are you doing that?'

Word order

The order in which words or larger constituents (PHRASES and CLAUSES) occur within a sentence. This is one of the major ways in which grammatical meaning is realized. 'Charlie hit Paul' means something very different from 'Paul hit Charlie', though the two sentences differ only in order of words.

Yes/no questions

Questions that call for *yes* or *no* in response, in contrast to WH- QUESTIONS, which ask for specific information. Yes/no questions typically begin with a finite auxiliary. '*Has* she gone?' '*Will* you get the project done on time?'

Bibliography

Recommended Source Books

Halliday, M. A. K. *An Introduction to Functional Grammar*. 2nd ed. London: Edward Arnold, 1994.

Huddleston, Rodney, and Geoffrey K. Pullum. *The Cambridge Grammar of the English Language*. Cambridge: Cambridge University Press, 2002.

Quirk, Randolph, Sidney Greenbaum, Geoffrey Leech, and Jan Svartvik. *A Comprehensive Grammar of the English Language*. London: Longman, 1985.

University of Chicago Press Staff. *The Chicago Manual of Style*. 15th ed. Chicago: University of Chicago Press, 2005.

Works Cited

Baldwin, James. 'Sonny's Blues'. *Going to Meet the Man*. Vintage, 1965.

Bambara, Toni Cade. 'The Lesson'. *Gorilla, My Love*. Random House, 1972.

Blake, William. 'Proverbs of Hell'. *The Marriage of Heaven and Hell. Complete Writings*. Ed. Geoffrey Keynes. London, New York: Oxford University Press, 1969.

Chomsky, Noam. 'Language and Problems of Knowledge'. *The Philosophy of Language*. 3rd ed. Ed. A. P. Martinich. New York, 1996. 558–77.

Cofer, Judith Ortiz. 'Silent Dancing'. *Silent Dancing: A Partial Remembrance of a Puerto-Rican Childhood*. Houston: Arte-Publico Press, University of Houston, 1990.

Dillard, Annie. *Pilgrim at Tinker Creek*. New York: Harper's Magazine Press, 1974.

Dillard, Annie. *The Writing Life*. New York: Harper & Row, 1989.

Doyle, Sir Arthur Conan. 'The Hound of the Baskerville's'. *Sherlock Holmes, the complete novels and stories*. New York: Bantam, 1986.

Erdrich, Louise. *Love Medicine*. New York: Holt, Rinehart, and Winston, 1984.

Halliday, M. A. K. *Introduction to Functional Grammar*. 2nd ed. London: Edward Arnold, 1994.

Halliday, M. A. K. and J. R. Martin. *Writing Science: Literacy and Discursive Power*. Pittsburgh: University of Pittsburgh Press, 1993.

Hawking, Steven J. *A Brief History of Time*. New York: Bantam, 1988.

Hayden, Robert. 'Those Winter Sundays'. *Angle of Ascent: New and Collected Poems*. New York: Liveright, 1975.

Hemingway, Ernest. *The Old Man and the Sea*. New York: Charles Scribner's Sons, 1952.

King, Martin Luther, Jr. 'I Have a Dream'. *A Testament of Hope: the essential writings of Martin Luther King, Jr*. Ed. James Melvin Washington. San Francisco: Harper and Row, 1986.

Kotlowitz, Alex. *There are no Children Here*. New York: Doubleday, 1991.

McPhee, John. *Coming Into the Country*. New York: Farrar, Straus, & Giroux, 1977.

Merwin, W. S. *Asian Figures*. New York: Atheneum, 1973.

O'Brien, Tim. 'How to Tell a True War Story'. *The Things They Carried*. Boston: Houghton Mifflin/Seymour Lawrence, 1990.

Orwell, George. 'Shooting an Elephant.' *George Orwell: A Collection of Essays*. New York: Harcourt, Brace, Jovanovich, 1953.

Paley, Grace. 'Some Notes on Teaching, Probably Spoken.' *Writers as Teachers, Teachers as Writers*. Ed. Jonathan Baumbach. New York: Holt, Rinehart, and Winston, 1970.

Rodriguez, Richard. 'Aria'. *Hunger of Memory: The Education of Richard Rodriguez*. New York: Bantam, 1983.

Sapir, Edward. *Language*. New York: Harcourt, Brace, Jovanovich, 1921.

Schuster, Edgar. *Breaking the Rules: Liberating Writers Through Innovative Grammar Instruction*. Portsmouth, N.H.: Heinemann, 2003.

Sommers, Nancy. 'Revision Strategies of Student Writers and Experienced Adult Writers.' *College Composition and Communication*. December, 1980.

Stafford, William. 'A Way of Writing' *Field*. Spring, 1970.

Tan, Amy. 'Mother Tongue'. *The Best American Essays, 4th College Edition*. Ed. Robert Atwan. New York: Houghton Mifflin, 2004.

Walker, Alice. 'The Black Writer and the Southern Experience' *In Search of Our Mother's Gardens*. New York: Harcourt, Brace, Jovanovich, 1983.

West, Cornell. *Race Matters*. New York: Vintage, 1993.

Wheeler, Rebecca S. Editor. *Language Alive in the Classroom*. Westport, CT.: Praeger, 1999.

White, E. B. *Essays of E. B. White*. New York: Harper and Row, 1977.

Wideman, John Edgar. The Language of Home. *The Winchester Reader*. Eds. Donald McQuade and Robert Atwan. Boston: Bedford, 1991.

Williams, Joseph M. The Phenomenology of Error. *College Composition and Communication* 32: 152–68.

Index